INDIA
DEFINITIONS AND CLARIFICATIONS

REGINALD MASSEY

HANSIB

Published by Hansib Publications in 2007
London & Hertfordshire

Hansib Publications Limited
P.O. Box 226, Hertford, Hertfordshire, SG14 3WY, United Kingdom

Email: info@hansib-books.com
Website: www.hansib-books.com

A catalogue record of this book is
available from the British Library

ISBN 978-1-870518-72-7 paperback
ISBN 978-1-870518-95-6 hardback

Printed and bound in the UK

For
Marcus Iqbal Ravi Massey
and
those of his generation

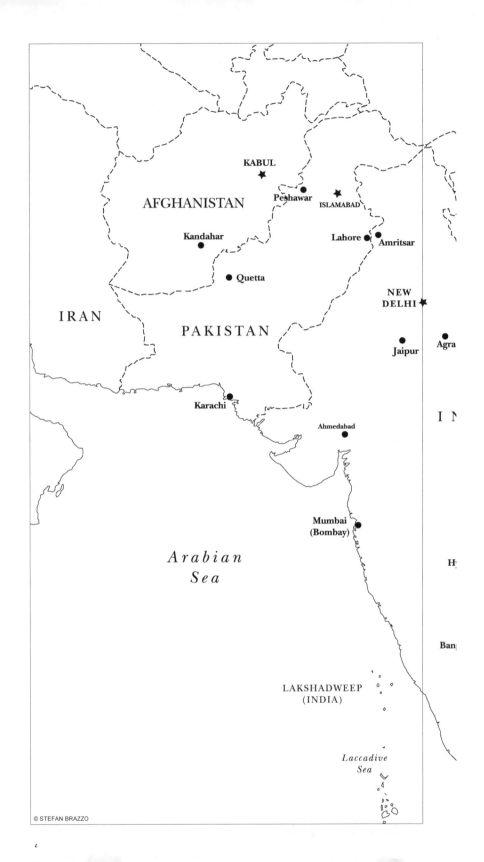

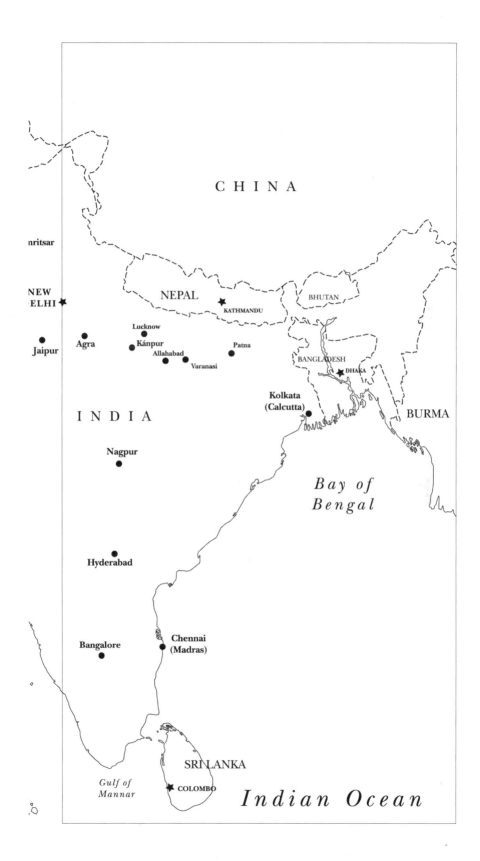

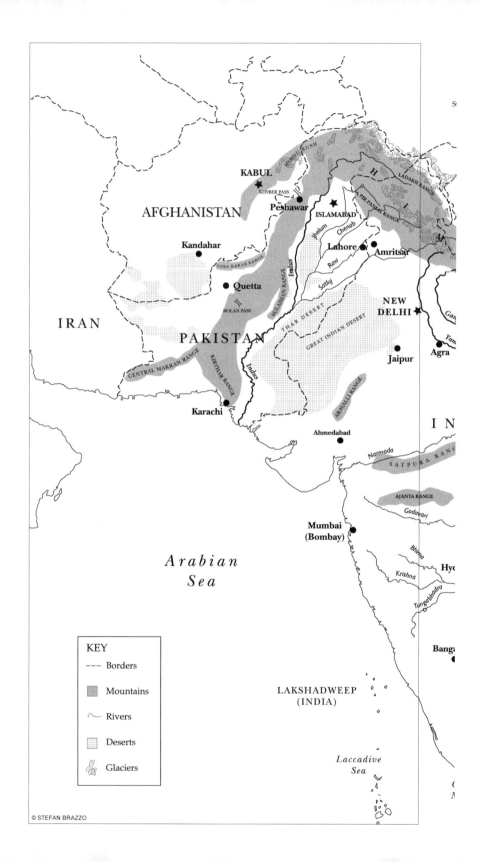

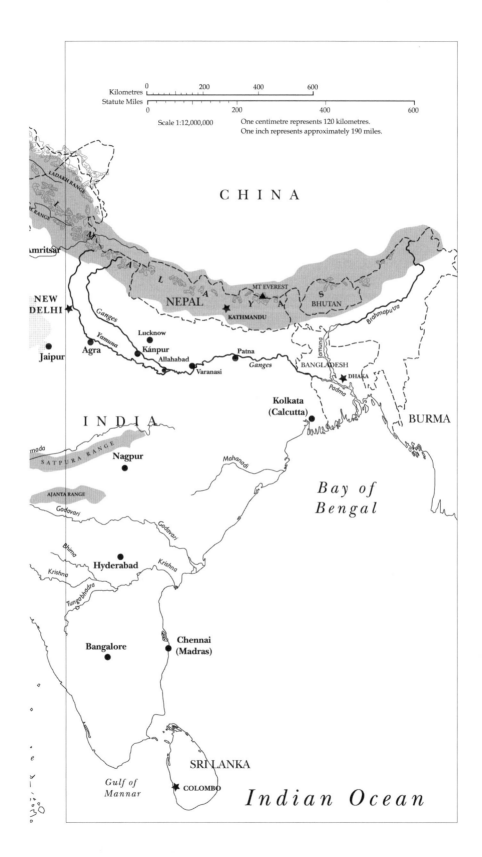

ACKNOWLEDGEMENTS

The author acknowledges the assistance and advice of several friends and colleagues, all over the world, too numerous to name individually. However, the essential editorial input of his wife Jamila Massey has been invaluable in the various stages of this book. Thanks also to Kash Ali of Hansib for his patience and professionalism.

CONTENTS

THE AUTHOR

Reginald Massey has authored many works on India. His books on Indian classical music and dance are required reading for all those who study these subjects. He wrote and produced *Bangladesh I Love You*, a film which starred the boxing phenomenon Muhammad Ali.

Azaadi!, his collection of stories and histories concerned South Asia after 1947, the year of India's independence and the creation of Pakistan. His poetry collection *Lament of a Lost Hero and Other Poems* chronicles subcontinental society in the post independence period.

Born in Lahore, in British India, he lives in Britain where over many years he has been journalist, critic, director-producer, broadcaster, lecturer and activist. He is currently completing *India: the Twenty-first Century and the Future*, a sequel to this book. In 2006, he was Visiting Professor of Creative Writing at India's Himachal Pradesh University.

His wife, actress Jamila Massey, collaborated with him on three books: *The Music of India*, *The Dances of India* and *The Immigrants*, a novel. He is a Fellow of the Royal Society of Arts.

INTRODUCTION

Why yet another book on India? Such a question might be asked with justification. Thousands of books on India have been written over the centuries. Most aspects of the Indian subcontinent have been commented upon and, quite often, misrepresented by propagandists posing as writers and experts, each with his or her own particular axe to grind. The perpetrators have been both Indians and foreigners. The worthy and authoritative books on India (and they are many) have, however, tended to concentrate on a particular subject and are thus narrowly focused and of use only to specialists.

This book is an attempt to present a wider scenario so that a clear, unbiased, overall picture emerges. There are no hidden agendas. Political correctness and politeness have been ruthlessly jettisoned in the interests of truth. No deliberate attempt has been made to humiliate or downgrade any person, ethnic group, society, state or religion. But facts are facts and it is not until we are in possession of facts that we can hope even to approach the portals of truth.

The epidemic of hate, greed, unashamed corruption and immorality that engulfs the whole of South Asia at the present time is due largely to the lies, misrepresentations and prejudices that have been systematically poured into the minds of successive generations. We know what our parents taught us; we are what our parents were. To echo the Bible, we have, verily, inherited the sins of our fathers. That is not our fault. The guilt must also be shared by teachers, mentors, politicians and religious leaders. Indeed, the guilt lies everywhere.

History is being rewritten to massage and bolster the national ego. In India there is a constant outpouring concerning the greatness of the Hindu past; in Pakistan the marvels of Muslim civilisation are likewise trumpeted.

The words of Tod, historian of the Rajputs, spring to mind: "Historic truth has, in all countries, been sacrificed to national vanity; to its gratification every obstacle is made to give way; fictions become facts..."

Those, such as me, who were born in an undivided British India, that is before 1947, were members of a subject race. Every Indian – even the fabulously rich Nizam, the powerful Maharajas and the cultured Persianised Nawabs – knew too well who wielded absolute and ultimate power in South Asia. The British were the superior race; indeed, many Indians believed (as did most British people) that the British were the most advanced race on earth, morally, politically and scientifically. This belief will certainly embarrass members of the present British government. Today, it is not the done thing to harbour such dirty thoughts, although, secretly, some still most certainly do. Public memory is notoriously short but "British is best" was on most lips when I was a boy.

The educational system that the British Raj implanted in India was primarily aimed at producing a subservient army of clerks, or 'babus' as they were called, whose sole purpose was to pen-push in the lower ranks of the complicated bureaucracy that administered the vast British Indian Empire. These 'babus' were not required to think; they had to learn to follow instructions, to work according to strict rules and to write English in a set pattern of Victorian officialese. After forty years of following instructions from their white bosses these men were well and truly neutered. They had little or nothing to bequeath to their sons in terms of intellectual nourishment. What they did pass on to their progeny was an unshakeable belief in the British Raj which meant, in effect, that everything Indian was inferior. The children of the 'babu' class were thus infected with a deep-seated inferiority complex. Their reading of Indian political and social history was limited, their ideas regarding Indian philosophy hazy and misleading. And since the ruling power was masterly in its 'divide and rule' policy, the Hindu-Muslim divide was actively encouraged. Animosities were instigated by the rulers and, to the delight of the British viceroys and governors, both the Hindus and Muslims foolishly participated in stirring up age-old hatreds. The British, therefore, were by no means solely to blame.

Such was the situation up to the middle of August 1947. The carnage was already in full swing before the creation of Pakistan (August 14) and the independence of India (August 15). The massacres, pillaging and raping continued with renewed ferocity after those dates. The whole gory business of blood has been well documented. The end result has been a complete impasse between the two countries. They have been abusing and blaming each other every single day for well over half a century. Currently, however, a game invented by their former white 'sahibs', masters, is being used to thaw relationships. 'Cricket diplomacy' and the restoration of air, bus and rail links coupled with trade talks might mislead many into believing that things are on the mend but the underlying core problems have hardly been touched.

India and Pakistan have fought wars against each other and have been involved in several major and countless minor skirmishes. Billions upon billions of dollars and pounds, not to mention trillions upon trillions of rupees, have gone down the drain. Some of the finest young men of the subcontinent have been sacrificed to the god of war. He is an ever hungry, voracious god and who can tell what he will demand in this new century?

The corrupt ruling elites of both India and Pakistan have done an excellent job in that they have succeeded in fooling the masses of their respective countries. Their success in this enterprise was, of course, assured since the majority of people on both sides of the border are poor, superstitious, gullible, illiterate and an easy prey to state propaganda and the poisonous rantings of religious bigots. One set of oppressors, the British, have been replaced by another, more dangerous, set of oppressors. To make matters worse, the elites of the entire subcontinent and the upwardly mobile classes have sold their bodies and souls to the multinationals.

The Brown Sahib has proved to be an unscrupulous bloodsucker; the White Sahib who represented a distant imperial power could on a personal level be just, even benign. Many British district officers had an acute sense of *noblesse oblige*. This statement will not be greeted with applause by the rulers of either India, Pakistan, Sri Lanka or Bangladesh. Even the good White Liberal will chip in with the trite slogan: "Good government is no substitute for self government". But go to any part of South Asia and speak to any poor landless labourer in his seventies or eighties. Ask only one question: "Were you happier under British rule?" I am quite sure of the answer you will get.

Those born after 1947 can have no idea of what it was like to be living under British rule in India. They have been told tales by their elders from one point of view or another. Let us be frank. The British were there to rule and to exploit. Only a minority were motivated by the altruistic desire to 'civilise the natives of Hindustan'. They were certainly not in India because they loved the snakes, the mosquitoes, the malaria, the torrential monsoons, the cholera, the dust and the scorching heat.

Having said that, let me give you one true example of Pax Britannica. In the 1930s, any Indian woman of any religion could be settled into a 'Ladies Compartment' of a train at Howrah Station, Calcutta, without the slightest concern about her safety or security. After a couple of days the woman would be received by her relatives perfectly safe and sound in the city of Peshawar in the distant North West Frontier Province.

In Peshawar the food, the language, the dominant religion, the dress and the culture was, and still is, radically different. The difference between Calcutta and Peshawar could be compared to that between Paris and Cairo. It is not my intention to sing the praises of British rule, but it is worth pondering the following: Which imperial power in history has been able to achieve anything like the above for its subject peoples?

Today, sixty years after the demise of the Raj with two boastful nuclear powers at each other's throats, no woman is safe on her own even in broad daylight in any city of the subcontinent. What, you might ask, is the price of independence? And who pays that price? It is certainly not the new ruling classes; they are the wealthy beneficiaries of the post-British era. Those who pay are the poor, the homeless, the despised, the oppressed.

The post-1947 generation has been taught nothing that would take away in the slightest from the glories of independence and the greatness of their respective national leaders. The ignorance even of those who are fairly well educated is appalling. This is because, immediately after 1947, in both India and Pakistan history began to be rewritten, twisted and mangled and presented in the form of a policy statement. The erstwhile imperial masters meanwhile patted themselves on the back; they believed that they had planted democracy on Indian soil and, indeed, had bequeathed to India a marvellous legacy. India was now 'the world's largest democracy'. Few, however, take the trouble to point out that it is an exceedingly odd democracy in which Brahmins vote for Brahmins and Dalits (the latest euphemism for outcastes) vote for Dalits and that votes are a saleable commodity.

In India, history initially became an anti-Pakistan exercise with Jinnah as the satanist, the arch enemy. Later, after the Nehru dynasty, it became distinctly anti-Muslim. Here it must be made clear that the Nehruvians were always at pains to point out that their Pakistan phobia was certainly not anti-Muslim. Thus, in order to prove their secular credentials the Nehruvians made Muslims ministers, governors of states and ambassadors (especially to Muslim countries). There were a few Muslim generals and the air force was once even led by a Muslim air chief marshal. How much all this was a matter of principle or a measure of expediency is open to debate. I personally believe that it was largely a matter of principle and caused Pakistan extreme embarrassment on several occasions.

When Nasser was the most important voice in the Arab world it happened that two brothers were ambassadors in Cairo. Both were

Muslims from a leading Punjab family. One represented India and the other Pakistan. At the time, as is well known, Pakistan was firmly in the American camp and Nehru, Nasser, Tito (Yugoslavia) and Sukarno (Indonesia) had joined hands in the Non-Aligned Movement. Hence the Indian ambassador, in contrast to the Pakistani ambassador, had Nasser's ear and so the ear of the Arab world.

The teaching and projection of history in Pakistan was, from the very beginning, starkly anti-Hindu and anti-India. All Pakistan's troubles, financial problems, water shortages and even floods were blamed on the Hindus. At school level, the subject called 'Pakistan Studies', still injects the virus of Hindu hate into the young. When I visited Pakistan in 1956 I was shocked to hear young men say that they wanted to join the army as their sole object in life was to kill Hindus. If they said that they wanted to kill Indians on account of the Kashmir problem, I might conceivably not have been so shocked.

Now that the Nehruvian era has passed into history, in India too the doctrine of hate is fast taking root. The Babri Masjid affair and the church burnings are symptoms of the times. In many ways, it must be said, the situation in India is far more lamentable. After independence, a whole generation of Indians believed that their republic was not only the largest democracy in the world but, more importantly, morally superior to every other country. After all, the young were taught, India was a country based on the Gandhian principles of peace, love, compassion, respect for all men and religious beliefs, non-violence and the search for truth. After the massacres of the Muslims in Gujarat, Indians themselves, as well as the world at large, now know better. The saffron clad Hindu fundamentalists of today are in no way different from their counterparts, the bearded brigade of Islamic fundamentalists. They are, in fact, the same people with the same base mentality; only their names and uniforms are different.

To Pakistan's credit, if it can be counted as a credit, it has to be accepted that few Pakistanis, including its founder Jinnah, ever attempted to take the high moral ground. From its very inception, Pakistan was unashamedly meant to be the homeland for Indian Muslims although Jinnah wanted constitutional rights for all and safeguards for the minorities. However, over the years the country has been hijacked by military dictators, corrupt politicians and fanatical mullah gangsters. Shias, Ahmadiyyas and Christians are persecuted. The Ahmadiyyas have been blatantly classified as 'non-Muslim'. Under mullah pressure, Pakistan has forgotten that two of its greatest sons (Sir Muhammad Zafrullah

Khan, the country's first foreign minister and acclaimed international jurist, and Professor Abdus Salam, the only Pakistani to have been awarded the Nobel Prize) were Ahmadiyyas.

The question might well be asked: "When this is supposed to be a book about India why is so much space being devoted to Pakistan?" The answer is that I was born in a country known as India which included the present day Pakistan, Bangladesh and even Burma. Moreover, most certainly, whether we like it or not the destinies of India, Pakistan, Bangladesh, Sri Lanka and Nepal as well, are inextricably bound together not only by the massive forces of history, culture and religion but also by the urgent demands of present day reality. Suppose India and Pakistan went to war yet again over Kashmir, can any one guarantee that the nuclear option would not be used? After all, the option is there, the missiles with nuclear warheads are ready for deployment. Neither of the two South Asian belligerents displays an impelling desire to take a quantum leap towards peace and mutual understanding. In short, how safe is South Asia?

The horrifying danger is that the holocaust can be triggered off in error. A rumour, a computer error indicating the approach of a guided missile, a nervous observer, or a commander suffering from delusions of power, anything can cause a catastrophe. It has happened before. During the Gulf war the American navy shot down an Iranian airliner with great loss of life. Their reading was that it was an enemy aircraft moving towards them. It later transpired that the airliner was actually moving away from the US warship. The Indian and Pakistani military, who have nothing approaching the sophisticated technology of the Americans, are prime candidates for bigger blunders.

On the present generation, that is all those under forty, rests a heavy responsibility for they are the ones who will shape the future. They must no longer trust the corrupt politicians, the experts, the heavy jowled generals, the exploitative multinationals and the so-called holy men. They must think for themselves and make up their own minds.

The coming of the computer age and the IT revolution is making the young in South Asia increasingly aware of what is happening in the world beyond their borders. They have realised that knowledge springs from the click of a mouse. And knowledge is power. This new aristocracy, the aristocracy of the internet, is open to all. It is universal. It knows no passport checks, no outmoded notions of nationality, no restrictions of race or religion and is no respecter of suffocating orthodoxy and meaningless ritual.

This is a time of infinite opportunity but also of immense danger. The next India-Pakistan war will certainly be waged with nuclear missiles; the fallout will be global.

I have great faith in the young of India, Pakistan, Bangladesh, Sri Lanka, and the other countries of South Asia. I also have great faith in those young people whose origins lie in South Asia but who were born abroad and are citizens of other countries. All these young people have their eyes to the future. They intend to move on and surely will. But I must tell them a simple story before I too move on.

There was in a far country a wise Old Man who had an intelligent, ambitious son. One day the young man turned to his father and said somewhat hesitantly: "My dear Father, you have taught me and imparted great knowledge to me. But this village is too small. I wish to go to the big city where I can use my knowledge and become rich and famous. May I leave this small, backward village and try my luck in the big world that beckons me?"

The Old Man, being wise with the passing of the years, knew that he could not hold his son back. Yet, he loved his only son greatly. With tears in his eyes the Old Man said: "Yes, my son, you are right. Go, and may the Almighty bless you."

The young man kissed his father and left the family home. He took the road to the great city about which he had heard so much. There, he was told, the streets were paved with gold. He walked with a determined step. After many days of travelling he came to a crossroad and there, to his confusion, he saw that several roads branched off in various directions. The young man was in a quandary. Which road should he take? He sat down on a nearby rock to consider his situation. His eyes wondered and some distance away he saw a signpost lying in the sand. It had been uprooted by the strong winds and had been blown about for days.

The young man ran over to the signpost and picked it up. It had the signs pointing in various directions; to one place and another place and yet another place. And one sign said: City of Gold.

The young man examined the signpost and smiled. But soon his smile vanished and tears came into his eyes. He had the signpost; but how was he to take the right road to the City of Gold? The signpost, he decided, was no good to him.

He was tired and he was hungry and as the moon rose in the star filled night he fell into a deep sleep.

The young man dreamt of his Father, so wise and so loving. And the Old Man said to him: "My son, have you forgotten what I always taught you? Remember, you will never get to your destination unless you know where you come from."

In the morning the young man picked up the post and positioned it so that the sign which gave the name of his small village pointed in the direction from which he had come.

And then, with a loud laugh, he confidently took the road which the signpost indicated would take him to the City of Gold.

You might know whither you are bound; but you'll never get there if you don't know whence you came. Hence this book for the younger generation whose roots lie in South Asia whether they live there or not. It will, hopefully, also be of use to those older Asians and Occidentals who want to learn the facts, some perhaps disturbing and uncomfortable, about one of the world's most interesting and fascinating regions.

THE DISTANT PAST

"All sects deserve reverence for one reason or another.
By thus acting a man exalts his own sect and at the
same time does service to the sects of other people."
(Ashoka the Great)

India's distant past is a tangled web and it would take many decades to sift the facts (very few and far between) from fiction and mythology. This chapter, therefore, has had to be written after reference to various chronicles and travelogues all of which are foreign. The authors were Greeks, Chinese and, later, Muslims and Europeans. Why should this be so?

"The Hindus had no sense of history," is a facile statement but is, nevertheless, true. A people who believed that man's sojourn on earth was only a short evolutionary stage leading to another existence, regarded the setting down of dates and events as irrelevant. History, as we know it, is a Greek invention. For the Greeks it became not only a record of the entire Hellenic experience but also an accepted and high literary form. The Romans, the heirs to the Greeks, established a great tradition of historical writing. This never happened in India.

Firstly, when we say 'India' we mean the whole subcontinent and not only the present day country known by that name. From this it becomes very clear that all the countries of the Indian subcontinent share a common past stretching back some thousands of years. Secondly, 'India' is not an Indian name; it will not be found in any of the several major native languages of India. Strictly speaking, neither is the word 'Hindu' an Indian word. In none of the ancient, and not so ancient, texts will these words be found. So how and when did these words appear?

The river Indus which is the very life blood of today's Pakistan was known as 'Sindhu' to the Aryans, the first foreigners to invade the subcontinent and to settle there. 'Sindhu' was later corrupted by the Persians and Greeks to become 'Indus'. The people living around and beyond the Indus were called 'Hindus' or 'Hidus' and hence their country became 'Hind', 'India' or 'Hindustan'. Thus 'Indus', 'Hind', 'Sindh', 'Hindu', 'Hindi', 'Hindustan', and 'India' are basically foreign names and labels. 'Hindu' pointed to a man's region rather than to his religion. When, for instance, a pre-Islamic Persian called a man a 'Hindu' he simply meant that the man hailed from the geographical area around or beyond the Indus river.

The earliest cities discovered on the subcontinent of India were Mohenjo Daro and Harappa in the Indus valley. Both lie in what is now Pakistan. Recently, other ancient sites have been discovered in the Indian states of Rajasthan and Gujarat. All these cities, planned and built by experts, had public baths, granaries, adequate housing, drainage systems and a good supply of drinking water. Even today vast areas of the subcontinent lack these basic facilities, or cannot equal the amenities available to the inhabitants of Mohenjo Daro, Harappa and the other cities and towns of ancient India.

Around 2000 BC the Aryans (they called themselves 'noble people') came into the subcontinent through the passes in the North-West and with their coming India entered the Vedic period of her history. The Rig-Veda, the first veda or book of knowledge, dates from this period.

Many theories about the coming of the Aryans to India have been expounded and demolished over the years. The most plausible seems to be the following: after leaving the region between the Danube and the Volga some Aryan tribes settled in Mesopotamia (Iraq), then pushed into Iran and, later, found their way into northern India. In any event, they do not seem to have had much difficulty in vanquishing and dominating the people of the Indo-Gangetic plains. When on the attack they had one great advantage: the horse. A single mounted warrior could cut through masses of foot soldiers. It was the Aryans who destroyed India's oldest known civilisation though some authorities now believe that floods and the shifting of the river courses were equally responsible.

Those native peoples who could not or would not be assimilated were driven into south India or found refuge in inaccessible forest regions. Those in south India were known as Dravids and the forest dwellers were called Adivasis. These terms still exist and are widely used.

Once the Aryans had settled in north India as masters of their new domains they began calling their country 'Aryavarta', the land of the Aryans. As the areas of which they took possession stretched from Afghanistan right down to the lower Ganges they often referred to the entire region as 'Sapta Sindhu', 'India of the Seven Rivers' or 'Lands of Seven Rivers' which clearly staked their proprietorship of both the Indus and the Ganges. Later, the term 'Bharat' was used. However, 'Bharat' had connotations of culture rather than of national boundaries for we know the names of numerous Aryan kingdoms and republics that had a common Vedic and Sanskritised culture. Much later, under Muslim rule, when Persian was the official language, India was called 'Hindustan' or 'Hind', both meaning 'the land of the Hindus'. And here lies the irony.

The earliest 'Hindus', who were Aryan foreigners lording it over the subcontinent, called the country 'Aryavarta' or 'Bharat'; but the Muslims, who were also foreign rulers and largely despotic, called the country 'Hindustan' or 'Hind'. Akbar, for example, was Shahenshah-e-Hindustan, 'Emperor of the Land of the Hindus'.

In Hindi, the officially proclaimed national language of present day India, the word for 'India' is 'Bharat'. But since the constitution of India was being written in English (the language which many nationalists detested) the framers of the constitution had a serious problem. Should they refer to the country as 'India' (the English word) or use the Hindi word? After much debate, for the promoters of Hindi dearly wanted the Hindi word, it was decided that both words be used. And thus rolled the sonorous declaration: "India, that is Bharat, shall be a Union of States." At all other times the country is called 'India' in the constitution.

Historically, however, 'Bharat' was a cultural Common Market that extended over vast areas of land and sometimes over the seas as well.

But back to the Aryans. They were a fair-skinned people whereas the indigenous inhabitants of the subcontinent were dark and so the 'master race' or 'noble people' set about organising the caste system in order to maintain their supremacy over all aspects of life. In Sanskrit, the language of the Aryans in which all their holiest books and laws were written, the word *varna* means both 'colour' and 'caste'. In short, the higher the caste, the fairer the skin. This, however, is not always the case. Many Brahmins are dark skinned and many low caste Hindus, especially those from the Himalayan regions, are extremely fair skinned. Nevertheless, from the very dawn of history the people of the subcontinent have been intensely colour conscious almost to the point of paranoia. South Asians are certainly more colour conscious than Europeans, north Americans and white South Africans.

This Aryanised society (founded on caste and sanctioned by holy books written by the Brahmins in Sanskrit which only they could read and understand) did undoubtedly generate great literature and scientific enquiry of the highest order. The Brahmins, the highest in the caste pecking order, were the hereditary priests and monopolised learning, astrology, philosophy and culture. They excelled, particularly, in mathematics and astronomy. They invented the zero and the decimal system.

There was always contact between India, Babylon and the ancient Egypt of the Pharaohs. According to Greek legend the Egyptian king Sesostris (Senusrit) who ruled in the second millennium BC extended his dominions to Arabia and India. It is claimed that he introduced into

India astronomy as well as a type of religion that prefigured Buddhism. The fabled queen Semiramis of Babylon, who is said to have co-founded Nineveh with her husband, Ninus, is also supposed to have attempted an invasion of the subcontinent in about 900 BC. It is said that she was struck with fear at the sight of the Indian war elephants and that her army was routed on the north-western borders of the Punjab.

During the 7th and 6th centuries BC there was intense rivalry and bloody conflict between the sixteen states, some of which were kingdoms and others republics, that then existed in north India. The leading kingdoms were Magadha, Kosala, Avanti and Kausambi and among the chief republics could be counted Vaishali and Kapilvastu which was headed by Suddhodana whose son became the Buddha.

The absence of a strong central government made the subcontinent an easy target for foreign invasions. The Persian empire of Cyrus the Great (6th century BC) included Gandhara, the region now comprising Pakistan's North West Frontier Province and the northern districts of Punjab Province. Later, Darius I (548-486 BC), best remembered for making Zoroastrianism the state religion of Persia, annexed Balochistan, Sindh, the plains of the Punjab and parts of Rajasthan. It is said that the revenues from his Indian dominions were greater than those from the rest of his vast empire.

In the 5th century BC there arose in north India a new religion which was founded by Siddharta of Kapilvastu. He belonged to the Sakya tribe which inhabited the border lands between present day India and Nepal. His father was what today would be called the President of the Kapilvastu Republic. In those days he had the title of Raja and so Siddharta had the status of a prince. Siddharta forsook family, riches and power and preached equality among all men. He came to be known as Buddha or the Enlightened One and, in due course, his teachings spread far and wide. Buddhism's most ardent champion was the emperor Ashoka the Great (3rd century BC) who sent missionaries to Lanka, Burma, Thailand, China, Afghanistan and Central Asia. Ashoka's civilising influence throughout Asia was immense.

Buddhism was very different from the Vedic religion which by that time can justly be called Brahminism since it had become an instrument of Brahminic domination and exploitation. The genesis and growth of Buddhism is a fascinating study. Essentially a puritanical religion, it was a reaction against ritualism and caste and it involved no gods. Buddhist monks and nuns took vows of poverty and chastity and devoted their lives to social service and education. The Brahmins, however, could not sit idly by and let their power over the people be eroded by this wave of dangerous egalitarianism and, after Ashoka's death, Brahminism began to reassert itself with vigour. The method used to blunt the reforming thrust of Buddhist evangelism was a characteristically clever one. The Buddha was accommodated and accepted as an avatar, reincarnation, of the god Vishnu and over a long period of time Buddhist zeal was diffused and dispersed. Outside India, of course, Buddhism had a far reaching and profound influence. But then, outside India, there were no Brahmins to contend with.

Jainism, another great religious movement which rejected the authority of the Vedas, was established by Mahavira, a contemporary of the Buddha. Jainism stressed non-violence and non-injury to all living creatures. It is a significant fact that both the Buddha and Mahavira were born Kshatriyas (members of the ruling warrior caste) and the doctrines they propounded were, without doubt, anti-Brahmin.

Throughout this time India had increasing commercial and cultural links with many other Asian countries, especially the Persian empire, since a sizeable part of the subcontinent was then ruled by Persian kings or their satraps. With Alexander's invasion of India in 326 BC there began, in the northern regions, an Indo-Hellenic style of art and architecture known as the Gandhara school. Even the images of the Buddha took on a Greek appearance; indeed, he began to be portrayed like a Greek god. It is probable that both Indian and Greek music also influenced each other.

Those who think that it was the Greeks who brought the light of culture to India are misguided. A people who could produce a religious leader and philosopher-saint like the Buddha centuries before Christ cannot be counted as backward. Equally misguided are those who believe that Alexander sent teachers from India back to his native Greece to instruct his barbaric compatriots. Let us not forget that Socrates and Plato were Greeks and that Aristotle had tutored Alexander.

In their several wars against the Greeks, the Persians often deployed Indian archers as well as infantry and cavalry. Herodotus, 'the father of history', writes that Hidus (Hindus) were in the army of Xerxes I when the Persian king ravaged Greece and sacked Athens itself. Even Darius III used troops from his Indian territories. Therefore, after subduing the Persians, Alexander thought it appropriate to teach the Hidus a lesson in their own land. To justify his over-riding ambition, if indeed justification were necessary, this was an understandable and perfect excuse for mounting an expedition into India.

When Darius III, the powerful Persian king, could not stop Alexander what chance had Raja Paurava of the Punjab? (The Greeks called him 'Porus'). Moreover, traitors such as Raja Ambhi of Taxila welcomed and assisted the invader. The Greeks crossed the Indus near Attock and defeated Paurava's army at Karri on the banks of the Jhelum. It was at Karri that Alexander's beloved horse Bucephalus was killed.

A well known story, based on fact, relates how the wounded king Paurava, reputed to have been seven feet tall, was brought before Alexander. The conqueror, impressed by the defeated king's demeanour, asked him how he expected to be treated. The proud ruler pulled himself up to his full height and replied: "Like a king." Never had Alexander met such a man. He accepted Paurava as a trusted ally and, always magnanimous to a brave adversary, appointed him governor of his eastern-most province which stretched across the rivers Chenab, the Ravi and right up to the Beas. Raja Ghazanfar Ali Khan, a leader of the Muslim League which in 1947 succeeded in creating Pakistan, claimed that his family were the descendants of Raja Paurava. If this is so, it must surely be a genealogical record.

However, by now the young conqueror's soldiers were tired of campaigning and longed to return to their wives and children in far off Greece. The heat of India was oppressive and the prospect of fighting the army of the powerful Nandas who ruled the Gangetic valley did not appeal to them. (The Nanda dynasty, incidentally, were of low caste, most probably Shudras.) In the meantime Alexander planted many Greek colonies in northern India and even sacked Multan. It was in Multan that he was badly wounded while personally leading a scaling party over the ramparts. He nearly died of his wounds.

After Multan the Greek rank and file decided that enough was enough. Both his generals and the soldiery informed Alexander that they were not going to march on into the hinterland of India. Alexander was forced to order a withdrawal. He never realised his dream which was to see the Ganges. He sailed down the Indus and left India.

While in the Punjab, Alexander was visited by the ambitious Chandragupta. This young man of "humble origin", according to the historian Justin, was known to the Greeks as Sandrakottos. He admired Alexander and longed to emulate him. However, he "offended Alexander by his boldness of speech". Later, with the assistance of his Brahmin mentor Chanakya he founded the Mauryan empire, the first powerful, centralised empire of India. Its capital on the banks of the Ganges was Pataliputra, now known as Patna. Chandragupta's dominions eventually stretched from the Bay of Bengal to Kabul and Herat. Chanakya, also known as Kautilya, wrote the Arthashastra which is a classic study of state craft and the conduct of war. Centuries before Machiavelli, Kautilya's book detailed the duties of princes, ministers, policemen, revenue collectors, soldiers and spies.

After the death of Alexander at Babylon in 323 BC his empire was divided among his generals. To Seleucus Nicator fell Babylonia, parts of Asia Minor and Bactria. He decided to repeat Alexander's invasion of India and crossed the Indus with a large army. But Seleucus, though an experienced general, was no Alexander and this time the Mauryan army was well trained and well led. The Bactrian Greeks were repelled and Seleucus sued for peace. The region up to Herat was ceded to the Mauryas and Seleucus gave his daughter in marriage to Chandragupta.

Megasthenes, the ambassador of the Bactrian Greeks at the Mauryan court, has left graphic accounts of life in India. It is clear from what Megasthenes writes, and he had no reason to be a PR person for Chandragupta, that the Mauryan empire was politically stable, well run, highly civilised and based largely on principles of justice. He makes a point of mentioning that the people loved beautiful objects and fine clothes.

Chandragupta's grandson, Ashoka, who ascended the throne in 273 BC, ruled most of the subcontinent (apart from a small area in south India) for almost forty years. He built roads, hospitals, centres of learning and instituted what today would be called a welfare state. A saintly king, he exhorted his subjects to lead a better, spiritual life based on deep compassion for all created things. His edicts were inscribed on rocks and pillars in various scripts all over the empire.

But Ashoka was not always thus. His reign started with wars of subjugation and conquest but it was the massacres which he had ordered in Kalinga, present day Orissa, that changed him forever. The sight of a hundred thousand bodies on the battlefield made him vow never to wage war again. He became a Buddhist in thought, word and deed. Ardent though he was about his own religion he proclaimed the following: "All sects deserve reverence for one reason or another. By thus acting a man exalts his own sect and at the same time does service to the sects of other people."

Taxila, about twenty miles from Pakistan's capital Islamabad, was a famous university before Ashoka became emperor but during his reign it became the chief centre of Buddhist studies and truly international in character. The imperial road ran from Persepolis in present day Iran right up to Taxila and students flocked to its colleges from as far afield as Central Asia and China. Buddhist art and architecture also flourished. H.G. Wells has written of Ashoka: "More living men cherish his memory today than have ever heard the names of Constantine and Charlemagne."

When a whole empire is guided by the vision of a single man, no matter how spiritually evolved, no one can guarantee what might happen when that man is no more. By stressing the virtues of non-violence, pure thoughts and good works, Ashoka can be accused of castrating the whole nation politically and militarily. The events that followed his death lend credence to that charge. There was a free for all. Evil men who had been biding their time silently while the great man was alive now showed their true colours. The last Mauryan emperor, Brihadratha, was murdered by the army chief Pushyamitra who belonged to the priestly Brahmin caste. Pushyamitra seized the throne for himself and established the Sunga dynasty. Kalinga, which Ashoka had conquered with so much bloodshed, rose in revolt and declared its independence. The Sungas were then themselves overthrown by the Kanvas. The frontiers were left unprotected and hordes of invaders poured in through the passes in the north-west.

The Bactrian Greeks under Demetrius marched right up to Pataliputra and were stopped with the greatest difficulty. Their king, Menander, however, was so impressed with the Buddhists he encountered in India that he embraced Buddhism and is known as Milinda. He followed in the footsteps of Ashoka. The Hellenic influence continued in north India with, for instance, the introduction of the Greek system of currency and town planning.

The Scythians (known in India as the Shakas) also invaded but they themselves were pushed further south by the Kushans who originated from the Chinese border in Central Asia. The Scythians occupied the deltaic region of the Indus river (which came to be called Scythia), Kathiawar and parts of the Deccan plateau. Their kings were titled 'Swami', a word which survives in the Sindhi language as 'Sain'. The Parthians also invaded. Their king Gondophares (1st century AD) made Taxila his capital and tradition has it that he was visited by the apostle Thomas. The recent discovery of a small Christian artefact in Taxila has caused considerable discomfort in Pakistan because it proves that there was a Christian presence in the Islamabad-Rawalpindi region centuries before the birth of the Prophet of Islam.

However, it was the Kushans who made the most lasting impression; their empire extended from Bengal to the Caspian and from the Arabian Sea right up to the Urals. It was their emperors who first used the imperial title 'Shao-nano-Shao' ('King of Kings') which in Persian later became 'Shahenshah'. The Kushans fostered economic growth, justice and peace among the various nationalities of their widespread empire. International commerce boomed and the Silk Route connected the Roman Empire to Central Asia and China. Their capital near Peshawar was, as it were, the headquarters of the United Nations. The second Kushan ruler, Kujul Kadphises, started a justly famous gold mint and Kanishka, the third ruler, convened the fourth Buddhist council which discussed and debated the differences between the two main Buddhist doctrines. It was chiefly due to the scholar Nagarjuna that Mahayana ('Great vehicle') was established in India and it was Mahayana that went to China. Hinayana ('Small vehicle') was accepted in Burma and Sri Lanka. Kanishka, apart from being a marvellous missionary for Buddhism, was a great patron of the arts. The Pakistani historian Ahmad Hasan Dani writes: "The period of the Kushans is the Golden Age in the history of the subcontinent when the Indus empire was at its most civilised peak."

The rapid growth of Sassanian power in Iran threatened the Kushans. It is probable, on account of their adherence to the Buddhist principle of non-violence, that their military preparedness was not as it might have been. And so when the Huns invaded, the Kushan empire crumbled surprisingly easily. Again there was chaos. In north India many petty kingdoms, based on feudal systems and dominated by Brahmins, rose and fell. Notable among these was the Brahmin Chach dynasty that ruled Sindh.

By the 4th century AD, Brahminism had finally superseded Buddhism. The Gupta dynasty was established by Chandragupta I in 320 AD and dominated northern India till the end of the 5th century. A number of exceptional monarchs (Samudragupta, Chandragupta II known as Vikramaditya, Kumargupta, and Skandagupta) established law and order and lavished their resources on literature, arts and the sciences. The leading universities were Nalanda, Sarnath, Taxila, and Ujjain.

Vikramaditya moved his capital to Ujjain, instituted a new calendar and erected the Iron Pillar in Delhi. This was a period of great Sanskrit drama in which poets such as Kalidasa flourished. Fa Hien, a Chinese scholar, visited India during Vikramaditya's reign. He and his countrymen Sung Yun, Huien Tsang and Yi Tsing have penned vivid descriptions of the country. These men, who came from a highly civilised society themselves, were greatly impressed with India's society and achievements.

By the mid-6th century, the power and glory of the golden Guptas had waned and history yet again repeated itself. This time the bloodthirsty

White Huns swarmed in with fire and sword. At this very same time they were ravaging Europe under Attila. In the subcontinent they were led by Toramana who took control of Kashmir, Punjab, Rajasthan and tracts of the Gangetic basin. His son Mihiragula, who set up his capital at Sakala (near present day Sialkot in Pakistan) was even more barbaric than his father. His name became synonymous with cruelty. The people rose in revolt and under the banner of Yashovarman of Malwa and, later, Harshavardhana of Kannauj the power of the White Huns was broken.

Harshavardhana (Harsha, for short) was a farsighted statesman, an outstanding military leader, a poet and dramatist of the first rank. He came to the throne at the age of sixteen when his brother Rajya Vardhana was murdered and through sheer ability and political acumen enlarged the area of his empire. He respected all religions and worshipped at the shrines of Shiva, Surya and the Buddha. All his subjects, therefore, identified with their greatly loved ruler.

A large part of north India was brought under Harsha's control and though he tried to extend his dominion over south India as well, he failed to penetrate beyond the Narmada river. His army was defeated by the Chalukya king Pulakesin II and Harsha wisely accepted the fact that south India was to stay independent.

It was during Harsha's reign that Huien Tsang came to India. He spent many years at Nalanda university, took a master's degree in law and was eventually appointed vice-principal. His famous book *Si-Yu-Ki* ('Record of India; the western kingdom') is essential reading for those who are interested in Sino-Indian relations. One is tempted to quote passage after passage from Huien Tsang's writings. Here, however, are a few remarks which encapsulate his assessment of Indians in general: "With respect to the ordinary people, although they are naturally light-minded, yet they are upright and honourable. In money matters they are without craft, and in administering justice they are considerate... They are not deceitful or treacherous in their conduct, and are faithful in their oaths and promises."

It was due to Huien Tsang's great respect for India and his influence at the Chinese imperial court that the T'ang emperor established diplomatic relations with Harsha.

Harsha died in 648 AD; his empire collapsed soon after and the subcontinent was yet again in disarray. In the Punjab was the kingdom of Jayapala; in the centre was the Pratihara empire comprising a number of Rajput clans (descendants of the Gurjaras who had invaded India after the Huns); in the east were the Palas; in the Deccan were the

Chalukyas and the Rashtrakutas, always at each other's throats; to the east of the Deccan was the Kalinga (Orissa) kingdom; and in the south the Pallavas had collapsed and the Cholas were back in power.

The history of three empires will throw light on the internecine wars and vainglorious ambitions of ruling dynasties that served to sap the energies of the ordinary people of India.

The Pala empire was founded in about 750 AD by Gopala who was succeeded by his son Dharampala. Though their power lay in the east, their great objective was to rule Kannauj which was the jewel in the crown of north India. Dharampala waged war against his two enemies, Vasantraja the Pratihara king and Dhruva the Rashtrakuta ruler, both of whom also coveted Kannauj. Dharampala was defeated but waged war again and managed to occupy Kannauj. Later, however, the Pratiharas fought back and Kannauj was lost to them. Dharampala's son, Devapala, had the sense to see that the Palas could not make territorial gains in either central or north India. He, therefore, turned his eyes elsewhere. After taking Orissa he pushed east and occupied Assam.

The Pratihara empire reached its defining moment when Bhoja took Kannauj in 836 AD. His attempts to occupy Malwa and Gujarat led to war with the Rashtrakutas. He, too, looked east and after his rival Devapala's death sought to move into Bengal. However, it was his son, Mahendrapala, who actually managed to take Magadha and territories in northern Bengal. Mahendrapala's son, Mahipala, as ambitious as his father and grandfather but without their military or political ability, was defeated by the Rashtrakuta ruler Krishna III. The Pratihara empire soon disintegrated into several minor states ruled by the chiefs of the many Rajput clans who were often at war with each other.

In the mid-8th century, the military adventurer Dantidurga, who owed allegiance to the Chalukyas, overthrew his overlord, the incompetent Kirtivarman II, and founded the Rashtrakuta empire. He was followed by the warrior kings Dhruva, Govinda III and Indira III who campaigned against enemies in both the north and south of India. Krishna III, mentioned above, occupied Ujjain. However, after his death this empire also disintegrated.

It was at this disunited and chaotic time for India that another great force was emerging, this time from the deserts of Arabia. When the forces of Islam appeared on the subcontinent the warring Hindu kingdoms and principalities had already been bleeding each other for a long time. The whole subcontinent had been ravaged by bloody conflicts with Hindus killing Hindus. A dispassionate study of 'Hindu India' (that is, before the Muslims appeared on the scene) shows that the Hindus were far from peace-loving. That they were always wedded to *ahimsa* (non-violence) is a recently created myth. The two greatest epics of India which have sacred status – the Ramayana and the Mahabharat – are about conflict and war.

The Islamic impact on the subcontinent will be considered in a later chapter. But now let us look at southern India.

THE SOUTH

*To this day the southern Brahmins pride themselves
on their exclusiveness, their intellectual attainments,
their artistic tastes and their fair complexion.*

From the last chapter it is evident that the earliest civilisations of the subcontinent originated in the north. The Aryan, the Brahminic, the Buddhist, and the Jainist beliefs began in the north. The sacred languages Sanskrit and Pali, as well as what came to be classed and termed Hinduism, evolved in the north. Yet so many northerners, Hindus particularly, have an inferiority complex when it comes to matters concerning south India.

On close examination it will be seen that when northern Hindus extol south India they actually have south India's intellectual elite, the Brahmin community, in mind. Also, many Brahmins of south India are fair-complexioned and this impresses all northerners, Hindus and Muslims alike. For the vast majority of southerners (who are very dark complexioned since they are of Dravidian stock) the northerners have nothing but dismissive scorn. For them all dark south Indians are *Kale Madrasi*, 'Black Madrasis'. The southern Brahmins, however, are held in high esteem because the northerners believe them to be vastly cultured, knowledgeable in Hindu philosophy and Sanskrit, and versed in classical music and dance.

Historically, moreover, the southern Brahmins were Aryans from the north. Though the main Aryan expansion into south India was checked by the mountain ranges and dense forests across central India, Aryan sages and missionaries spread into the whole of Dravida, south India, and converted the inhabitants to the Aryan way of life. These missionaries and their families formed the nucleus of the south Indian Brahmin castes. Knowing that they were surrounded by a sea of dark, hostile Dravidians, the south Indian Brahmins have always preserved their identity more fanatically than their Brahmin brothers in the north. Their situation, in fact, was analogous to that of the whites in southern Africa or the whites in the southern states of the USA.

To this day the southern Brahmins pride themselves on their exclusiveness, their intellectual attainments, their artistic tastes and their fair complexion.

The famous statuette of the dancing girl found at Mohenjo Daro clearly shows Dravidian features. This has led to the justifiable belief that the people of the Indus valley were dark skinned and were pushed southwards by the aggressive Aryan whites. However, some remnants of the Dravidian heritage linger on. Brahui, still spoken in the Pakistani province of Balochistan by Muslims who owe allegiance to the Khan of Kalat, has been identified as belonging to the Dravidian family of languages. But this example is exceptional. Apart from the Dravidian tribes who were forced to hide and lead isolated lives in the deep forests, the Aryanisation of north India was complete and thorough.

In order to maintain their supremacy the Aryans organised the caste system and invested it with permanence and reverence by giving it the sanction of religion. It is thus that the curse of the Hindu caste system was born.

The Brahmins who went to Dravida subjugated the natives of the south not with the sword but with a weapon infinitely more potent: fear of the wrath of the gods.

The kings and petty chiefs of the south did nothing without first consulting their Brahmin priests and astrologers. The Brahmins told them what to eat, what to wear, how and when to pray, when to venture out and when and where to wage war. The ruling class, therefore, was stifled and stunted. The south had nothing to compare with the majesty of the Mauryas, the mighty kingship of the Kushans or the glory of the Guptas. It was much later that dynamic ruling dynasties emerged in southern India. These were the Satvahanas, the Andhras, the Chalukyas, the Pallavas, the Cheras, the Pandyas, and the Cholas. It was the Pallavas who colonised south-east Asia and Hindu influence can still be seen in the culture and art of many countries in that region. There was, however, constant warfare between the Pallavas and the Chalukyas of the Deccan who, in their turn, were challenged by the Rashtrakutas. This almost permanent state of friction was conducive to neither economic welfare nor national integration. To compound the malaise the divisiveness of the caste system within Hinduism itself made the country an easy prey to foreign invasion.

The first of the important southern dynasties, that of the Chalukyas of Badami, was founded in 540 AD by Pulakesin I. In the previous chapter reference was made to his grandson Pulakesin II who put an end to Harsha's southern ambitions at the Narmada river. Pulakesin II also vanquished the Gangas of Mysore, the Mauryas of Konkan and the Kadambas of Vanavasi. Later, he himself was killed in a battle with

Narasimhavarman I, the Pallava king. Thereafter, for generations there were bloody wars between the Chalukyas and the Pallavas. Eventually, Vikramaditya II, who ascended the throne in 733 AD, captured the Pallava capital Kanchi. He also defeated the Pandyas, the Keralas and the Cholas and evicted an Arab expedition which had invaded the north of his empire. His son, Kirtivarman II, was overthrown by Dantidurga, one of his own feudal chieftains.

The Pallava domains were situated between the Krishna and Kaveri rivers. Their best known rulers were Sinhavishnu (6th century AD), Mahendravarman (who lost much territory to the Chalukyas), Narasimhavarman I (who avenged his father's defeats with interest), and Narasimhavarman II who is justly famous as a patron of the arts and builder of great temples. Among the many luminaries at his court was Dandin the celebrated Brahmin scholar.

There was a sudden decline after the death of Narasimhavarman II. At the end of the 9th century the Cholas triumphed over the Pallavas and annexed their possessions. The last Pallava king was Aparajita.

It was becoming the set pattern for subordinate chiefs to stage *coups d'etat* and take over empires. The foundations of the Chola power base were similarly laid. A chief named Vijayalaya, who owed allegiance to the Pallavas, took Tanjore in the year 850. His successors, Rajaraja and Rajendra I, were extremely able men. The former expanded the empire by invading Sri Lanka and the Maldive Islands and by defeating the Chera king of Kerala and the Pandyan king of Madurai. His army even conquered Kalinga in eastern India. The Chola policy of expansion was carried further by Rajaraja's son, Rajendra I, who completed the occupation of Sri Lanka. The Tamils established their base in what is now known as Jaffna. Even today several families in Jaffna trace their ancestry to the original twenty-two aristocratic families of Thondaimandalam in south India who established fiefdoms in Sri Lanka. These 'upper class' Tamils go to great lengths to distance themselves from the 'coolie class' Tamils who, much later during British rule, went to Jaffna as labourers and craftsmen.

The armies of the autocratic Rajendra I penetrated as far as Madhya Pradesh to the north and Bengal to the east. Across the seas, the Cholas established their presence in Burma, the Malay peninsula, Indonesia and other parts of south-east Asia. This was the heyday of Hindu imperialism which, most significantly, thrust out from south India.

Rajadhiraj and Rajendra II were involved in wasteful wars with the remnants of the Chalukyas. After this period the Cholas were a mere shadow of their former glory. The *coup de grace* for them and for the Pandyas came in 1310 when Malik Kafur swooped across the Deccan and plundered south India on the orders of his master, Ala-ud-din Khilji, the sultan of Delhi.

The Hindu states of the south had been so busy warring with each other that when the armies of Islam invaded they were too weak and ill prepared to face the foreign onslaught. Also, the caste system had fractured south Indian society, and a fractured society is a weak society. The historian Panikkar deplored the "system of division and sub-division" which made it difficult for the Hindus to develop a feeling of community. The philosopher Radhakrishnan, too, was conscious that India's culture was not conducive to the development of a high civic or national sense. A Madras Brahmin, Radhakrishnan's rigorous mind gained him an international reputation; a professor of Eastern Religion and Ethics at Oxford, he also became President of India. It is a pity that Hindu writers today tend to shy away from the intellectual honesty of thinkers like Radhakrishnan.

The observances and rituals of the caste system were always stricter and more heartless in the south than in the north. The difference is that, to a varying extent and right across the caste divide, the Hindus of north India have been influenced by Islam. Many northern Brahmins, especially from Kashmir, eat fish and meat. For the southern Brahmin the very thought of eating fish or meat is anathema. Indeed, in the north the Brahmins never exercised economic power or any kind of intellectual stranglehold. It was always the ruling caste, the Kshatriyas, who led in the north. They viewed the poor Brahmins with disdain since it was the priests who came with begging bowls and had to be fed on occasions of ritual importance. Hence the derogatory term *Bhookay Brahmin*, ('Hungry Brahmins').

In south India a Brahmin would be polluted even by the shadow of an Untouchable. The low castes were forbidden from entering Brahmin temples and hence they took to worshipping the lesser god or demi-god Murugan, a son of Shiva, rather than the major gods and goddesses so favoured by the Brahmins. This practise prevails even today, especially in the rural areas of Tamil Nadu. Many priests of Murugan temples in the villages and small towns are non-Brahmins. The statues of Murugan are also revealing; he is never depicted wearing the sacred thread, the *jane'u*. In other words, those who worship him do not include him in the two top castes, the Brahmin and the Kshatriya.

The ill-informed believe that Hinduism is 'purer' in south India than in the north simply because the rules and regulations of caste and food prohibition are far more rigid in the south. This results in the lower castes having to worship their own deity rather than worshipping the deity of the upper castes. Hence the admiration.

The Hinduism of the south was certainly more orthodox, ritualistic, Brahmin dominated and exploitative. Recently, however, there has been a dramatic change and the Brahmins of south India are paying a heavy price for the atrocities of their forefathers.

The anti-Brahmin animosity in the south Indian states and in the Tamil areas of Sri Lanka is growing. Hindu society is now sharply divided into two sections: Brahmins and non-Brahmins. The Brahmins being in the minority and having lost the advantages they once had in higher education, the learned professions, the sciences and the arts, are on the defensive and, frankly, on the run. Powerful non-Brahmin politicians such as Karunanidhi, the Chief Minister of Tamil Nadu (he named his son 'Stalin'!) have made no secret of their aim to Tamilise society. In other words, they are intent on weeding out the Brahmins with their traditional Sanskritic culture. Tamil, the native Dravidian language, is being actively promoted and Sanskrit words that were introduced into Tamil by the Brahmin intelligentsia are being relentlessly rooted out. International Tamil Conferences are convened and delegates from far-flung corners of the world such as Fiji, Mauritius, the West Indies, South Africa, Malaysia, the USA, the UK, Canada, Sri Lanka and the United Arab Emirates attend in droves.

Southern Brahmins in the higher cadres of the civil service prefer to serve in other states where their lives cannot be made unbearable by lower caste ministers who get a perverse pleasure in humiliating them. Once a southern Brahmin is fortunate enough to get to Delhi and procure a posting in a central ministry, he prefers to stay there and on retirement continues to live there. He hears no call beckoning him to return home to Madras, now Chennai.

A beautiful and highly talented woman, a classical dancer of repute, told me a few years ago somewhat proudly, that she had got a professorship in Madras University "in spite of being a Brahmin". As if being a Brahmin today were some sort of a curse! The southern states are thus depriving themselves of exceptional talent and important posts are going to second-raters who are also corrupt. Their main qualification is that they are non-Brahmins and hence *Bhoomi Putras* ('Sons of the Soil'). Ironically, this Sanskritic term is often used by Muslims in Malaysia to justify jobs and scholarships going to poorly qualified Muslim Malays rather than to highly qualified Tamils or Chinese.

The two drugs of present day India, money and power, are coming into the caste equation. Before independence no Brahmin woman would countenance the company of a low caste man. On the other hand, it was acceptable for a Brahmin woman to marry a foreigner. Rukmini Devi, the famous dancer and founder of Kalakshetra, the renowned cultural centre, was married to George Arundale, a well known Theosophist. Today, however, people pretend they have not noticed when on rare occasions a low caste minister, industrialist or film producer keeps a Brahmin mistress. Also, though 'inter-caste' and 'love' marriages are certainly discouraged and frowned upon they no longer provoke murder and riots.

CASTE AND COLOUR

*"The duties of Brahmins, Kshatriyas and Vaishyas,
as well as Shudras, are divided according to the
qualities born of their respective natures."*
(Krishna in the Gita)

The India of theory is very different from the India of daily living. Very few Europeans, north Americans or others of European extraction such as Australians and New Zealanders can ever understand this fact because a white person in India is a special person. He or she is always treated differently, even preferentially. Every Indian has two faces; one for his fellow Indians and the other, ever smiling and hospitable, for foreigners who are white. The average foreigner can have no notion of how alive the question of caste and colour still is in India.

To be more accurate, the whole of South Asia is even today caste conscious to a degree that is staggeringly unbelievable. Caste has transcended the confines of Hinduism and insinuated itself into the fabric of society as a whole. All South Asians, no matter what religion they might profess, are conscious of both caste and skin colour. As explained in a previous chapter, caste, colour and ethnic origin are intimately intertwined.

Nice educated Indians and Pakistanis will assure you that caste no longer matters, that it was important in the past but now in this new age of science and technology no one takes it seriously. All this is eagerly accepted by western visitors to the subcontinent. White liberals and other India lovers are particularly naive in these matters. The silly statements made by westerners who participated in the Khumb Mela during the first few weeks of this century only go to prove how pernicious blind love can be.

A Pakistani friend of mine who is proud of being a Rajput (a Hindu term meaning 'Son of Kings') often declares that in the 17th century his Hindu ancestors "had gladly accepted Islam so that they could escape from superstitious Hindu beliefs and evil social practises". From worshipping stone idols they wisely accepted Allah, the one and only True God to whom all men are equal. So far, so good. And then, half an hour later, he informs me with even greater pride that in Pakistan every respectable Rajput father is on the look out for a good Rajput son-in-law. "We don't give our daughters to Pathans and Sindhis and certainly not to kummis!" *Kumm* means 'less' and hence *kummi* means 'lesser being'; usually a poor, serf-like landless labourer.

When Nawaz Sharif, the deposed and disgraced prime minister of Pakistan, was in power no one spoke about his background. Now that he has been proved guilty on several counts and dishonourably exiled one often hears remarks such as: "Blood will tell. After all, he is a lohar!" *Lohars* are blacksmiths, a low caste occupation.

When Islam, a religion ostensibly based on brotherhood, has failed to change the mentality of south Asian Muslims, what can be expected of Hinduism which has never even pretended to preach equality? From time immemorial the religion, the society, the life style, the food and the clothes of Hindus, even the length and upward curl of their moustaches, have been governed by caste which means a set ordained hierarchy with a few at the top and the many at the bottom. True, it was the Aryans who instituted *varna* but it was classical Hinduism, more accurately Brahminism, that erected the edifices, the iron laws and the instruments of social and economic exploitation. So deep has the consciousness of caste sunk into the Hindu psyche (and, by extension, insidiously seeped into the thinking of all South Asia's inhabitants) that it will take a thousand years or more to heal the afflictions of exploitation.

No other great civilisation has yet conceived of anything as ingenious and diabolical as India's caste system. It is, laments Swami Sachchidanand, a contemporary Brahmin commentator, "the root of our downfall". The tyranny of the Chinese Mandarins, Roman Patricians, Prussian aristocrats, Russian feudal landowners, America's slave owners, Hitler's Nazis, and even the Afrikaners' apartheid laws were tawdry, temporary and miserable in comparison. This is because Hinduism made caste an integral part of religion and invested it with the sanction of divine law. No other religion has done that. Religion itself was called Varnashram Dharma, that is, belief, duty and action based on caste.

Several present day Hindu apologists are making a strong case against caste on the grounds that it was a social institution imposed by the upper castes and had nothing to do with the divine purity of their religion. Yet in the Gita, the holiest scripture of the Hindus which many of them claim as their Bible, Krishna states unequivocally:

"The duties of Brahmins, Kshatriyas and Vaishyas, as well as Shudras, are divided according to the qualities born of their respective natures."

"All varnas have been created by me."

"One should not abandon one's duty which attaches to him from his very birth, even though defective."

Thus, even today, in the 21st century, no Hindu can truthfully say that he is untouched by caste. If he tells you that he is unconscious of, or untouched by, caste he is either being devious or is woefully ignorant of Hindu history. It is not possible to call oneself a Hindu without subscribing to the caste system.

Every Hindu is born into a caste. He may in his lifetime choose to break all caste injunctions as a matter of personal principle, or be forced into breaking them. Present day urban living makes it impossible to observe the rules of caste. In a crowded bus, for example, an upper caste Hindu, whether he likes it or not, has to sit close to and even actually touch a fellow passenger who might well be an Untouchable. In the office or factory canteen who knows whose hands have prepared the food. Be that as it may, when a Hindu dies he dies as a member of his caste.

In all the ancient texts of India, human beings are never considered as individuals – that is, simply as human beings in themselves. A person is not a person until his caste is specified. Caste, in essence, is what defines the person. A well known example will illustrate this.

Nehru never made any secret of the fact that he disliked the trappings of Hinduism; and though as a Brahmin boy he underwent the sacred thread ceremony, in adult life he never practised any of the hundred and one Brahminic rituals. He was a confirmed, card carrying agnostic, possibly even an atheist. "Yes, he may say what he chooses and write whatever he wishes," I was told by an orthodox friend. "But he was born a Brahmin whether he likes it or not! And he can't change that!"

Hence he was called Pandit Nehru by both friend and foe though he was uneasy with the honorific 'Pandit'. It not only proclaimed his Brahmin caste (embarrassing for a man who considered himself a socialist and a man of the people) but also gave the impression that he was a learned scholar of the Vedas which he was not.

In his will, Nehru had stated, "I do not want any religious ceremonies performed for me when I am dead." In spite of the prohibition, he was given a Hindu cremation befitting a Brahmin. To compound the disregard for his express wishes, the prime minister who succeeded him attended the funeral ceremony. The general feeling that day in India was: "O Brahmin, you strayed! But in death Hinduism reclaims you." Significantly, Shastri, the new prime minister, was not a Brahmin.

Among the Hindus there is no such thing as a surname. They use the name of their caste instead. In a word, the Hindu tells you his caste the moment he gives you his surname. Those who know the Hindu castes, which all Hindus are supposed to, get the message. To a considerable extent this is also true of Muslims and Sikhs.

To wield such immense control caste must obviously have a long history. It certainly has. In a hymn of the Rig-Veda, the most ancient text of the Hindus, the creation of the castes is described. From the god Prajapati's mouth came the Brahmins (priests and philosophers), from his arms the Kshatriyas (rulers and warriors), from his thighs the Vaishyas (traders and shopkeepers), from his feet the Shudras (cultivators, manual workers or various sorts, servants and slaves). Beyond the pale of these established castes were the pariahs, the Untouchables. To them were allocated the most unpleasant tasks such as cleaning latrines, garbage collection and disposal, and the skinning of dead animals.

The Brahmins, being the highest caste, are expected to have the fairest skins. And so if a Brahmin has the great misfortune of being dark complexioned he has serious problems. He is called a '*Kala Brahmin*' ('Black Brahmin') and a well known saying in Hindi goes, "Never trust a Black Brahmin". The suggestion is that his family are not real Brahmins or that his mother must surely have slept with some low caste black man. Chanakya, the author of the famous treatise and guru of the first Mauryan emperor, was said to be ugly and dark skinned. His detractors and enemies labelled him 'The Black Brahmin'. He is also known as Kautilya, an unfortunate name which derives from the Sanskrit word for crookedness, fraud and deceit.

The accident of birth determined a man's position and status in life and the doctrine of reincarnation tied in with the caste system giving it a logical legitimacy. Hindu theorists, the Brahmins, propounded an amazing belief system which even the Untouchables subscribed to. It was this: a man was born into an upper caste because in a past existence he had fulfilled his *dharma* (a word with multiple meanings but here 'duty' will do). A man was condemned to a lower caste or to Untouchability because in a previous life he had failed to fulfil his *dharma.* It followed that in order to better one's chances in the next reincarnation a human being must accept his current condition and perform his duty according to the prescriptions of the caste system. Beliefs such as this shackled the minds of the illiterate masses and, it must be conceded, succeeded admirably in keeping down dissent and social unrest.

Natural calamities such as earthquakes and floods, personal tragedies such as the death of a close relative, inherited and acquired ailments and even national disasters such as defeat in war could be explained away by the *dharma* (duty) *karma* (deed) equation. Even Gandhi blamed the Bihar earthquake (January 1934) as divine retribution for the "sin of Untouchability". When the poet Tagore questioned this amazing statement by asking why, if that were the case, so many Untouchables and innocent children were also killed, Gandhi made no reply.

Manu (a Sanskrit name meaning 'man') is credited with having written the Manu-smriti which systematised the caste structure. No one can give you his dates and it is claimed that the Laws of Manu are a compilation, set down over generations, with the main author being a Brahmin named Vaivasvata. However, even today, the Manu-smriti forms the foundation of Hindu society. A few sentences typical of this sacred text are well worth quoting:

"... a Brahmin, whether a fool or scholar, is a great God."

"Anybody who offends powerful Brahmins will be destroyed."

"... Brahmins are worthy of respect by all even after perpetrating the most obnoxious acts because they are like God."

"The Shudras should not be given knowledge ... If anybody advises a Shudra to keep a fast and imparts to him religious instruction, he, along with the Shudra, goes to the dark hell named Asambrat."

"The Brahmin can appropriate the property of the Shudra without any hesitation because the latter owns nothing. All his property belongs to his master, that is the Brahmin."

"To kill a Shudra is as simple a sin as to kill a cat ..."

"The Brahmins are the masters of everything in this world, because since birth they are the best."

"The Brahmin is respectable even if his character is bad; the Shudra is not respectable even if he has overcome his base instincts."

"No sin on this earth is greater than the killing of a Brahmin."

The Ramayana, 'The Life Story of Rama', is revered by all Hindus and one of its introductory verses assures the faithful that he who reads and repeats "the holy, life-giving Ramayana is liberated from all sin and attains heaven".

In this sacred book when the hero Rama returns victorious to Ayodhya after sacking Sri Lanka and establishes Ram-rajya, the ideal Hindu state ruled by Rama where peace prevails, he is approached by a Brahmin carrying his dead son. The Brahmin is reproachful. He claims that a great sin has been committed in the kingdom and that is why his son has died. A sage tells the king that it is obvious that some low caste Shudra is studying the Vedas. Rama goes in search of the culprit who has dared to commit such a crime. In a distant hermitage he discovers Shambuk, a Shudra, who has been studying the scriptures. The Shudra does not attempt to deny his crime. The infuriated Rama slays Shambuk for breaking the laws of caste and the people of Ayodhya sing the praises of their just king.

Ironically, in modem times, Gandhi always advocated the establishment of Ram-rajya in India. He must, surely, have known of Shambuk's fate. He renamed the Untouchables and called them 'Harijans', beloved children of God. Gandhi was a Vaishya, the third tier of the Hindu hierarchy who were denied the sacred thread and not regarded favourably by the two upper tiers. However, he was fervently convinced that the caste system was the very bedrock of Hinduism but that it had to be tidied up; and one of his urgent tidying up exercises was his crusade to rid Hinduism of the iniquity of Untouchability.

Gandhi believed that a man could not change his caste merely by changing his occupation. He dismissed the claims of Hindu thinkers and missionaries that caste was merely a convenient method of dividing labour and, therefore, at a particular time in India's long history, made economic sense. He wrote: "... disregard of the law of heredity will create confusion of caste ... varna is intimately, if not indissolubly, connected with birth."

The Gandhian view was actually supported by commentators such as Sir George Birdwood who maintained that: "So long as the Hindus hold to the caste system, India will be India." This says all that has to be said of the west's India lovers who do not have to endure the inhumanities of a system that has emasculated millions upon millions of India's inhabitants for centuries.

The Mahabharat, the epic which contains the Gita, gives an account which exemplifies the strength of caste beliefs. Drona, the great Brahmin *acharya* (teacher) realised that a Shudra named Eklavya was a far better archer than even the Kshatriya hero Arjun. This was clearly unacceptable to the teacher. Drona, therefore, told Eklavya to sever his thumb and present it to him as a *guru-dakshina*, gift to the guru. The Shudra, who also accepted the divine validity of the caste system, did as Drona demanded, thus obediently sacrificing his unique ability.

The question that Hinduism always had to contend with was the following: Where in the caste set-up were all the foreigners and invaders to be accommodated? As a general rule the priests among the invaders were accepted as Brahmins, the warriors became Kshatriyas and so on. Those who could not, or would not, be accepted became *mlechh* (uncivilised and unclean foreigners). Those with unusual fighting abilities were quickly given high-sounding caste names and divine genealogies by the Brahmins. An example is the case of the Rajputs. They came late to the subcontinental scene and were descended from Central Asian tribes though some seem to have intermingled with the warlike forest dwellers of Madhya Pradesh in central India. The Brahmins quickly installed the Rajputs as superior Kshatriyas with Solar and Lunar lineages. Their dynasties and clans became the custodians of Hinduism against the onslaughts of Islam though they later became the staunchest supporters of Akbar, the Great Mughal. And even when some of them converted to Islam they tenaciously held on to their caste names and Hindu titles.

The caste system was always inflexible in spite of what some writers try to maintain. Power and wealth could, of course, always tip the scales and make a difference. Shudras (though not Untouchables) could rise in status though they were never allowed to forget the fact of their low caste. It has already been mentioned, in a previous chapter, that during the time of Alexander's invasion, the Nanda kings of eastern India were most probably Shudras. It is believed that Valmiki, the poet of the Ramayana, was not only of an Untouchable but also a brigand. This is the reason why in India many colonies (*bustees*) of Untouchables, mainly scavengers and latrine cleaners, are called Balmikinagars (Valmiki towns). The 'v' in the demotic and in Bengali becomes a 'b'.

Several of the Maratha rulers were also low born: the Holkar of Indore's ancestors were goatherds, the Scindia of Gwalior was descended from a menial servant, the Gaikwar of Baroda's ancestors were cowherds. The founders of these dynasties must have been extremely remarkable men but their descendants were ever reminded of their origins. This is the problem with caste; rather than being praised for their ability, those who rise successfully from the lower castes are humiliated in subtle, and not so subtle, ways. Ability and achievement are darkened by the shadow of low birth.

Many years ago, I knew the son of a well known Brahmin family of Indore whose members occupied high positions at the then Holkar's court. My friend told me, not without some pride, that though his family were loyal to the Holkar they would certainly never eat at his table. Wouldn't it be an honour, I asked, to have dinner with the Maharajah? Certainly not. He was, after all, a Shudra.

Shivaji is the most outstanding figure in Maratha history and yet the Brahmins caused him endless problems when he asked them to perform the rituals for his coronation. They contended that as he, the man who had mauled the mighty Mughals, was a Shudra he had no right to kingship. There was much wrangling and consultation with shastraic scholars. Eventually, Pandit Gaga Bhatt, a famous authority on the scriptures was bribed and he dutifully worked out that Shivaji was actually a Rajput of the Sisodia clan and hence a Kshatriya. First, however, the Hindu hero had to be invested with the *jane'u*, the sacred thread that only Brahmins and Kshatriyas are permitted to wear. Only after this ceremony was performed, was Shivaji installed on the *gaddhi*, the Hindu equivalent of the Muslim *takht* (throne).

At the height of Nehru's socialist and secular experiments in India a few Shudras and even Untouchables were recruited into the Indian Administrative Service, the successor to the erstwhile Indian Civil Service. It is interesting to note that even Nehru could not detect the oddity that when Indians assumed power they were 'administrators' whereas the British were content to be 'civil servants'. A presentable young man (an Untouchable but in Gandhi's anodyne terminology a 'Harijan') came to Simla – now Shimla – as Deputy Commissioner. As head of the district he had immense power, but he did nothing, he played safe, he didn't want to offend anyone. If anything went wrong, and his high caste assistants would make sure that something did, he would be blamed. On his way to the office every morning and on his way back in the evening he would have to go past Scandal Point, the central hub of the town. Here, the policeman on duty was expected to salute the Deputy Commissioner and it became a subject of Simla gossip that the town's policemen always had an excuse for not being on duty at Scandal Point at nine in the morning and five-thirty in the evening. In those days no Untouchables were recruited as policemen. One could not fail to see the strain and the deep feeling of failure on the Deputy Commissioner's face.

On the Mall, the town's promenade, members of Simla's high society could be heard to say: "This is what independence has brought us, a *choora* (lavatory cleaner) now heads this district." And in a fit of Raj nostalgia the prince of a tiny hill state, a Rajput, would chip in: "The British used to send their best men to rule this country. Now it's come to this. From British Raj we've descended to Bhungi (sweeper caste) Raj!"

The chief architect of the constitution of India was Ambedkar, an Untouchable, who had campaigned for his people even during British rule. A man of immense intellect and learning he was also practical and down to earth. Knowing full well that the caste system had suppressed his people spiritually and materially for centuries, Ambedkar wanted separate electorates for the Untouchables just as the other minorities had during British rule. Gandhi, however, wanted to keep the Untouchables within what he called the "benevolent Hindu fold". He believed that the fabric of Hindu society would be torn asunder if the Untouchables were allowed to drift away.

Gandhi was also acutely aware of the mathematics; if the Untouchables were permitted to leave, the Hindu majority would be reduced by about 50 million. The bargaining position of his Hindu majority Congress Party would thus be considerably diminished. This did not augur well for the future especially when the Congress claimed to represent all Indians irrespective of caste or creed. At the same time Jinnah's Muslim League was gaining strength as it claimed to represent all the Muslims of India. In such circumstances Gandhi could not allow the Untouchables to move away from Hinduism – or be classed as non-Hindus – and he was prepared to pay the price.

In 1932, the British Prime Minister, Ramsay MacDonald, announced the Communal Award which gave all minorities the right to elect their own representatives to the various legislatures. The Untouchables (officially the Depressed Classes) were also given the same right. This meant that the British had recognised the Untouchables as a minority distinct from the corpus of Hinduism.

In order to persuade his opponents to his way of thinking, Gandhi went on a hunger strike which he declared would continue unto death unless the Award was changed. Ambedkar called Gandhi's fast a "political stunt". Later, under pressure from influential leaders such as Malaviya, Ambedkar came to an agreement with Gandhi. This was the infamous Poona Pact. The end result was that in theory the Untouchables agreed to be classed as Hindus but in practice they were given some seats that should have gone to caste Hindus. This was the price that Gandhi paid. In reality it meant that the Untouchables had been handsomely bribed to stay within the Hindu fold.

Some hailed the Mahatma ('Great Soul') as the saviour of Hinduism while others, mainly Brahmins, called him Mahabhungi ('Great scavenger'). Ambedkar escaped abuse. Had he stuck to his guns, Gandhi might have died from his self-inflicted starvation. In which case Ambedkar would have been reviled throughout India as 'that Untouchable who murdered the Mahatma.'

The Mahatma was murdered. Not by an Untouchable and not by a Muslim, but by a Brahmin.

Nehru appointed Ambedkar independent India's first minister of law. He was also the driving force behind the new republic's constitution. This was, no doubt, well thought out as a timely corrective since several centuries ago it was the Brahmins who had framed the repressive Laws of Manu. Ambedkar once said: "The Hindus wanted an epic, and they sent for Valmiki who was an Untouchable. The Hindus wanted a Constitution, and they sent for me."

The new laws ushered in an era of positive discrimination in favour of all those who had been disadvantaged on account of their low-caste or Untouchable origins. But there soon began vociferous complaints from upper caste Hindus. They complained that it was now they who were being ill treated and persecuted. They took to the streets. When V.P. Singh was prime minister there were instances of upper caste Hindus soaking themselves in kerosene and burning themselves to death to protest against government policy. In Uttar Pradesh and Bihar there were, and still are, bloody caste wars. The facts about Phoolan Devi, the low caste 'Bandit Queen', are too well known to recount here.

The Untouchables have tasted blood. They now know that no bolt from heaven will smite them down should they kill a Brahmin or shoot a high caste landlord. They have thrown overboard the patronising term Harijan and call themselves Dalits ('members of an army or organised group'). This has given them an acute sense of unity, solidarity and awareness. Some, like the Dalit Panthers, have become experts in assassination and Nazi-type bullying tactics.

Little did the constitutionalist Ambedkar know that his people would take this path. At the end of his life he converted to Buddhism saying that he was escaping from the hell of Hinduism. About Gandhi himself he was sceptical: "Mahatmas have come and Mahatmas have gone, but the Untouchables have remained Untouchables."

Ambedkar advised all Untouchables and Shudras to follow his example and become Buddhists. Many did but the stigma remained. Today in India when a man says he is a Buddhist it is taken to mean that he is of low caste, possibly even an Untouchable. Gandhi's base treatment by the whites in South Africa was as nothing when compared to Ambedkar's daily humiliations at the hands of high caste Hindus in India.

The influence of the caste system has extended beyond Hinduism to the Christians (about 2.5 percent of the population) and the Sikhs (slightly less than 2 percent). Both religions claim to be based on the highest principles of mutual respect and brotherhood, but an examination of these minorities will give some clue to the Indian way of thinking and attitudes to caste.

Many Indian Christians believe that Saint Thomas, the apostle Doubting Thomas of the Gospels, brought the Christian message to India almost 2000 years ago. There are in the south-west Indian state of Kerala many 'Saint Thomas Christians' or 'Syrian Christians'. They have an ancient liturgy and certainly belong to a very old tradition of Christianity. In their services can be heard Aramaic, the language that Jesus spoke. Their church is undoubtedly older than the Roman church. These Christians like to believe that Thomas baptised only Brahmins. Hence, Syrian Christians regard themselves as well above their 'brother' Christians.

When the Portuguese arrived they were surprised to see Christians already living in India. But these Christians did not recognise the Pope as the supreme pontiff and so the Portuguese took it upon themselves to persecute the heretics. They also converted many low caste Hindus to their particular brand of Christianity which was Roman Catholicism. Hence, Roman Catholicism in south India became synonymous with low caste. But here also there are wheels within wheels. The Mangalorean Catholics, many of whom have Portuguese ancestry and are quite fair complexioned, regard themselves as 'Brahmin Christians'. This term is also used in Goa where 'Brahmin Christian' families still tend to marry within their own community.

A Roman Catholic priest, Father Desouza, once informed me quite casually: "Well you see, I come from a family of Brahmin Christians". Such is the consciousness of caste that even today in south India there are some churches where 'Dalit Christians' are not welcome. Not long ago it became a matter of much public and press comment when it was announced that a Dalit had been appointed an archbishop of the Roman Church. It is not surprising, therefore, that Dalit Christians are now finding common cause with other Dalits.

In Bengal and north India, Christian families who were converted from the upper castes always proclaim the fact. They do not wish to be mistaken for low caste converts. This, of course, defeats the whole idea of becoming a Christian in the first place. But the Christians of India cannot see it that way. The concept of caste is inexorable. And so the Eric Ajit Chatterjis, Kenneth Kumar Shuklas and Malcolm Malaviyas still flaunt their Brahmin caste surnames.

Many scavengers, Untouchables, converted to Christianity attracted by the obvious advantages. They were, to use the term much used by Hindu fundamentalists, 'rice bowl Christians'. Their children were decently fed, clothed and given free education in Christian schools and colleges. The youngsters usually worked hard and took advantage of the facilities they were offered. Full marks to them. University education being the key to progress, many did well and got good jobs.

Now, with notions of Hindutva (consciousness of a new Hindu identity) so widespread and heady there is a strong movement in India to bring the converts back into the embrace of Hinduism. A case in point is that of an Untouchable whose parents had become Christians and who had a doctorate in philosophy. But in Hindu India it is not natural for an Untouchable, professing no matter what religion, to become a teacher, a repository of knowledge and a Guru. The philosophy lecturer was, therefore, approached by Hindu groups and was told that the past was to be forgotten; bygones were bygones, and he was most welcome to return to the Hindu fold should he wish to do so. He had made it up the economic ladder; now he could make it up the caste ladder as well. Also, there were career prospects and promotions to be considered and there was much mileage in a 'Christian intellectual' returning to his 'mother religion'.

At a public ceremony, with the press and television covering the event, saffron clad holy men washed the feet of the lecturer and begged his forgiveness for the iniquity of Untouchability. The washing of feet was an effective piece of drama following as it did the example of Jesus. The doctor of philosophy was taken back to the bosom of Hinduism. And since he was a highly educated man, he was instantly made a Brahmin.

Gandhi, the Father of the Nation, would certainly not have considered him a Brahmin. And neither, for that matter, would the Eric Ajit Chatterjis, the Kenneth Kumar Shuklas or the Malcolm Malaviyas. However, when the learned young philosopher decides to take a wife, I wait to hear which Brahmin family gives him their daughter.

Nehru's special assistant was a Christian from Kerala named Mathai. This is what he wrote about his mother: "Despite almost 2000 years of Christianity behind her, she practised Untouchability with as much conviction as Pandit Madan Mohan Malaviya. She would not allow a Harijan to draw water from our well in summer when water was generally scarce. She would rush for a bath if an Untouchable came within twenty feet of her."

Mathai, I get the distinct impression, did not pen this in shame or sorrow but rather as a matter of some pride. He related the above to Ambedkar and his message to the great man was: "Don't take me for an Untouchable Christian! I'm a Brahmin".

The Malaviya that Mathai refers to was an important figure in the independence movement, a famous enlightened educationist and a leading light of the secular Congress party. It was he who persuaded Ambedkar to sign the Poona Pact. Malaviya publicly practised Untouchability and even disliked sharing a railway compartment with Muslims and Christians. When Benaras Hindu University disallowed a girl student from taking a course in Vedic studies on the grounds that she was not a Brahmin, Malaviya did not utter a word. He would certainly have disapproved of Mayawati, a Dalit woman, becoming Chief Minister of his home state Uttar Pradesh.

Nanak, the founder of the Sikh religion, was a Punjabi Hindu. He was born in 1469 in a village about forty miles from Lahore into a family of Bedis (those who studied the Vedas). Much influenced by Muslim *sufis* and Hindu *bhagats*, he preached peace and tolerance and made a genuine attempt to combine the best elements of Hinduism and Islam. His first disciple was Mardana, a Muslim minstrel who followed him faithfully all over the subcontinent. Nanak's teachings made a great impression on both Hindus and Muslims and the Mughal emperor Akbar visited Amar Das and Arjan Dev, the third and fifth Gurus respectively, to pay his respects.

Much later Prince Dara Shikoh, the eldest son of the emperor Shah Jehan, visited Har Rai, the seventh Guru. Dara Shikoh and two of his brothers were put to death by their fourth brother Aurangzeb who, after he had seized the throne, began perpetrating the worst atrocities on the Hindus of the empire. It was during Aurangzeb's reign that the Sikhs became a martial people.

The tragedy of India is that even a forward looking, modern religion like Sikhism (in which *langar*, communal eating, is an important feature) could not rid itself of the curse of casteism. From its earliest days there was consciousness of caste with Bedis, Sodhis (the last six Gurus were Sodhis), Ramgarhias, and several others jostling each other. In 1699, Gobind, the tenth and last Guru, initiated the Khalsa ('the society of the pure') regardless of caste or class. Every Sikh male was elevated to the status of 'Singh' (Lion) and every Sikh female became a 'Kaur' (Princess).

However, the sheer weight and historicity of Hinduism had the last word because, after all, most Sikhs were originally Hindus. There was a time when it was considered obligatory for the eldest sons of Punjabi Kshatriya families to be 'given up' to Sikhism. There was always inter-marriage with Hindus and many Sikhs retained their original Hindu caste names.

Tegh Bahadur, the ninth Guru, was summoned to Delhi by Aurangzeb and ordered to renounce his faith. The Guru refused and was executed in Chandni Chowk, the main square of the old city. So terrified were the assembled people that no one, not even his faithful Sikh followers, would come forward to claim the saint's body. It was three Untouchables who stepped forward reverently and carried away the corpse. Gobind Singh, the tenth Guru who was Tegh Bahadur's son, thereupon welcomed the three Untouchables and their descendants into the brotherhood of Sikhism.

Unfortunately, those Untouchables who later converted to Sikhism in the hope that they would achieve status and equality in a free society were to be disappointed. They were labelled 'Mazhabi Sikhs', that is 'Sikhs by Religion', a euphemism for 'Untouchable'. They worshipped in their own temples and married amongst their own kind. Today, even in England, there are Mazhabi Sikh temples. Significantly, most of the discrimination directed against them comes from the Sikh Jats, the cultivator caste who are, in fact, Shudras.

The infantry regiments of the Indian Army, since Raj times and even after the proclamation of a sovereign, socialist, secular and democratic republic, were based on the principle of caste and race. So far as the Sikhs were concerned, the Sikh Regiment was recruited from among Sikh Jats. The Sikh Light Infantry, on the other hand, was composed of Mazhabi Sikhs. There was no question of Sikh Jats and Mazhabi Sikhs sharing the same barracks let alone eating together. Incidentally, Gandhi himself strongly disapproved of inter-caste dining or marriage. He said that the notion of inter-caste dining was a strange, foreign idea imported from the west.

Among the Rajputs, however, the situation was slightly different. In the Rajputana Rifles ('Rajrifs') there could be a mixed battalion with, for example, three companies of Hindu Rajputs and a company of 'Mian' (Muslim) Rajputs known as Ranghars. The companies, needless to say, had their own messing and barrack room arrangements.

The ancestors of the vast majority of subcontinental Muslims were converts from Hinduism. There were, without doubt, those who were forcibly converted but many accepted Islam happily and willingly. Islam offered self-respect, equality and brotherhood to millions of low caste Hindus, particularly in eastern India and Bengal. The missionary work and the selfless example of the Sufis has not yet been fully appreciated. On conversion, however, the poor neo-convert though now equal with his Muslim rulers in the eyes of Allah in heaven, did not rise automatically, socially or economically, on Allah's earth. The Muslim ruling classes, whether of Arab, Turkish, Persian, Afghan, or Mughal origin, always kept the dark skinned Hindustani Mussalman in his place.

The white Muslim aristocracy, who were of foreign origin, lived and operated in Hindustan within their own elite society. Firstly, they were the rulers and had absolute power over millions of *kaafirs*, non-believers; secondly, they believed that their religion was superior in every way to any of the world's religions, past, present or future. Hinduism, with its idol worship, castes, food taboos and Brahmin dominated exploitative society, they regarded with particular contempt. The Muslims were the only rulers of India thus far who had no intention of being Hinduised like, for example, the Scythians or the Kushans. In fact, they felt that they had brought the light of civilisation to India.

To this day the Turks, Arabs, Persians and even Afghans openly display a haughty and superior attitude towards all Indians, Pakistanis and Bangladeshis. They have not forgotten that even before the British they were the rulers and the top dogs of south Asia. So far as Turks, Arabs, Persians and Afghans are concerned all south Asians, irrespective of their religious affiliations, are somewhat inferior people. This is because Hindustan was once ruled by them, the Muslims.

Just after the creation of Pakistan in 1947, many Pakistanis went to work in the Middle East (the more accurate term is West Asia) as they thought that their Muslim religion would endear them to their Arab employers. They were disappointed. Not only were they badly treated by their Arab masters but what offended them most of all was that their Arab bosses referred to them as 'Hindi'. That cut them to the quick.

The United Arab Emirates does not grant citizenship to foreigners even though they may be Muslim. This means that no Pakistani or Indian Muslim can become a citizen of the UAE. So much for 'Islamic Brotherhood'. However, it seems that a Hindu family, originally from Sindh, are citizens of the UAE. Many years ago, before the creation of Pakistan and before the Arabs were rich and power drunk with oil wealth, a Hindu merchant from Karachi had been kind to the Sheikh of Abu Dhabi. As a token of gratitude the *kaafir* had been granted citizenship.

Apparently, the Arabs have pay scales depending on race. A white nurse, for example, from the USA or Britain is paid much more than a nurse, with equal qualifications, of Indian, Pakistani, or Bangladeshi origin. This applies to doctors and engineers and others right across the professional spectrum.

If this happened in Britain or the USA there would be cries of "Islamophobia!" and "Racist and religious discrimination against Muslims!". And yet no British Muslim (or Pakistani, Indian, Bangladeshi or Sri Lankan Muslim for that matter) has dared to raise his voice against the Arabs. Why? They have a deep-seated inferiority complex (the Prophet of Islam was an Arab) and they do not wish to get on the wrong side of their 'Arab brothers'.

Hindus, Christians and Sikhs from India who go to work in Arab countries have the further disadvantage of belonging to the wrong religion. A Brahmin surgeon of my acquaintance, with British qualifications, was not only paid less than his white British colleagues but he and his family had to make sure that they took no tokens of their religion with them – no copy of the Gita, no pictures of Hindu gods and goddesses and certainly no idols.

Yet the government of India, which proclaims its secular policies so loudly, does nothing about this blatant racial and religious discrimination against its citizens. India's foreign policy in this respect coincides neatly with that of its Islamic neighbour Pakistan. And so, though India and Pakistan are prepared to wage war against each other, neither is prepared even to point a finger at the Arabs. In fact, they compete with each other in an effort to keep the Arabs happy. The state visit of Abdullah, Custodian of the Holy Places of Islam and King of Saudi Arabia, to India and Pakistan showed up the moral bankruptcy of South Asia. The governments of both India and Pakistan were eager to ingratiate themselves with the Arab monarch. However, when Abdullah made the useful suggestion that India be given observer status at the Organisation of Islamic Countries, on the basis that there are more Muslims in India than there are in Pakistan, there was an uproar in Pakistan. But it was an uproar marvellously tempered with expedient sobriety. No India haters marched to demonstrate in front of the Saudi Embassy in Islamabad.

But back to history. The majority of Indian Muslims have lived side by side with Hindus for centuries. Those who had been converted from the upper castes retained their caste names so as to distinguish themselves from low caste converts. And so Muslim Rajputs, even in Pakistan, use surnames such as Chauhan, Rajput, Janjua and Bhatti. Some even sport Hindu titles such as Raja, Rana and Rao. In western India, many Muslim Memons and Bohras, who were originally Brahmins, retain a number of Brahmin practices. A Muslim sect, the Atharavadis, use the caste mark on their foreheads and do not have their sons circumcised. Those Brahmins who became Shia Muslims proudly call themselves Hussaini Brahmins. In Uttar Pradesh, the high caste Muslims are known as Ashrafs and they include Mughals, Syeds and Pathans. The list is long.

In their beliefs and caste rituals, millions of Muslims in the countryside have been influenced by Hinduism. Here are only a few examples. The Memons in the Kutch region of Gujarat always get a Saraswati Brahmin to name their new born children. Many Muslim peasants in West Bengal and Bangladesh offer prayers to both Allah and Kali. I know of a well known family of Muslim musicians who originally came from east Bengal (now Bangladesh) who offer sacrifices to Kali as well as offering their *namaz* (Muslim prayers). The Meos of Haryana do not eat pork and neither do they eat cow's meat. The Urdu-speaking Sahib Muslims of Tamil Nadu do not marry low caste Tamil-speaking Muslims such as the Lebbais. The Moplahs of Kerala have adopted many Hindu superstitions. In no Islamic country does there exist the South Asian Muslim practise of lighting *deevas* (oil lamps) on graves.

It should, therefore, come as no surprise that the original Muslims of West Asia regard south Asia's Muslims with not a little suspicion.

In the Urdu language, the abusive term *badh-zaat* is often used. It means bad or low caste. This only goes to show how pernicious has been the influence of caste on the Muslims of South Asia.

The British learnt to their cost, and this was in the 19th century when Britain was the most powerful world power, that none dare tinker or play games with caste in India. In Vellore, south India, in 1806 there was a bloody mutiny of the sepoys (Indian, then termed 'native', soldiers) because, among other injunctions, an unthinking commander had passed an order which forbade the wearing of caste marks. In 1824, at Barrackpore, a regiment of sepoys mutinied because they were ordered to take ship and join the British assault on Burma. Many upper caste Hindus believed that they would lose caste if they crossed the seas. And then, of course, the uprising of 1857 was sparked off by the issue of a new type of cartridge to the sepoys. The cartridge had to be ripped open with the teeth before the gunpowder was poured into the rifle barrel. It was rumoured, and with good reason, that the cartridge cover had been made waterproof with a mixture of cow and pig fat. This fraud, it was claimed, was being perpetrated by the British so that Hindus would lose caste and the Muslims would be thoroughly polluted. And thus the sepoys would have no option but to convert to Christianity.

Matters came to a head in 1857 but discontent had been simmering among the sepoy ranks for a long time. British officers, especially those who had come out fresh-faced from England, were insensitive to Indian caste consciousness. For instance, it was asking for trouble to reprimand a Brahmin or Rajput in the presence of low caste sepoys. Losing face in South Asia is tantamount to death. And it was playing with fire to call a Muslim sepoy a "filthy pig" or a *"sur ka bucha"* ("son of a pig").

The British, undoubtedly with the best intentions, sought to cleanse and civilise India. There was Bentinck's war on the thugs who, in the name of the goddess Kali, murdered travellers. In 1829, he banned the practise of *sati* and made it a crime of murder. Many caste Hindus held *sati* up to be a glorious institution. They quoted the Skanda-purana in which the goddess Sati ('true wife') had burnt herself to death, thus setting an example to all true and pure Hindu wives. It was widely believed that a woman could do nothing nobler than die with her Pati-dev ('Husband-god').

A few Hindu widows did voluntarily commit self-immolation on the funeral pyres of their dead husbands. Most, however, were either forced or blackmailed by their relatives to the burning *ghats* (cremation sites near river banks) or were tied down to the pyres with ropes. There are horrifying accounts of the wailings and loud cries of widows being burnt to death by the banks of the Hooghly near Calcutta.

Bentinck also took measures against infanticide. In 1850, a law was passed which permitted a son who had changed his religion to inherit his father's property. This was seen as a British ploy to encourage Indians to convert to Christianity. It is significant that the Hindu Widows Remarriage Act came into effect only a year before the 1857 uprising. Thus far, a Hindu widow could not contemplate marriage; her lot was an unhappy one and the higher her caste the more hellish was her life. In India even today, especially in the rural areas, a Hindu widow has insignificant status.

Orthodox Hindus, with the exception of a few such as Ram Mohan Roy, believed that the British reforms were an organised attempt by a 'crusading' Christian power to destroy the very foundations of Hindu society.

Most people do not know that amongst themselves the British too operated a caste system in India. Like the caste system of the Hindus it was based unashamedly on theories of racial superiority. The uppermost caste consisted of WASPS (White Anglo Saxon Protestants). There was a multiplicity of layers and sub-layers dependent upon their original status back home in Britain, their background and connections, their education and that touchstone of British caste, namely accent.

The Muslims had *badh-zaat* and the British coined a term with the same meaning. It was *chee-chee* which in Hindi means human excrement. The term was used to describe Eurasians, then known by the derogatory term 'half-castes'. This was the community that the common British soldiery (often Scots, Irish and Welsh) had fathered when they slept with Indian women who were usually Untouchables. It was much later, in the early 20th century, that Eurasians began to be called Anglo-Indians.

The original Anglo-Indians were a small community of white British families who had lived in India for generations. Few of them had ever seen what they liked to call 'home' (Britain) and, with Indian independence in 1947, many of them left for Rhodesia (now Zimbabwe), South Africa, and Kenya where they could continue their accustomed lifestyle with servants, clubs, ballroom dancing and cocktail parties. In the post-war period, Britain still had rationing, there was hardly any central heating and there were no domestic servants. Hence, few Anglo-Indians made for 'home'; those who foolishly did, soon moved to warmer climes. Many eagerly migrated to Australia since at that time Australia allowed in only white immigrants under its 'White Australia' policy.

It is worth observing here that the *nouveau riche* of India, Pakistan and, to some extent, Bangladesh, have stepped into the Anglo-Indians' shoes with the greatest alacrity. The Brown Sahibs of India, particularly, are religiously adhering to Anglo-Indian culture. Members of this new caste are happier speaking English and pay mere lip service to the slogans of fundamentalist Hinduism which are now fashionable and politically correct such as the use of an increasingly Sanskritised Hindi language, the absolute sanctity of ancient mythology now presented as history, herbal curatives and vegetarianism, etcetera. In reality they worship only one god: money. Hence it can be claimed with some justification and not without a touch of sarcasm that the modern Hindu is now, verily, a monotheist.

What has been called the Indian Renaissance would never have happened if India had not been exposed, on account of British rule, to Western value systems which were, to a large extent, founded on Christian idealism and nourished by ideas of the 18th century European Enlightenment. Hence, though British imperialism-capitalism looted India mercilessly, the British, in spite of themselves, were obliged to permit notions such as the Rights of Man, the Rule of Law, humanity, justice and representative government to filter down to their Indian subjects. The English language, which was introduced to facilitate the imperial agenda and the governance of India, became a channel for the inflow of intellectual invigoration. It is only by allowing this to happen that the imperialists could justify to themselves their presence on Indian soil.

The earnest declarations of the earliest Indian reformers, mostly high caste Hindus, on the marvellous benefits of British rule to the people of India are both revealing and, frankly, sickening. The British may have inadvertently opened the eyes of the upper castes but the vast majority of the masses were exploited as never before.

Ram Mohan Roy, widely accepted as the Father of the Indian Renaissance, was greatly influenced by Islamic monotheism and Christian social values. His Brahmo Samaj movement was a worthy attempt to cleanse Hinduism of polytheism, idol worship and superstition. He saw that some of the best educated Brahmin families of Bengal, such as the family of the poet Michael Madhusudan Dutt, were converting to Christianity in droves and that the fault lay primarily with Hindu decadence. With like-minded friends such as Dwarkanath Tagore, the poet Tagore's grandfather, Roy sought to cleanse Hinduism in order to stem the drift to Christianity. He could not and, in fact, did not wish to upset the Brahminic applecart too much. And so, though Brahmo Samaj meetings involved no offerings to idols, the services were conducted by Brahmins. Suitable arrangements were made to keep the prayers and chants pure and untainted. In other words, they made sure that the prayers and chants were not polluted by entering the ears of Shudras and Untouchables.

In 1830, Roy, who was proficient in Persian, Sanskrit, Arabic, Bengali, Urdu and English, went to London as ambassador of the Mughal emperor Akbar II to make representations against the East India Company. Before he set sail he underwent all the Brahminic rituals that were prescribed for high caste Hindus before they crossed the oceans to the lands of the *mlechh* (the unclean). He took two Brahmin cooks with him so that the food he ate in England was untainted; for by the mere act of touching the utensils a non-Brahmin would have polluted the great man. And yet this same man appealed for educated Englishmen to be brought to India in large numbers so that his countrymen could benefit from the fruits of European learning, science and culture.

The Brahmo Samaj, started with the best intentions and the highest motives, floundered on the caste question which came to the fore when Keshub Chandra Sen, a non-Brahmin, came to head the movement. He wanted the officiating priests to rid themselves of their sacred threads which proclaimed their high priestly caste. There was heated controversy and the movement split into two factions along caste lines: Brahmins and non-Brahmins. The Sen faction was accused of becoming not only non-Hindu but anti-Hindu.

For many years Sen, like other Hindu reformers, had campaigned against child marriage and yet, when the opportunity arose, he married his daughter, a minor, to the prince of Cooch-Behar. When confronted about this he said that he had received an *adesha* (order or message) from God himself which sanctioned the marriage. This *adesha*, which many thought was suspiciously timely, caused yet another split in the movement. Not only did Sen lose all credibility but the Brahmo Samaj itself was ridiculed.

Other outstanding Hindu reformers were Swami Dayanand and Swami Vivekananda both of whom espoused 'Hindutva', a return to pristine Hindu values. The former crusaded for a purer, nobler Hinduism and in 1875 started the Arya Samaj (Aryan Society) sect in north India. Swami Dayanand claimed to be a social and religious reformer and yet he constantly referred to the Manu-smriti. He also initiated the Shuddhi movement which aimed to bring back to a renewed Hinduism all those who had unwittingly strayed away or had been enticed to Islam and Christianity.

Swami Vivekananda, a disciple of the saintly Ramakrishna, was an inspired revivalist who made a great impression at the World Parliament of Religions held in Chicago in 1893. He spoke vehemently against both Christianity and Islam. Whereas, he said, "Christianity wins its prosperity by cutting the throats of its fellow men ... today the Muslim sword is carrying destruction into India". Hinduism, on the other hand, he said was "based on the laws of love". In Hinduism, said Vivekananda, the word "intolerance" was nowhere to be found. He established centres abroad for the study of Hindu culture and philosophy. Many of his acolytes and supporters were foreigners.

However, in spite of their zeal, neither Swami Dayanand nor Swami Vivekananda thought it prudent or even necessary to consider surgery on the cancer at the core – namely, caste. In fact, both revivalists, like Gandhi after them, fully accepted the conventions of caste.

In recent post-independence years, Dalits have been converting to Christianity and Islam in increasing numbers. This has triggered violent reaction from the proponents of Hindutva who believe that these 'non-Indic' faiths are disrupting Hinduism (read caste) thus causing, according to them, social upheaval and unrest. The paranoia is that, on conversion, the Dalits will acquire ideas above their station. Christian missionaries, doctors, teachers and nurses (now overwhelmingly Indian) who work among the most disadvantaged sections of the population such as the Adivasis, are often harassed and beaten up by right-wing Hindu groups led by the well organised Sangh Parivar and the Vishwa Hindu Parishad. The burning of churches in secular India is not unknown. However, it must be said at this point that the position in Islamic Pakistan is vastly worse. The persecution of Christians, many desperately poor, in Pakistan ('country of the pure') has reached alarming proportions.

In India, Christians have been accused of seducing Dalits by offers of money, jobs and free education for their children. This may well be true in certain cases but, in the end, if a man wishes to change his faith for whatever reasons – spiritual or material – it is ultimately his choice. If the religion into which he was born treated him like a human being there would be no reason for him to be 'seduced', 'bribed' or even 'tricked' into Christianity. Becoming a Christian or a Muslim does not necessarily make a Dalit a better person; it does, it cannot be argued, give him a little dignity.

The Indian constitution, no mean document by any standard, guarantees the citizen the right to practise and preach his religion. It also gives the citizen the right to change his religion. However, fine lines are now being drawn between the right to practise, the right to preach and the right to convert. Some states, such as Tamil Nadu and Gujarat, are taking determined steps to prevent free citizens from changing their religious beliefs.

A positive result of this highly charged and controversial situation is that some upper caste Hindus have realised that the inherent iniquity of the caste system is the root cause of conversion to other faiths and so some minor reforms have been initiated. A few Dalits have been trained for priesthood so that they can conduct the rituals for their fellow Dalits in the Dalit temples. However, there is no question of them being made the equal of the Brahmin priests. And, in an effort to prove that Hinduism is a religion of equality, the Shankaracharya of Kanchi (the highest dignitary of Brahminism in south India) visited a Dalit temple in November 2002.

No one has recorded or reported how many baths, penances and purification rituals the Shankaracharya had to endure after his visit to the 'Untouchables'. Even today many Brahmins in south India, especially those in rural areas, feel polluted should even the shadow of a pariah (a word from the Tamil language) fall on them.

The frustration of the Hindutva apparatchiks is vented on the Christians who are a small minority and who cannot, or will not, react with violence. After all, Jesus (known in India as 'Bhagwan Isa') taught his poor and disinherited followers to be meek and to turn the other cheek. The Muslims, whose faith does not recommend turning the other cheek, are treated very differently. Muslim missionaries and religious schools (*madrassas*) funded with Saudi money, expand their activities without any interference. The Hindutva activists are well aware that Islamic radicals have an unpleasant habit of murdering devout pilgrims in the mountains, evicting Brahmins from the Kashmir valley and bombing innocent worshippers in the holiest temples of the Hindi hinterland.

One has only to glance at the matrimonial columns of the newspapers (not only in India but even those published by and for Asians living in the UK, Canada and the USA) to see the persistent power of caste and colour. The vast majority of the advertisements specify the religion and caste required; many ask for a fair-complexioned bride. If a white man, English, American or German inserted such an offensive colour conscious advertisement he would be instantly vilified. Very few matrimonial advertisements state "C&D no bar", meaning that caste and dowry would not be taken into consideration. It is a well known fact that even today, throughout South Asia irrespective of religion, the parents of a dark skinned girl have great difficulty in finding her a suitable husband. The darker she is, the higher the dowry demanded from her parents.

Everybody knows that dowry has been banned in India and that the law stipulates severe punishment. In practise, however, it still operates as there are many diabolical ways of getting round the law.

Parents who are poor or those who have a dark skinned daughter fervently pray that some man will fall in love with her and thus take their girl – an awful embarrassment – off their hands. Indian men are so conditioned, however, that they are not attracted to dark complexioned girls; they prefer *gora rung* (a fair complexion) or *saaf rung* (a clear complexion).

Very often, if there is an 'inter-caste' marriage, 'love' marriage, or even a 'Hindu-Muslim' marriage, the young man (madly in love) never expects a dowry and that lets the parents off the hook. Among the urban middle classes if there is a 'Hindu-Muslim' marriage it is most probably a Hindu girl marrying a Muslim man. In such cases there is no question of a dowry as the parents pretend that they have already done the Muslim a great favour by 'giving' him their daughter. If they had made too much of a fuss the girl would have eloped in any case, but her parents always act as if they have been terribly hurt and have been forced to make a great sacrifice.

Needless to say, they sigh in quiet relief. Later, they happily inform their relatives and neighbours that their Muslim son-in-law is a Muslim only in name. After all, it was only by chance that he was born into a Muslim household. Since he lights fireworks during Dewali, the Hindu New Year, and eats 'Hindu' sweets he is, at heart, a Hindu. Significantly, similar comments were made about Akbar in the 16th century when the Brahmins wanted to deify the Mughal emperor. One saw the same mentality in operation with regard to the recently retired President of India who is a low born Muslim from Tamil Nadu. Since the President was a strict vegetarian and read the Gita rather than the Qur'an, many claimed that he was no ordinary Hindu; he was, they alleged, an Iyer Brahmin at heart or must surely have been one in a previous life. Hence, it was highly appropriate that he be the Rashtrapati, 'father of the nation'. Abdul Kalam is certainly a much loved and respected individual. His retirement was lamented and many wept when 'Abdul Kalam Iyer' departed from Delhi.

The same sort of thing happens when a girl falls in love with and marries an Englishman, an American or any other foreigner. It is proudly proclaimed that the foreigner is actually more Hindu than a native Hindu. Marrying a white man, apart from substantial savings to the family because of no dowry being involved, has another practical and more immediate advantage. The girl goes to live abroad and acquires, as a right, foreign nationality. The doors then open up for other members of her immediate family to travel to foreign countries and even to settle abroad.

Today, so far as the urban English-speaking middle classes of India are concerned, to marry outside one's caste or even religion no longer presents a very serious problem. The crucial concerns are salary, professional qualifications, status and career prospects. It is in this context of stark 21st century economics and urgent upward mobility that the grip of caste is beginning to loosen a little.

WOMEN

*"Like a Shudra, a woman is entitled to
only one sacrament and that is marriage."*
(Manu-smriti)

Manu, the great lawgiver of the Hindus, enunciated the fundamental text for all Hindus. Manu equates women with Shudras – the caste born with no rights. A woman's position, like that of the Shudras, was always to be one of subservience. As a girl she was under the authority of her father, as a married woman under her husband, and as a widow under her son. Indeed, her husband was her Pati-dev ('Husband-god') and had to be worshipped by a faithful wife even though he might be "destitute of virtue" or seek "pleasure elsewhere". Women, like Shudras, were not entitled to education, property or independence.

A man, according to Manu, was permitted to take as many wives as he wished. A woman was only permitted to marry once in her lifetime and hence there was no question of her marrying again should her husband decide to leave her or should he happen to die. In fact, it was believed that the wife was blameworthy if her husband died before she did. A widow, especially a young one, was regarded as evil. If she were a faithful, virtuous wife why would her Pati-dev have died?

In Mathura and Varanasi, both sacred cities, there are to this day asylums for high caste widows. In an effort to make these places respectable the asylums are called *ashrams,* hermitages. The inmates have their heads shaved and wear white *dhotis* (cheap cotton saris). They survive on a meagre diet and are expected to spend the rest of their condemned lives chanting mantras. It is an open secret that the young, attractive ones are used for other purposes – but then it is impossible to get proof. Which woman from 'a good family' is likely to go into a police station and make a complaint that she has been forced into prostitution? Moreover, the Indian police, particularly in the rural areas and small towns, are notorious for molesting girls who go to them to register complaints of rape.

Incidentally, even prostitution in India is caste based. In the brothels and shady hotels of the large cities, fair skinned girls (usually Nepalese, girls from the higher Hindu castes, Muslims and Anglo-Indians) command higher fees for their sexual favours than dark skinned prostitutes from the lower castes.

Wife beating is common in India, more so in the villages where most Indians live. However, a good Hindu wife, especially one from a 'respectable, high caste family' never talks about the beatings she receives at the hands of her husband or the sexual abuse she might have to endure from his senior male relatives. Girls from their very childhood have been taught by their mothers that family honour (*izzat*) rests primarily in the hands of the women. If a woman has to suffer then that is her fate; she must keep her mouth shut so that the honour of the family is unsullied.

The Laws of Manu sanctioned wife beating "with a rope or a split bamboo". The edict, in an effort to be even-handed, did specify that a man could mete out similar punishment to his son, his slave, his pupil and his younger brother.

Because low caste women had to go out to work in order to supplement the family income they were, in an odd way, freer than high caste women who were, until quite recently, largely house-bound. Men from the Brahmin and Kshatriya castes thought it quite natural to exercise their *droit de seigneur*. Any winsome low caste girl, married or unmarried, was fair game. Indeed, the girl herself was sometimes all too flattered that the eyes of the Panditji or the Thakur Sahib of the village had settled on her. Her husband or father, too, would be silently flattered but would pretend not to know what was afoot. However, when the time came for him to pay his rent or settle his debt, he knew that he would be generously treated.

Whenever you speak to or question an authority on Hinduism or ancient India, you will invariably be given a lecture on the great wisdom of the *rishis* (sages) and how pure and glorious was India before it was polluted by the *mlechh* Muslims and, later, the unclean Christians. You will be bombarded with quotations from the holy books to 'prove' every fantastic claim. Indians love to rely on the divine authority of age old texts.

In ancient India the birth of a female child was an unhappy event. Most Indian families even today have not changed in this regard. In the past, the killing at birth of a baby girl was a common event. The practise was most prevalent among the Rajputs. Modern technology has made murder more efficient. It is a well known fact that in the cities of India doctors and clinics in possession of scanning machines are minting money. Pregnant women have their scans done only to ascertain the sex of the child. If it's a female foetus, an abortion is arranged. In a country that proclaims non-violence, love for all creation and vegetarianism, murder most foul is being perpetrated on a massive scale. A recent report by Professor Jha's team in Toronto, based on years of research, documents that in India half a million female foetuses are aborted annually. Indian law prohibits such abortions; but abortion is still big business.

This is happening in a country where in New Delhi there would be mayhem and murder if a single stray cow, scraggy and hungry, were shooed away with a stick by a 'wicked beef-eating Muslim'. Why does Indian, specifically Hindu, society allow this to happen? It is simply because India has been conditioned over many generations to accept certain norms. And one of them is the belief that women are devious, basically untrustworthy and sexually promiscuous.

To quote from the Laws of Manu:

"Through their passion for men... through their natural heartlessness, they become disloyal towards husbands however carefully they may be guarded."

"Women do not care for beauty... they give themselves to the handsome and the ugly."

"One should not sit in a lonely place with one's mother, sister or daughter..."

"It is in the nature of women to seduce men."

Though it was accepted that nature had made women faithless (and therefore, logically, it was not their fault) the penalty for a woman guilty of adultery was extremely severe. She was to be devoured by dogs in a public place. There was no such penalty for men whom nature had made superior and endowed with multiple virtues. The sages of old were not as wise as they are made out to be.

Because the holy texts are so revered their influence is still strongly prevalent in the rural areas. A girl is considered a liability and her family home (more correctly, her father's home) is only a temporary staging post until a husband can be found for her. It is then, to the relief of her parents and family, that she is sent off to her 'own home'. However, even then it is not her home; she becomes part and parcel of her husband's extended family with, most often, her husband's father very much as the patriarchal and dictatorial head. Indeed, the daughter-in-law always covers her head in the presence of her father-in-law and never dares to look him in the eye when he addresses her. Her submission is a mark of her gratitude.

It is her father-in-law who has selected her from among the many girls he has considered for his son. He has given her a roof over her head and the respectable status of a married woman. She can now apply *sindoor* (vermilion powder) in the parting of her hair to proclaim that she is a married woman. Of course, her status in relation to the other daughters-in-law depends strictly on two factors: firstly, how much dowry she brought with her and, secondly, how many sons she will produce.

The Hindu holy books provide countless examples of women being nothing more than the property of men. In the Mahabharat the five Pandav brothers share one wife, Draupadi, which simply tells us that not only was polygamy sanctioned but polyandry as well. The eldest brother, Yudhishthira, stakes all he has in a game of dice. He even stakes Draupadi. He loses, and the wife is taken by the Kauravs, the wicked cousins of the Pandavs.

Rama, the ideal god-man and king, invaded Sri Lanka and recovered his wife, Sita, the ideal Hindu wife, from the clutches of Ravana, the demon king. During her lengthy imprisonment Sita spent her time concentrating on her husband and her marriage vows. However, when Rama repossesses Sita he begins to suspect his wife's fidelity. Later, even though she proves her chastity by undergoing an ordeal by fire, Rama banishes her.

Krishna, the god who delivered the Gita, married off his sister Subhadra with a huge dowry. The dowry included a thousand beautiful girls for the pleasure of his brother-in-law who, when he tired of any of them, had the right to gift them to his friends and favourites. The Ramayana recounts that when Rama married Sita, his father-in-law, Janak, presented him with female slaves (*dasis*). And in one of the Upanishads a king presented his daughter as a slave to his teacher in payment for the knowledge that he had received. The sage happily accepted the deal. This is cited as an example of how highly regarded was the acquisition of knowledge in India's golden age! Statements such as this come very easily to those who have made it a lucrative business touring the world, first class and five-star, singing the praises of India's past while collecting funds for well appointed centres devoted to meditation, vegetarianism, vedic studies and yoga.

According to the ancients it was essential for a man to have a son because it was only a son who could perform the final funeral rites for his dead father. One of his duties is to make sure that his father's skull has been properly shattered. On the funeral pyre, because of the flames and intense heat, the skull usually bursts open and the boiling brains spill out. But if, for whatever reason, this does not happen the son is expected to pick up a log and smash open the skull. The belief is that it is only when the skull is broken open that the soul is released. Therefore, this gruesome duty is enforced upon the eldest son who is already devastated by the death of his father.

In India's cities there are now crematoriums and cremations are both thorough and cleaner; moreover, no educated Hindu today could be coerced into smashing open his dead father's skull. However, most Hindus are not educated and these funeral rites continue unabated throughout rural India.

After assisting his father's soul to a better existence elsewhere or to eternal peace, a son is expected to assume his family responsibilities such as looking after his mother and marrying off his sisters. The second duty is the more onerous since each sister has to be provided with a suitable dowry. Many a good Hindu family has been ruined by the dowry system which still operates in devious ways even though the state and various social reformers have endeavoured to get rid of it. In short, daughters impoverish the family; sons, on the other hand, bring in dowries and are a source of wealth. Therefore, the more sons the better.

So much are sons wanted that wives are ill-treated and looked down upon if they fail to produce male progeny. It is solely the woman who is blamed, science notwithstanding, for giving birth to girls. And if, after several failed attempts, a son is eventually born there is no stopping the father and his family from spoiling him. Even his mother, sisters and aunts are guilty in this respect; they give in to the boy's wants, whims and tantrums and contribute to him becoming a conceited, self-centred and thoroughly unpleasant individual. Many a family has been ruined by such over indulged sons.

The necessity of having a male heir was paramount. The Manu-smriti advised a husband who was either impotent or could not produce a son to send his wife to a sexually active man to be impregnated. The man had to be the husband's *sapinda* (kinsman) and this permissible adultery was called *niyog*. However, it was stipulated that though the man was free to enjoy the pleasure of sexual intercourse the woman, since she was another man's wife and hence belonged to him only, must not enjoy the experience in any way. If she did, she was guilty of infidelity and no better than a harlot.

A woman's function, therefore, was primarily to be a producer of sons; her needs, feelings and desires were of no consequence. Here let me bring in Aryabhatta, the renowned Indian mathematician-astronomer of the 5th century who, quite naturally, set his pupils (all males) the task of calculating the price of a twenty-year-old female slave given that a sixteen-year-old could be bought in the open market for a specified amount. He might just as well have got them to work out the price of cows, goats, horses, cotton or grain.

The degradation of Indian women and their exploitation by men was at its worst in the temples. As late as 1927, there were 200,000 temple prostitutes in the Madras Presidency alone. This was a British-ruled province and thus a part of British India. There were many more temple prostitutes (known as *devadasis* – servants or slaves of the gods) in the south Indian princely states. In utter disgust, Gandhi wrote: "There are, I am sorry to say, many temples in our midst in this country which are no better than brothels."

Temple prostitution goes back a very long way in India and has divine sanction in the ancient texts. The worship of the sun-god, Surya, demanded the services of girls in the temples to sing and play instruments in honour of the god. Their function extended to dancing and sacred prostitution. The Padmapurana recommends that the dedication of girls to the temple of Surya is one of the surest ways of gaining Suryaloka, the heaven of the sun-god. The Chinese scholar Huien Tsang noted the large number of prostitutes in Multan's famous Surya temple.

The influence of Buddhism checked sacred prostitution and there are numerous stories in Buddhist literature of how fallen women were reclaimed to a state of grace and thenceforth led lives of asceticism. This is borne out by the existence of orders of nuns and almswomen, called Bhikshinis, instituted by the Buddha himself. However, with the reassertion of Brahminism, temple prostitution again became socially acceptable. In fact, it became thoroughly respectable for the best families to dedicate their daughters to the service of the gods. They became *devadasis* who were trained to sing and dance. *Devadasis* were an integral part of all the great temples. Not only did they sweep, clean, cook and minister to the needs of the priests but they also danced before the idols and, most importantly, the earnings from their prostitution swelled the temple coffers.

The 9th and 10th centuries saw the most glorious period of temple architecture and it was during this period that the temples of south India, still famous today, were built. The Chola king Rajaraja installed 400 *devadasis* in his temple at Thanjavur (Tanjore). They were housed in luxurious quarters and granted tax-free lands. Officially they were 'married' to the temple deity and they were thus highly regarded. This 'marriage' took many forms and varied from region to region. However, after the marriage ceremony, a Brahmin priest representing the god consummated the marriage.

As a *devadasi* was married to a god it meant that she could never be a widow, that worst possible condition for a Hindu woman. Hence, a *devadasi* was considered lucky; her presence at weddings and births was regarded as a good omen. *Devadasis* were always invited to the best houses on important occasions.

Domingo Paes, a member of the Portuguese Embassy to the southern Vijayanagar kingdom in the early 16th century, has left a vivid description of the temple prostitutes. He says that any high-born man could visit these women without censure and is wide-eyed with wonder at their wealth. ("Who can describe the treasure these women carry on their persons? ... One woman in this city is said to possess 100,000 parados... and I can believe this from what I have seen.") Methwold, an Englishman who visited the Muslim kingdom of Golconda, also in south India, during the reign of Elizabeth I, remarks that these women were invited to formal public functions as well as to "circumcisions, weddings, ships' arrivals, or private feasts ..." Since circumcisions are a particularly Muslim practice this is evidence that Muslim society also had come to accept the temple courtesans as harbingers of good luck.

Like society in general, the *devadasis* too operated a caste system amongst themselves. The *valangai* would only go with 'right-hand' (upper caste) men; the *idangai* were not selective and consorted with 'left-hand' (low caste) men. Neither would go with an Untouchable. The Malayali devadasis from Kerala considered themselves superior to the Tamil devadasis and would not even eat with them. Likewise, the temple prostitutes of Maharasthra (*murals*) and Andhra (*vasabs*) had their own conventions and customs.

In general, the offspring of the temple prostitutes had only one, very limited, choice. The daughters followed their mothers and became *devadasis*; the sons became musicians and dance conductors. However, since the children were usually fathered by Brahmin priests – though it was often impossible to identify the exact father – the sons and daughters of the *devadasis* became a caste unto themselves. They mostly took the caste name of Pillai or Mudali which, though not Brahmin names, were regarded as respectable enough for them.

Apart from the free sexual services offered by the *devadasis*, the priests were allowed other perquisites. It was an accepted practise throughout India, till quite recently, that if a husband failed to make his wife pregnant he would send her to the temple. A Brahmin would lie with her and, with luck, she would return home impregnated. The child, when born, would be considered truly God-given.

The Venkateshwara temple at Tirupati attracted Vishnu devotees from far and wide to its annual festival and pilgrims brought expensive offerings. After accepting the gifts the priests went out among the crowds and picked out the best looking women and girls. The husbands and parents were informed that the deity had honoured their wives and daughters; they had been selected for service in the temple. Indeed, the husbands and parents themselves had been blessed by the god. Whereupon the married women and girls were joyfully handed over to the priests.

When after a few years a sex slave had served her purpose and was either old or diseased she had to leave the temple. Her breasts and thighs were branded with the mark of Vishnu and she was handed a testimonial to the effect that she had been the god's wife. This testimonial would be brandished when she solicited for alms.

A Nambudri (Kerala Brahmin) could have any Nayar woman that caught his fancy. Indeed, it was the custom amongst the Nayars to present their most beautiful virgins to the Nambudris to be deflowered. Then there was an institution called *sambandam* which gave the Nambudri the right to have as many Nayar concubines as he wished. The Nayar woman lived in her own house and the Nambudri would visit her and stay overnight. He would sleep with her but, incredible though it might sound, would not eat with her. The food cooked in a Nayar's kitchen was polluted and so the Nambudri ate only food that was prepared in his own kitchen by his faithful Brahmin wife.

What, it will be asked, did the Nambudri's wife think of her husband's behaviour? She accepted it as the done thing. As a girl she had seen her father and uncles leaving at sunset for the homes of their Nayar concubines. Now her husband and brothers were doing the same and, in time, her sons would be continuing the tradition. What is perhaps shocking is that when Nambudri women gossiped amongst themselves they boasted about the number of *sambandams* that their husbands had with Nayar women.

Since the socio-economic structure was constructed by and for the Nambudris, the children of these liaisons had no claim to the Brahmin's property or caste.

Even the ruling families of the past, who were Kshatriyas, were proud to have their girls 'honoured, blessed and purified' by the Nambudris.

Thus, not only were the Kerala Brahmins the biggest landowners and the intellectual and religious elite but, because power is the ultimate aphrodisiac, they were also sexually the most predatory.

The movement for the emancipation of Indian women started with the introduction of British-style education and the efforts of the Christian missionaries. Here, mention must be made of the pioneering crusade of Pandita Ramabai, a Maharashtrian Brahmin woman who converted to Christianity. She was a scholar and a woman of impeccable character who fought the good fight for all Indian women. Today, few know her name.

Hindu reformers such as Ram Mohan Roy were also concerned about the lot of Indian women. Gandhi, while engaged in the freedom campaign, fought at the same time for the dignity of Indian womanhood. After independence, the Indian constitution and the passing of the Hindu Code Bill finally granted Hindu women equality with men. However, what is on paper does not necessarily translate into action. It is not easy to jettison a whole culture.

There is no doubt that Indian women today are in a better position than their grandmothers and great grandmothers. But the changes are mainly restricted to the urban, English-speaking middle classes. Working women have economic independence and access to the media. They demand their rights and they get them. In the villages, however, the old ways persist. Newspapers often report bride burning, the killing of female children at birth and even the occasional case of *sati* in the rural areas.

The best documented *sati* of recent years was that of the young bride Roop Kanwar in 1987. Dressed in her bridal finery she was burnt to death on her husband's funeral pyre. Roop Kanwar was eighteen. Women's groups protested but Hindu zealots hailed her death as a return to the days of India's glorious past.

The practise of demanding a dowry may have diminished but is still prevalent. Surprisingly, it persists among the newly-rich commercial and industrial classes. A multi-millionaire proves his love for his daughter by providing her with a vast dowry. Also, it is a signal to her in-laws that her father is a man of means and hence has power and influence.

The term 'bride burning' is an original Indianism. If a girl brings a dowry with her and dies the husband is free to marry again and collect another dowry. Often the husband's family is actively involved in the mysterious deaths of young brides. The girl is usually doused in kerosene oil and set on fire, almost always in the kitchen. The news is then given out that by accident her sari caught fire while she was cooking.

We have thus far considered Hindu women because they constitute the vast majority of India's female population. The position of Muslim women in South Asia presents a very different picture since Muslim society is based on Sharia or Islamic law.

The position of women is clearly stated in the Qur'an which Muslims believe to be the Word of God. Here are a few relevant verses:

"Marry women of your choice,
Two, or three, or four;
But if ye fear that ye shall not
Be able to deal justly with them
Then only one ..."

"From what is left by parents
And those nearest related
There is a share for men
And a share for women ..."

"Ye are forbidden to inherit
Women against their will.
Nor should ye treat them
With harshness ..."

"Men are the protectors
And maintainers of women ..."

"As to those women
On whose part ye fear
Disloyalty and misconduct,
Admonish them first
Next, refuse to share their beds,
And last, beat them lightly ..."

It is clear that Islam permits polygamy under certain conditions; that women have property rights and rights of inheritance; that men are expected to protect and support their womenfolk; and that it is a man's duty to discipline his wife or wives whenever necessary.

In short, though Muslim women do, in theory, get a better deal they are not by any means equal to their husbands. Muslim society is male dominated and, like traditional Judaism and Christianity till only a few generations ago, very patriarchal. The man is indisputably the head of the family but is expected to be benevolent towards the weaker vessel.

Though a man could divorce his wife comparatively easily, the woman could not though, again theoretically, she also had the right to demand a divorce. Similarly with sexual misdemeanours. In Muslim society, like Jewish society, women guilty of infidelity could be stoned to death.

A Muslim widow was encouraged to remarry and, in fact, it was considered a virtuous deed for a man to marry a widow and become her protector. This may stem from the historical fact that the first of the Prophet's many wives, Khadija, was a widow. She was, incidentally, older than him and a wealthy, successful businesswoman.

Though, as we have seen earlier, South Asian Muslim society was affected by the sheer weight of Hinduism surrounding it, Muslim women could own property and conduct business in their own right and no Muslim woman was ever prostituted in a mosque. The brothels of South Asia did, nevertheless, have their fair share of Muslim whores.

Where Muslim women have really suffered, and been at an enormous disadvantage, is in the field of education – even though Islamic apologists advocate the education of women. However, Muslim women are now beginning to fight for their rights. Asma Jehangir of Pakistan, Taslima Nasrin of Bangladesh and Ayaan Hirsi Ali from East Africa, now living in the United States, are in the vanguard of this crusade. Ali has challenged the Islamic fundamentalists. She quotes chapter and verse from the Qur'an which she believes sanctions the suppression of women, and advocates an Islamic reformation and reinterpretation in the 21st century. She is under sentence of death by Muslim fanatics. However, the problem of education has also affected Muslim men and will, therefore, be considered in a separate chapter.

The custom of the veil is often taken to be a Muslim importation into the subcontinent. This belief is only partially true. Even before the advent of Islam, upper caste Hindu women covered their heads and faces in public. It was not only a sign of modesty but a mark of distinction. And, in any case, low caste men had no right to gaze at the beauty of upper caste women. When the Muslims conquered the country they did not want the non-believers and infidels (*kaafirs*) to gaze at their womenfolk. Hence, their women took to the veil with greater dedication than, for instance, Muslim women in Iran and Turkey. The effect of this was that Hindu converts to Islam also accepted the practice. They had to keep in step with their co-religionists who also happened to be the rulers. The *burqa*, the totally enveloping, loose-fitting, tent-like garment with lacy apertures for the eyes, was certainly a Muslim invention. Hindu society never imposed the *burqa* on its women.

However, during times of Muslim hegemony, aristocratic Hindus had to prove that they were equal to the occasion. Their women, too, were sometimes made to observe the intricate protocols of *purdah*, the segregation of women and the observances of the veil. Even today women who hail from the old Rajput families always appear in public with their heads graciously covered. It is a social signal which says: We are ladies of class, of good breeding, of good family.

The millions upon millions of poor peasant women who toil in the arid fields of the subcontinent cannot afford the luxury of veils. In parts of south India the rural poverty is such that many women in the villages find it hard to cover even their breasts. In central and eastern India, the Adivasi women who have not been Hinduised or Christianised are often unconsciously and innocently bare breasted. The Adivasis, the original inhabitants of the Indian subcontinent, are the worst exploited of India's peoples. And, as always happens, it is the women who are the most exploited.

There were great women in India's past, but they were rare exceptions. It is only now, after several decades of western-type education, that Indian women are beginning to discover their potential and overtly exercise their power in substantial numbers. Pratibha Patil has recently become the first woman President of India. The women of Pakistan, however, have still a long way to go because the axis of feudal and male-dominated Muslim fundamentalist interests in that country militates against women's rights.

Sharia law imposes horrendous punishments on women and these are still carried out in many Muslim countries, notably Saudi Arabia. Muslim theologians and jurists, not only in Pakistan but elsewhere in the Muslim world as well, will sooner or later have to examine and reconsider the whole question of retribution, the position of women and the humane dispensation of justice. Islam will, in effect, have to delete the medieval mode. There are today some liberal thinkers in the Islamic world who are paying a heavy price for their perceived 'sins'. They are the true heroes and martyrs of Islam.

THE ISLAMIC IMPACT
AND HINDU REACTION

*"The Hindus became like the atoms of dust and scattered in
all directions… Their scattered remains cherish of course
the most inveterate aversion to all Muslims." (Al Biruni)*

In the early 7th century a charismatic leader emerged from among the
disorganised, warring tribes of Arabia. Muhammad, the Prophet of Islam,
'submission to the will of Allah', created a nation out of a lawless,
disparate people who were sunk in *jahalat* (ignorance and barbarism).
He proclaimed himself not only a messenger of God but declared that he
was the last of a long line that included Jesus and the prophets of the
Jews. In other words, Muslims, those who 'submit to Allah's will', believe
that Islam is the final revelation of the entire Judaic-Christian tradition.
They also believe that Jews and Christians are in serious error but they
are, nevertheless, accepted as 'People of the Book'.

The Prophet was the religious, political and military leader of the
Arabs. After him the Khalifas (Caliphs), the supreme leaders of the
Muslims, took on the same responsibilities. This means that Islam from
its very inception did not separate religion from politics. Therefore, a
Muslim, by the very nature and history of his faith, finds secularism an
uncomfortable and difficult concept. However, many Muslim states in
west Asia and India, though theocracies in theory were, in practical terms,
fairly secular. Baghdad, when the Khalifas themselves were ruling there,
was a glittering example of a forward-looking, progressive society. After
the First World War, Kemal Ataturk abolished the Khalifate and declared
Turkey a secular state. In Christian terms this was the equivalent of
abolishing the papacy and, in Hindu terms, it would mean getting rid of
the Shankaracharyas and others who make pronouncements on Dharma.

Islam is an uncompromisingly monotheistic faith as well as a social
and political philosophy. From the earliest days of Islam it became the
sacred duty of Muslims to spread their beliefs among the non-believers.
Jihad, the struggle in Allah's cause, meant many things and took several
forms: it could be a man's fight against the evil within him, it could be
conducted through words, good deeds or writing and, if necessary in
exceptional circumstances, it could be conducted by the sword. The
principle of jihad gave the new religion dynamism and a puritanical
driving force. It propagated, in effect, a condition of renewable revolution.

To give one's life for Islam was an honour; all *shaheeds* (martyrs) were promised the pleasures of paradise for all eternity.

There was also the concept of the earth being divided into Dar-ul-Islam (those parts where Islam was the prevailing religion and where, for Muslims, peace reigned) and Dar-ul-Harb (those parts where non-believers were the rulers and, hence, for Muslims, an area of strife). India, obviously, fell into the second category.

The whole Indian subcontinent at the time of Islam's birth was undergoing long periods of disunity and political rivalry as was west Asia. The Byzantine empire (in the area that is now Turkey, Syria and Israel) was Christian. The Byzantines and the Persians, whose established religion was Zoroastrianism, had bled each other with costly wars. Both were economically rich and had huge, well-trained armies, greatly experienced though somewhat jaded. The Arabs, although lacking large armies and wealth, were invigorated by a new faith and ideology, and that made the difference. The Arabs took Palestine and Syria from the Byzantines and at Qadesiyeh in 636 AD sealed the fate of the Persian empire. Persia was soon converted to Islam. Thus, within only a few decades, the Arabs had conquered and dominated their neighbours with amazing ease.

Coincidentally, the year 711 marks a turning point for both Europe and India. In that year, Tariq crossed the narrow strip of water that separates Africa from Europe and, after defeating the armies of Spain, established Islamic rule in that country. (Gibraltar, both the Rock and the Straits are named after Tariq). The Muslim armies crossed the Pyrenees into France and sacked Bordeaux. Panic seized Europe as no Christian army seemed capable of stopping the invaders. Many began to believe that the cross of the Christians was no match for the crescent of Islam. However, in a fateful battle fought between the cities of Poitiers and Tours, the Muslim armies were defeated. The Christian hero was Charles Martel, known as 'The Hammer' and sometimes as 'The Bastard'. The first sobriquet he earned on account of his ruthless generalship; the second was his by birth.

Tariq's counterpart in India was Muhammad bin Qasim, a very young man but a military leader of the first rank. With a relatively small army he traversed the difficult terrain of southern Persia and the coast of Makran and invaded Sindh. The port of Daibul was sacked and many were put to the sword. It was at Daibul that the first mosque was built on Indian soil. Some now claim that Kerala had a mosque before Daibul.

At that time, Sindh was inhabited by both Buddhists and Hindus but the king, Dahir, was a Brahmin who belonged to the Chach dynasty. He was, by all accounts, able and courageous but dissident elements within the country went over to the enemy. Four thousand Jats, obviously smarting under Brahminical rule, joined the invaders and this seems to have tipped the balance. Dahir met the Muslim army at Rawar. He was killed and his forces scattered. Qasim occupied his capital, Brahminabad, and marched northwards. Multan, with its fabulously rich Surya temple, was taken.

It was at Multan that Qasim received news of the death of Al-Hajjaj, his close relative and patron who was the governor of Iraq and all the Arab territories in the East. Soon afterwards he learnt that Khalifa Al-Walid, who was well disposed towards Qasim's family, had also died. The new Khalifa favoured a rival family and charges were trumped-up against Qasim. He was put in chains, taken back to Iraq and put to death.

For almost 400 years, Sindh and southern Punjab formed part of the Arab empire under successive Khalifas. Colonies of Muslims, mostly Arabs, were settled in these territories and the culture of these regions became increasingly Islamic. There were conversions from the local Hindu population but non-believers were tolerated. It is interesting, though confusing, that Al-Hajjaj, very probably with the approval of Khalifa Al-Walid, instructed Muhammad bin Qasim to deal humanely with Hindus and Buddhists and to treat them with consideration on a par with 'People of the Book'. This ruling, however, has no theological basis. Hindus and Buddhists follow texts, cultural traditions and practices that are vastly different from the Semitic religions. Hence, to bracket Hindus and Buddhists with Jews, Christians and Muslims is doctrinally an error.

It is quite possible that an attempt was being made to secure the allegiance of the *kaafirs* and to make them more amenable to Muslim rule; in which case it was merely political expediency rather than an example of tolerance. Economic expediency was certainly the main reason why the Arab administrators did not destroy the Surya temple. This temple attracted large numbers of devotees who, apart from their offerings, spent money when visiting Multan on their pilgrimages. The authorities, moreover, imposed a tax on the temple's huge income, thus giving rise to the conundrum of a Muslim government making money from the offerings to an idol. Surely, in the eyes of any honest Muslim such money is *haram* (forbidden). But when large amounts of money are involved most men, irrespective of religion or race, tend to shut their eyes.

There was also a very practical reason why the temple was, so to say, 'protected' by the Arabs. Whenever the Pratihara empire of central India tried flexing its muscles in a menacing manner the Arabs would let it be known that they might reconsider their 'protection' of the Surya temple. It was a threat that worked. There was, nevertheless, relative peace between India and the Arab world and trade flourished. Arab sailors took advantage of the monsoon winds and established trading posts along the west coast of India. Many Arabs settled permanently in Kerala and married Indian women. Their descendants are known as Moplahs.

Muslim missionaries, too, started coming to India and were permitted to preach and spread the message of Islam by the Rashtrakuta kings. There was also much cultural traffic between India and the Arab world. Sanskrit works on mathematics and astronomy were translated into Arabic and the Arabs adopted Indian numerals and the amazing Indian concept of the zero. In Arabic the word for 'number' is 'Hindsa', meaning 'from Hind'. The Arabs introduced this Indian system into Europe and, in error, the Europeans called it 'Arabic numerals' although for several years many people in Europe, spearheaded by the Pope, mistrusted the very idea of the zero which they regarded as un-Christian and satanic.

Baghdad became a world centre of learning and Indian scholars were invited there by Al-Mansur, the 8th century Khalifa. Indian doctors practised in Baghdad and it is recorded that it was Manak, a Brahmin *vaid* (physician) who was sent for when the famous Khalifa Haroun Al-Rashid was taken ill. Greek scholars were also made welcome and there was much intellectual intercourse between East and West. The Arab empire stretched from Spain to India and Baghdad was the cultural epicentre.

However, within the Muslim world, as elsewhere, there were dissensions and rivalries. There was, firstly, the split between the Sunnis and Shias, the latter sect rejecting the first three Khalifas. The Arabs were largely Sunnis, the Persians predominantly Shias. There were also many smaller sects who were regarded as heretics. In time, the Arabs lost the leadership of the Muslim world to other nationalities – some quite recent converts to Islam. The turmoil within the body politic of the Muslim world had a spill-over effect on India. Also, the disunity of India was an open invitation to Muslim adventurers of all races.

In central Asia, India acquired the dubious reputation of being an easy prey. It became the favourite hunting ground for those intent on plunder. Often the plundering was accomplished with impunity, the marauders carting away as much as they possibly could. Moreover, the Muslim marauder could salve his conscience with the belief that he was robbing and killing *kaafirs*. Thus, while enriching himself, he was also doing Allah's good work on earth. Divine mission as a cloak for banditry has been used throughout history all over the world.

During the early part of the 11th century the rape of India began in earnest. Mahmud, the sultan whose capital was at Ghazni in Afghanistan, raided India seventeen times or more over a period of twenty-seven years. Mahmud's father was a Turkish slave from central Asia who had secured a kingdom that included Afghanistan and parts of Iran.

Many central Asian tribes were known generally as Turks; they are not to be confused with the people of present day Turkey who are descendants of the Osmanli Turks. Mahmud, who paid only token allegiance to the Khalifa in Baghdad, spread a reign of terror wherever his armies marched. The temples of India were his prime targets, for in them were stored untold treasures. The idols, since they represented heathen gods, were melted down and the bullion carried away.

For the Brahmin priests, Mahmud had nothing but hateful contempt as he demonstrated when he sacked the fabulous temple of Shiva at Somnath in Gujarat. The priests offered him anything he wanted provided he spared the huge idol in the temple. Mahmud refused. He drew his sword and struck the idol declaring that he wished to go down in history not as Mahmud who could be bought with bribes but as Mahmud the destroyer of idols. This incident is now disputed, but the fact remains that Mahmud did carry away the treasures of the temple.

Mahmud knew that girls were prostituted in the temples and that, in the name of religion, the priests were exploiting their own people to accumulate wealth. He relished the thought that he was Allah's sword sent to destroy the heathen bloodsuckers. What Mahmud failed to see was that he, too, was exploiting his religion. He was a thief in the name of Allah.

The Brahmins of India had thus far never had to endure such indignities; here was a *mlechh* (unclean) Muslim who enjoyed eating the holy cow and could, at his will and pleasure, spit on them, kill them, rape their wives and daughters and plunder their temples. All this he did with Shudras and Untouchables looking on. The Brahmins had lost face; their superiority, so lucidly enunciated in the holy books, was exposed as illusory. Herein, perhaps, lie the roots of the hatred harboured by most Brahmins towards Muslims.

Al Biruni, the eminent scholar and linguist who was of Persian origin though he hailed from Khiva in central Asia, saw the slaughter and the mayhem. He described the plight of India in these words: "The Hindus became like the atoms of dust and scattered in all directions... Their scattered remains cherish of course the most inveterate aversion towards all Muslims."

After almost a thousand years, the last thirteen words of Al Biruni ring true even today when Hindu activists (mostly upper caste Hindus) rant about wanting to 'Indianise' and 'nationalise' the Muslims of India in the name of 'cultural integration' and 'communal harmony'. Mahmud of Ghazni and the temple destroyers that followed him sowed dragon's teeth in the soil of India. Today's Indian Muslims are paying a high price for the sins of their foreign co-religionists.

With centuries of the good life behind them the upper castes of India had become comfortable, self-satisfied and, worst of all, arrogant. Al Biruni makes the penetrating remark: "They believe that there is no country like theirs, no nation like theirs... no science like theirs." He describes them as "haughty, foolishly vain, self-contained, and stolid". A millennium later, his brilliant and accurate summing up still applies to many well-off Indians, Pakistanis, Bangladeshis and Sri Lankans, bloated as they are with money and servants to cater to their needs.

Mahmud, it must be said, did not indulge in forced conversions; perhaps, in his imperial hauteur, he was convinced that Islam was too good a religion for the depraved people of India. After he had annexed Sindh and the Punjab to his kingdom he did, however, raise an army of Hindus under the command of Tilak, his favourite Hindu general. In fact, he used his Hindu commanders and troops very successfully against Muslim tribes in central Asia. The last years of his life were spent campaigning against the Seljuk Turks who were his co-religionists.

This man, who robbed India mercilessly, had another side to his character. He transformed Ghazni into a centre of learning and the arts, financed with the loot from India. Palaces, buildings and public works were constructed by masons and workers brought from India. At his court, among other luminaries, were Al Biruni and the Persian poet Firdausi who composed the Shah-namah, the classic *Book of Kings.*

For about 150 years after Mahmud's death there were no Muslim invasions. But when Ghazni itself was sacked during a fierce struggle in central Asia which brought the Ghurids to power, the situation changed. The Ghurids looked eastwards to India. If Mahmud could rob that country, why not they who now ruled Ghazni? They also attacked Khorasan which lay westwards and was inhabited by their brother Muslims. Their forces, led by Muhammad Ghuri and Qutb-ud-Din Aibak, first attempted to enter India by the southern route through the Gumal Pass. The march across the desert exhausted them and they were confronted by Mularaja II, the

Chalukya ruler of Gujarat, who defeated them decisively. They retreated and after regrouping entered India via the northern route through the Khyber Pass. In north India the Ghurids hammered the local Muslim rulers first and captured Peshawar, Sialkot and Lahore.

During what has been called the Muslim Period, there was no clear-cut Hindu-Muslim contest. During the Hindu Period, before Islam came to the subcontinent, we know that Hindus massacred Hindus. Those historians and commentators who harp on religious wars tend to cloud the real issues. Invaders invade, and if they have to mow down their co-religionists they do so. A thug does not scrutinise his victim's religion too closely. Indian history is a bloody history with Hindus killing Hindus, Muslims killing Muslims, and Hindus and Muslims killing each other. In several battles there were Hindus and Muslims in both the opposing armies.

Those who view the history of the subcontinent in terms of a Hindu-Muslim conflict are misinformed, blinkered and prejudiced. The Muslim Mughals did not take the throne of Delhi from the Hindus. They wrested it from the Lodis who were fellow Muslims.

The man the Ghurids had to contend with was Prithvi Raj, king of Delhi and leader of the Chauhan Rajputs. He was fearless but had offended a few of his fellow Rajputs, especially Jaichandra of Kanauj whose daughter he had carried off. There was, therefore, at this critical time, disunity, even war, among the Rajput clans. After taking Multan, Muhammad Ghuri advanced on Delhi. In 1191, at Tarain, the Rajputs defeated the Ghurids who were forced to retreat to Afghanistan. The next year the invaders returned with a larger army. Prithvi Raj urgently appealed to the other Rajput chiefs but, mainly on account of Jaichandra's intrigues, the support Prithvi Raj received was less than wholehearted.

The inevitable occurred. Again, at Tarain, the armies met and Prithvi Raj was beaten with heavy losses. He was put to death and Delhi fell to the Ghurids. The brave Prithvi Raj was the last Hindu king of Delhi. Thereafter, for well over 650 years, Muslims of various nationalities sat on the throne of Delhi.

Muhammad Ghuri had to leave India in haste as trouble was brewing back home. He left behind Qutb-ud-Din Aibak, who was, in reality, his slave, to look after his Indian possessions. At Andkhus, in 1205, Muhammad Ghuri's army was destroyed by the non-Muslim Qara-Khitai Turks and he himself was later assassinated. Seizing the opportunity, Qutub-ud-Din Aibak proclaimed himself sultan of Delhi and inaugurated what is called the Slave Dynasty. However, his master had left behind other slave generals and they too wanted the throne. For a long time there were battles, intrigues and conspiracies.

Qutub-ud-Din Aibak is well known for starting the victory tower, the Qutb Minar of Delhi, which celebrated Muslim domination over the northern regions of the subcontinent. He, too, met an early death when he was thrown from his horse in a polo match. His successor was his son-in-law, Altumash (often spelt Iltutmish), who had once been his slave. The new sultan inherited two serious problems; the conspiracies of the old Turkish landed nobility in India who hated being ruled by former slaves, and the Rajput chiefs who represented a constant threat to Muslim rule. On three occasions the sultan's armies were mauled by the Rajputs and this encouraged uprisings by both Hindus and Muslims. These problems, however, were overshadowed by a far greater threat which emanated from the depths of central Asia.

The Mongol hordes, led by Temujin (known as Chengiz Khan), swept in from the windblown wastes of Asia and, it is conservatively estimated by some scholars, massacred during the period of their depredations at least eight million Muslims. The Mongols were shamanists who believed in spirits and the power of shamans (priests) and witch doctors with mysterious powers. To some extent they were influenced by a degenerate and corrupt form of Buddhism. Nehru was amused by this and remarked on the irony that the bloodthirsty conqueror Chengiz Khan was "probably some kind of Buddhist."

City after city – marvels of Islamic architecture and culture – were reduced to rubble and Chengiz Khan's successor, Hulagu, even sacked Baghdad. Master horsemen, the Mongols had perfected the tactics of encirclement and slaughter. Their campaigns, wrote Liddell Hart, surpass any in history. Caravans of Muslim refugees, fleeing the bloodthirsty Mongols, poured into north India and Altumash had to give them succour; but the sultan had to be careful as he could not afford to offend the Mongols. If the Europeans, the Turks, the Arabs and the Chinese had crumbled before the swift moving Mongol cavalry, what chance had the sultan of Delhi who was, in any case, insecure? His cautious approach succeeded.

The Mongol army did enter India and slaughtered indiscriminately – but it stopped at Lahore. The sultanate of Delhi managed to survive, due largely to a group of slaves, known as 'The Forty', who had sworn loyalty to the family of Altumash.

The sultan, contrary to Islamic injunction, nominated his daughter, Razia, to succeed him. By doing this he followed the example of the

Sassanid kings of pre-Islamic Persia who, being Zoroastrians, allowed their daughters to occupy the imperial throne. The Delhi sultans even celebrated the pre-Islamic Persian festival of Navroz.

Razia was a woman of strong will. Her open affair with Yakut, an Ethiopian slave, and her appearance in public without the veil, gave orthodox Muslims all the ammunition they needed. There was an uprising in which she was defeated and then murdered in her sleep.

'The Forty' installed Altumash's son, Nasir-ud-Din Mahmud, as the new sultan. He was a safe choice since he was otherworldly and of a quiet, pious disposition and left the administration to the deputy sultan, Balban – one of 'The Forty'. Balban was conspicuously competent and kept the Mongols at bay while, at the same time, managing to keep the various competing factions busy plotting against each other. Since the Mongols had severed India's contacts with the Turkic peoples of central Asia, he started recruiting Afghans and Indian Muslims into the army and the bureaucracy. After twenty years as deputy, Balban became sultan. Under him court life and ceremonials became even more pre-Islamic Persian both in content and style. Balban gave many of his family legendary Persian rather than Muslim names. Like the Sassanid rulers, the sultans wished to be considered representatives of the divine on earth. This was un-Islamic, but an absolute ruler can always find learned jurists and theologians who, for gold, lands and titles, are willing to justify his position. Henry VIII resorted to the same tactics when he excised the Pope from English Christianity and made himself head of the Church of England.

Amir Khusro, poet and the first great Muslim musicologist of India who called himself a Hindu Turk, graced Balban's court as did other artists, wits and scholars. With the decline of Persia itself, on account of the Mongol invasion, Delhi became a haven for Persian culture and etiquette.

Balban's decadent grandson, Kaikobad, was enthroned against the express wishes of the dying king. Bughra, Kaikobad's father, not particularly concerned to be denied the throne of Delhi, promptly set up an independent kingdom in Bengal.

While these Muslims of foreign origin were busy carving kingdoms for themselves in India what, one must ask, were the people of India – the Hindus – doing? They comprised, after all, the overwhelming majority of the population. There were a substantial number of Hindu landowners in north India and the trade and commerce was largely in Hindu hands. The Muslim upper classes, being the rulers, considered business demeaning and below their high status; and so a whole class of Hindu traders, the *banias*, had begun to accumulate considerable wealth. The *banias* were concerned with making money and were prepared to do business with anyone. They lacked status, but that didn't bother them – and who ruled their country did not concern them. Lending money on interest (*sood*) was legitimate for the *bania*; for the Muslim it was a sin. Over the years, the *banias* became richer and in comparison the Muslims became poorer. The properties of many Muslim aristocrats were mortgaged to *banias*.

Many Khiljis, a tribe of Turkish stock who had been living in Afghanistan, had entered India as mercenaries and adventurers. It is recorded that Qutb-ud-Din Aibak had, in effect, licensed one Bhaktiyar Khilji to conquer Bihar and Bengal which in those days were prosperous kingdoms. The soldier of fortune did just that. A former slave, now the ruler of Delhi, permitted a freebooter (both foreign Muslims) to ravage lands ruled by indigenous Hindu kings and chieftains. During this period, when Muslims were carving out kingdoms for themselves in India, none of the scores of Hindu rulers all over the Indian subcontinent seem to have been unduly disturbed by what was happening. There was, quite clearly, no such thing as Indian nationalism even as late as the 13th century. Indian nationalism, in fact, is Britain's gift to India.

Another Khilji, Jalal-ud-Din, a veteran of the north-west frontier where he had confronted the Mongols, now comes on the scene. Since Kaikobad was incapable of discharging his duties, thanks to his other passions (wine, women and song), the general was summoned to Delhi. With great efficiency, Jalal-ud- Din set about putting matters right. This was not liked by the nobles. He was accused of being over ambitious and there were several conspiracies against him. In the end Jalal-ud-Din decided that he himself was the only man fit to rule Delhi. He had Kaikobad killed and his body, wrapped in a carpet, was thrown into the Yamuna river. Kaikobad's young son was put into prison and died there.

The sultanate of Delhi now passed to the Khilji dynasty in the face of fierce opposition from the nobility who accused the Khiljis of being racially inferior. The people at large were also unhappy; but, significantly, most resentment came from the *ulema* (the Muslim clerics). Kishori Saran Lal, an authority on the period, writes: "Whatever the Khiljis did or undid for the country, they at least showed to the Muslim world that the State could not only exist but vigorously function without religious support – an unprecedented phenomenon indeed."

Jalal-ud-Din had to contend with revolts, the worst being one led by Malik Chhajju Khan who was aided and abetted by powerful Rajput princes as well as a number of disaffected Turkish noblemen. He also dealt mercilessly with a conspiracy, hatched by a religious leader named Sidi Maula, which nearly succeeded. The sultan's expedition to capture Ranthambhor, the stronghold of the Chauhan warrior Hammir, was a failure. Yet again, the Mongols invaded and Jalal-ud-Din managed to defeat them and stop them at the Indus. He concluded a treaty with their leaders and married one of his daughters to Alghu, a descendant of Chengiz Khan. Alghu embraced Islam and became known as Ulugh Khan. He and thousands of his followers, who also converted to Islam, were granted lands near Delhi. Since in India the Mongols were known as Mughals, their settlement near Delhi was called Mughalpura.

As the sultan grew older the achievements of his brilliant nephew, and son-in-law, Ala-ud-Din began to be noticed. It was Ala-ud-Din who had helped to quell Malik Chhajju Khan's rebellion and he was rewarded with the governorship of Kara which had been the rebel's fiefdom. Kara, on the Ganges, was a safe distance from the capital. It was here, far from the king and the interfering queen, that Ala-ud-Din contemplated his future. With further military successes, his ambition soared.

In search of glory and gold and without obtaining prior permission from the sultan, or even informing him as a matter of courtesy, Ala-ud-Din marched southwards and attacked the powerful Devagiri kingdom which was ruled by the respected Ram Chandra of the Yadava clan. The Yadavas claimed that they were descended from the god Krishna himself and had, in the past, subdued many of the surrounding Hindu principalities. Ala-ud-Din, however, was unimpressed by Ram Chandra's divine lineage. Also, as luck would have it, he discovered that Singhana Deva, Ram Chandra's son, had marched off with his father's best troops on an expedition against the Hoysalas of the south. The rich city of Devagiri was, in effect, unprotected. So sure were the Yadavas of their invincibility that they had even neglected the moat around the fort; there was no water in it.

Hearing that Ala-ud-Din was threatening Devagiri, Singhana Deva abandoned his southern adventure and rushed back to assist his father. In the meantime, Ram Chandra had submitted to a humiliating treaty with Ala-ud-Din. The hot-blooded son repudiated the treaty that his father had signed and, in a rude manner, challenged Ala-ud-Din. There was a bloody battle and both Ram Chandra and Singhana Deva were routed. Ram Chandra gave his daughter in marriage to the victorious general and agreed to send him the annual revenues of the rich province of Ellichpur. The indemnity which Ram Chandra had to hand over to Ala-ud-Din was staggering. The historian Ferishta gives the following list: 600 maunds of gold, 1000 maunds of silver, 4000 pieces of silk, 2 maunds of diamonds, sapphires, rubies and other precious stones as well as a vast quantity of pearls. As a maund equals about 40 kilos it is not surprising that many important people in Delhi were impressed by and jealous of Ala-ud-Din. This vast treasure was his and he was not obliged to share it with anyone, not even with the sultan himself.

Jalal-ud-Din had lost the respect of his subjects mainly because of the way in which he had kow-towed to the Mongols. He had beaten them in battle but when it came to signing a treaty with them he had behaved as if he were the defeated party. He had not only given his daughter to a Mongol but had brought in thousands of neo-Muslim Mongols who were generally regarded as barbarians.

Ala-ud-Din took it upon himself to get rid of the sultan. In an apologetic letter he asked the king to forgive him for plundering Devagiri without Delhi's permission. He begged the king to come to Kara, to bless him and to accept personally all the treasures of Devagiri from his faithful nephew and son-in-law. Jalal-ud-Din, against the best advice of his courtiers, fell into the trap. As soon as the royal boat touched the bank of the Ganges, Ala-ud-Din rushed forward and fell at his uncle's feet. As the old king spoke kindly to him and took his hand, Ala-ud-Din's men suddenly struck down the king and beheaded him.

The 'faithful nephew' thereupon made for Delhi, seized the throne and became the most successful sultan of Delhi in spite of various internal and external threats. The Mongols attacked again; the Rajputs were ever on the warpath and, nearer home, the sons of his uncle Jalal-ud-Din had their eyes on the throne. One of Ala-ud-Din's own nephews tried to assassinate him and nearly succeeded.

Ala-ud-Din's sacking of Ranthambhor and Chittor – both indescribably brutal – mark him out as a man of blood. Jalal-ud-Din had failed to take Ranthambhor and Ala-ud-Din decided, therefore, that he had to succeed where his uncle had failed. Furthermore, he now had an excuse. Raja Hammir had welcomed two Mongol fugitives to his court and the sultan demanded that they be handed over to him. Hammir flatly refused saying that if the sultan wanted the fugitives so much he'd have to come and take them. He added, for good measure, that it was not the practise of the Rajputs to betray their guests. Ala-ud-Din beseiged the fort and literally starved out the defenders. The women committed sacrificial suicide (*jauhar*) on funeral pyres and the men, led by Hammir, dashed out to meet the enemy. Fighting by Hammir's side were

Muhammad Shah and Khebru, his Mongol guests. But the desperate Rajputs were cut down. Hammir died fighting and Muhammad Shah, on Ala-ud-Din's orders, was trampled to death by an elephant. The sultan's soldiery then proceeded to pillage the Rajput stronghold. The temples with their gold idols and treasures received special attention.

Ranmal and Ratipal, the ministers who had betrayed Hammir by deserting their master, were also executed. Ala-ud-Din declared that if these Rajputs were traitors to their own king, it was impossible for them to be faithful to him.

The sultan now turned his attention to Chittor. Its fortress was considered impregnable and Rana Rattan Singh, the ruler of Chittor, was regarded as the bravest Rajput of them all. Ala-ud-Din, who had begun to suffer from delusions of grandeur, could not resist the challenge. He surrounded Chittor but despite all his attempts could not breach the defences. Eventually after a siege of eight months, the Rajputs were forced to capitulate but not before the royal ladies, led by Rani Padmini, had consigned themselves to the flames. Some sources claim that Rattan Singh was taken prisoner and humiliated by the sultan; others that he died fighting, sword in hand. Angered by the defiance of the defenders and the long, frustrating siege, Ala-ud-Din ordered a general massacre. Amir Khusro, who witnessed the scene, describes the death and destruction graphically. Thirty thousand Hindus were "cut down like dry grass" before the sultan rushed back north as he feared another Mongol invasion.

The bards of Rajasthan still sing the praises of Padmini, declaring that Ala-ud-Din attacked Chittor because he wished to possess her. Other stories tell of his infatuation and how he persuaded her husband Rattan Singh to let him have a glimpse of her in a mirror. The 16th century Hindi poet, Muhammad Jaisi wrote an epic romance titled *Padmavat* into which he embroidered the story of the ravishingly beautiful Padmini, of Ala-ud-Din's mad passion for her and the mirror episode. None of this is true and, in any case, Jaisi wrote his popular poem almost two and a half centuries after the sacking of Chittor.

With the most powerful Rajput states (Ranthambor, Chittor, Jaisalmer, Jalor, Sevana, Bundi, Mandore and Jodhpur) under his control, Ala-ud-Din considered himself emperor of Hindustan. In the west, his armies had reached Ghazni; in the east, his power extended up to Varanasi. On coins he proclaimed himself the second Alexander and, in his wilder moments, talked about promulgating a new religion with, of course, himself as its leader.

Having heard of the fantastic riches of south India, Ala-ud-Din ordered his ablest general, Malik Kafur, a former slave who had been castrated, to plunder the southern kingdoms. Since the Hindu rajas failed to unite under a single banner they all fell, one after the other, in quick succession. Many rajas assisted Malik Kafur with men, supplies and war elephants; notable among these were the sultan's faithful vassal Ram Chandra, raja of Devagiri, and Ballala Deva, a ruler of the Hoysala dynasty. Ballala Deva became so helpful that he guided the invaders into the heartland of the Pandya territories in the deep south. Scores of the richest religious shrines were looted; the famous Chidambaram temple was plundered and the Mahadeva-lingam idol was smashed. Malik Kafur returned to Delhi laden with treasures. Ballala Deva accompanied him and both were honoured by Ala-ud-Din.

For the first time the whole subcontinent recognised the overlordship of a single individual. Ala-ud-Din was, without doubt, a callous king but it has to be said that his callousness was even-handed. None was spared; be he Muslim, Hindu or Mongol. Even Il-Khan Khuda Banda, the shah of Iran, experienced Ala-ud-Din's anger. In 1310, the shah sent an embassy to Delhi and in a conciliatory message of goodwill suggested that a marriage tie could cement their harmonious relationship. Perhaps, the message continued, the daughter of the sultan of Hindustan might prove a suitable match for the shah of Iran? Furious at the impudence of the shah, Ala-ud-Din ordered that the eighteen members of the embassy be arrested and trampled to death by the imperial elephants. The sultan's elephants were, incidentally, war booty from the Hindu rajas his armies had routed.

Perhaps the most disgraceful massacre was perpetrated on the neo-Muslim Mongols who had originally been brought to Delhi by Jalal-ud-Din. A few disgruntled neo-Muslims had plotted against the sultan but when the conspiracy was discovered the whole community was blamed. Ala-ud-Din had between twenty to thirty thousand of them put to the sword. Nevertheless, the subcontinent as a whole owes a debt of gratitude to the ruthless sultan because it was he who kept out the rapacious Mongols. Had it not been for him the whole subcontinent would have been laid waste. They invaded India many times and every time he mauled and humiliated them. On December 30, 1305 near Amroha, for instance, the invading Mongol army was cut to pieces and their generals, Ali Beg and Tartaq, were paraded in chains before the populace of Delhi. Eight thousand Mongols were beheaded and their skulls cemented into the towers of Siri fort which were then being built. Amir Khusro wrote: "They (the Mongols) give blood to new buildings."

Kakka Suri, author of the *Nabhinandana-jinodhara-prabandha,* an account of the times from a Jain perspective, compared Alavadina (as the Hindus and Jains called Ala-ud-Din) with the Hindu god Indra. Describing how the sultan dealt with the armies of the Kharparas (Mongols), Suri writes: "He dealt with them in a manner that prevented their return... Resembling Indra in prowess... who can count the strong forts that he captured?" A Hindu writer who composed a Sanskrit inscription at Jodhpur praises Alavadina's "god-like valour". The sultan's general, Ghazi Malik, carried the war to Kabul, Ghazni and Qandahar where he destroyed the Mongol bases; he boasted, with good reason, that he had routed the enemy no less than twenty-nine times.

Long before Akbar, Ala-ud-Din envisaged a state in which both Hindus and Muslims could share in the administration. Many of his troops were non-Muslims and one of his best generals and Master of the Horse was Malik Naik, a Hindu.

With age and deteriorating health, the sultan depended increasingly on Malik Kafur and the former slave, as often happens with self-made men, began to settle old scores. As soon as Ala-ud-Din died, from a draught of poison administered by Malik Kafur, there was chaos in Delhi. Malik Kafur immediately appointed himself regent and installed the six-year-old Umar as the puppet sultan. Umar was Ala-ud-Din's youngest son; his mother was the daughter of Ram Chandra, raja of Devagiri. And then, in spite of being a eunuch, Malik Kafur married Umar's mother and so became the stepfather of the new king.

Three sons of the late sultan were blinded and then put to death. Khizr Khan, the preferred son of Ala-ud-Din, was a tragic figure. Spoilt by his mother, he had fallen hopelessly in love with Deval Rani, a Hindu princess, and eventually married her. Deval Rani stayed with her husband till the end and witnessed his bloody execution.

However, one of Ala-ud-Din's sons, Mubarak Khan, managed to outwit the powerful regent. He hired assassins who broke into Malik Kafur's chambers and murdered him. Mubarak Khan made himself regent and began to cultivate the nobles. As soon as he felt secure he had the boy king (his half-brother) blinded and took the crown for himself. He assumed the title Sultan Qutb-ud-Din and embarked on a life of pleasure and debauchery. The most competent minister in the government, upon whose shoulders the whole administration rested, was Khusraw Khan, a Hindu from Gujarat who had recently converted to Islam.

Earlier, Khusraw Khan had proved his worth in the Deccan and the south by robbing the rajas and despoiling the temples and so, he believed, his Muslim credentials were impeccable. His master trusted him and readily granted all his demands. Like Malik Kafur, he too had risen from the ranks by dint of courage and ability, and he now saw that the kingdom was within his grasp. One night when Qutb-ud-Din was in a drunken stupor, Khusraw Khan and an associate murdered the sultan.

Next morning, Khusraw Khan, with the backing of both Muslims and Hindus, occupied the throne as Sultan Nasir-ud-Din. The name was carefully selected in the style of the previous monarchs. The populace was relieved to see the end of the dissolute Qutb-ud-din, the last of the Khiljis. But now, as always in India, caste considerations came into play. The new king, though a Muslim, belonged to the Barvar caste of Gujarat, the majority of whom were still Hindus. Several of his Hindu relatives and friends, seeing that one of their own was now the sultan, streamed into Delhi. They lived luxuriously in the palace and swaggered about the capital behaving as if they owned the city. Their unsophisticated provincial manners and language aroused the resentment of the nobles as well as the ordinary inhabitants of Delhi.

Many Barvaris brought their idols with them and installed them in convenient niches in the royal palace. Hindu prayers and chants were heard emanating from imperial residences and the perfume of *agarbattis* (joss sticks) filled the air. Also, on the advice of some puritanical Hindu friends and relatives, the sultan banned the slaughter of cows. The cow is holy for Hindus whereas Muslims eat the cow. Indeed, even today in secular India, the cow is a creature of great contention; a bloody Hindu-Muslim riot can start with a mere rumour that Muslims in a particular village or district had ritually slaughtered a cow in order to eat it. Human beings are often killed in honour of the cow.

However, even more foolishly, the sultan failed to punish his brother and his friends who had entered the palace *zenana* (women's quarters) and violated many Muslim ladies, some of royal blood. The honour of their women is a matter of great pride for all Muslims and Hindus. Worst of all, rumours started circulating in the mosques and bazaars that in the palace itself the Qur'an was being ripped apart and burnt by Muslim-hating Hindus.

Muslim fanatics raised the righteous cry "Islam in danger!" The sultan, they alleged, was smuggling in the rule of the *kaafir* by the back door. Nothing, of course, could have been further from the truth. Khusraw Khan, son of the soil, was only doing his duty. Hindus would say, fulfilling his *dharma*. He was simply doing the best that he could for his own family and friends. The successful head of every Asian family does just that.

The man who now emerged as Khusraw Khan's greatest enemy was Ghazi Malik who, it will be recalled, terrified even the Mongols. He took it upon himself to restore, so he made known, Muslim supremacy. Most of his requests to the governors and nobles asking for support were met with indifference. A few did pledge help but not very enthusiastically. Nevertheless, Ghazi Malik prepared for war and marched on Delhi.

Ghazi Malik wanted the throne and the way to get it was by raising the flag of Islam against 'the infidel sultan'. However, the universally respected sufi saint Nizam-ud-Din Auliya categorically refused to bless his enterprise.

What is interesting is that while one Muslim noble, Malik Yaklakhi, decided to fight against Ghazi Malik and in doing so was killed, two Hindu Khokhar chiefs, Gul Chandar and Sahaj Rai, joined the *jihad* against Khusraw Khan. The Khokhars were notorious predators and saw this as a timely opportunity to partake in the plunder of Delhi.

Khusraw Khan mustered his forces. All his generals were Muslims with one exception: Maldeva, the Rajput rana of Chittor. The armies met near Delhi. The result was in the balance from hour to hour but finally Ghazi Malik broke through his enemy's defences. Khusraw Khan, sultan for a short time, was captured and beheaded.

The Tughlak dynasty now commenced with Ghazi Malik ascending the throne. He took the style and title of Ghias-ud-Din Tughlak but he reigned only five years repelling, during that period, another Mongol incursion. His main achievement was the subjugation of Bengal which he had long coveted. Bengal was ruled by independent Muslim kings and this rankled Ghias-ud-Din. Without much difficulty he brought Bengal under the rule of Delhi. On his way back, near Delhi, a wooden structure, under which he had to ride, suddenly collapsed. He was killed, and his son Muhammad bin Tughlak became sultan. There is no proof that Muhammad was involved in the accident but over the centuries suspicions have been cast in his direction.

However, in his long reign of twenty-six years Muhammad bin Tughlak spent most of his time trying to expand the territories of the sultanate. He looked to the Deccan and the south, saw the local states in disarray and decided that direct rule from Delhi was the solution. Independent and semi-independent states were made provinces and members of the Turkish nobility – of whom the sultan wanted to be rid – were sent out from north India as governors, administrators and military commanders. This policy of centralisation was to prove fatal. Muhammad would have been far better advised to keep only parts of north India under his direct control and to exert his imperial authority over the rest of the subcontinent through tributary rajas and nawabs. This is exactly what Akbar did many years later with remarkable success, as did the British till 1947.

In an effort to control the south, Devagiri was made the second capital and renamed Daulatabad. A sizeable portion of Delhi's population was moved to Daulatabad. This decision was bitterly opposed by Hindus and Muslims alike. The sultan's preoccupation with the south meant that the north was neglected. And so when, yet again, the Mongols attacked they swarmed right up to the walls of Delhi without encountering opposition. The sultan had to pay them a huge tribute to spare the city.

The evidence that Muhammad had feet of clay led to rebellions in almost every part of the kingdom. The Muslim governor of Ma'bar, the former kingdom of the Pandyas in the southernmost part of India, declared his independence and Ma'bar became the sultanate of Madura. Many Hindu states, including Vijayanagar, were founded at this time as was the Muslim Bahmani kingdom. Both Bengal and Gujarat rose in revolt. Muhammad spent years quelling insurrections in various parts of the subcontinent. He died in 1351 while campaigning against a rebel in Sindh.

In his personal dealings Muhammad bin Tughlak was courteous. As the fount of imperial justice he was scrupulously impartial. The Arab writer and historian, Ibn Battuta was at the sultan's court and has left vivid accounts of life in mid-14th century India. In fact, the sultan sent Ibn Battuta as his ambassador to China. Though blessed with a vast vision, Muhammad bin Tughlak's abilities could not match his grand ideas. His cousin, Feroz Shah Tughlak, whose mother was a Hindu princess, inherited the crown. A pious Muslim, Feroz set about doing good works. He is remembered for his hospitals, Islamic colleges, roads, rest houses for travellers (*serais*) and irrigation works. One of the canals he built was 150 miles long – for its time a marvel of civil engineering. But politically he proved a failure since he gave in to the Muslim fundamentalists, stopped appointing Hindus and even converts to high office and allowed the nobility too much autonomy.

Feroz Shah's death resulted in virtual civil war and a cousin, Muhammad Shah, eventually assumed power. Muhammad Shah's youngest son Mahmud, a precocious boy of ten, succeeded him but power lay in the hands of a general named Iqbal Khan.

The whole of north India was in chaos with warlords – both Hindu and Muslim – fighting, jostling, intriguing.

It was at this time (1398) that Timur struck like a thunderbolt. Known to the western world as Tamerlane (from Timur-e-Leng, meaning 'Timur the Lame'), his name still strikes fear. On his mother's side he was descended from Chengiz Khan. His father, a central Asian Turk, was amir (chief) of a clan called the Gurghans (from *gurg*, meaning wolf). Contemporary astrologers claimed that at his birth there was an auspicious conjunction of the planets; hence his title Sahib-e-Qiran, 'Master of the Conjunctions'. However, during his life of nearly seventy years, Timur's arrival anywhere was regarded as anything but auspicious.

Timur had to fight both internal and external enemies and it was while subduing the Sistanis in Afghanistan that his foot was pierced by an arrow; hence 'Timur the Lame'. Shakespeare's contemporary, Marlowe, in his powerful drama *Tamburlaine*, fixed in the popular imagination the terror evoked by Timur's name.

The Mongols had a propensity for adopting the culture and religion of the peoples they conquered. From the Turkish Uigars they took their laws and alphabet and when Kublai Khan, the grandson of Chengiz Khan, became emperor of China, he made Buddhism the state religion. Kublai Khan, the Mongol, perhaps outdid Ashoka in spreading Buddhist thought. The Great Khan's influence stretched from the Arctic Ocean to Malaysia and from Korea to the borders of Hungary. Marco Polo, the Venetian, who served Kublai Khan for many years, was not unaware that the splendours of China, which he had seen and recorded, were achieved under a foreign emperor.

Those Mongol and Turki tribes which conquered the civilised Muslim states of western Asia settled in their new territories and soon accepted Islam. Timur's tribe was one such. However, as the Indian Muslim scholar Humayun Kabir has perceptively remarked, a man can change his religion but changing his culture is another matter. Timur proves the validity of that statement. Though professing Islam in pious statements when it suited him, he was as bloodthirsty, if not more so, than Chengiz Khan.

After conquering most of Persia, Georgia and the Tatar regions and establishing his capital in Samarkand, Timur looked to India. Reports of the disarray in Delhi prompted him first to send his grandson. He followed soon after and spread fire and desolation wherever he went. Timur's claim was that he had invaded India to punish the idol worshippers; the truth is that he put both Hindus and Muslims to the sword. At Bhatnir he butchered a combined army of Muslims and Hindus and it was at Bhatnir that there occurred something never before recorded in the history of Islam. Within the fort, before their men-folk rode out to certain death, Muslim women, like the Hindu women, consigned themselves to funeral pyres.

At Tohana and all along the march to Delhi, Timur singled out the Muslim Jats for punishment. He regarded them as infidels. By now Timur had taken a vast number of prisoners (about 50,000), and they had become a liability. There was always the danger that, in the middle of an engagement, they might break out and join the enemy; also, they had to be fed. Timur's solution was to have them all slaughtered.

Just outside Delhi the army of Sultan Mahmud was vanquished after a hard-fought battle and Timur entered the city in triumph. In the name of the conqueror, prayers were offered in the main mosque and victory messages were sent to Samarkand, Herat, Shiraz and the other cities of the Timurid empire. During the victory celebrations a quarrel broke out in one of the markets of Delhi. It soon turned into a riot with Timur's soldiers looting shops and killing people. More troops poured into the city and started a massacre. This went on for three days and the situation got out of control. Timur ordered that those who had taken refuge in the mosque be brought out and executed. Delhi was then put to the sword and the corpses were stacked in the streets as a warning to the people of Hindustan.

Never having had any intention of staying in India, Timur moved swiftly on to Meerut where he defeated Ilyas Khan. Here, again, Muslim women immolated themselves. He pushed on to Haridwar, the place of Hindu pilgrimage, and caused havoc. Like a whirlwind he moved on, ravaging the fertile land through which the Ganges flowed. Then he turned westward, skirting along and looting the Himalayan foothills up to Kangra and Jammu. He had received intelligence that there was a Christian uprising in Georgia and that the ambitious Bajazid (sultan of Turkey) had occupied Mesopatamia (Iraq). Timur was now in a hurry to leave. Moreover, he had no wish to suffer the sweltering heat of India. In March 1399, he held his last *durbar* (court) on Indian soil. He announced that he was leaving behind Khizr Khan Sayyad as his viceroy in India; and perhaps as a final farewell, had a Muslim chief who had displeased him, publicly executed.

The treasures he took back to Samarkand were nowhere near the quantity nor quality that Mahmud of Ghazni had taken, but he did take with him masons, artists, craftsmen and jewellers and because of them Samarkand was transformed. Timur, who considered himself the ultimate sword of Islam, annihilated the Turks at Angora and took sultan Bajazid prisoner. So far as his Indian expedition is concerned, he spelt disaster for the Muslim kingdom of Delhi. It is little wonder, then, that Indian Muslim theologians such as Hafiz-ud-Din Bazazi and Ala-ud-Din Bukhari declared that Timur must be considered an infidel.

The Hindus of the north did suffer from Timur's incursion but not to the same extent as the Muslims. In fact, there is no evidence that Timur destroyed any temples. He had idol worshippers and fire worshipping central Asians in his army and could not afford to alienate them. It is significant that Timur went to see the Jwalamukhi temple in Kangra where there is a constant flame fed by an emission of natural gas.

There were no great Hindu states in the north. Thus, by destroying Muslim power in north India, Timur managed to make the Hindu states of central and southern India comparatively strong when measured against the depleted condition of the Delhi sultanate.

Khizr Khan Sayyad, the conqueror's viceroy, became, in time, the sultan of Delhi. The easy-going Alam Shah, one of his successors, handed over the affairs of state to Bahlul Lodi, the Afghan king of the Punjab, with these words: "I consider you my elder brother... I have therefore made over the government to you... Would to God the sultanate of Delhi might prosper under you." Whereupon, Alam Shah retired to Badaon, a provincial town. Some historians have branded him a coward and an imbecile – but he was no fool. Since no one considered him a threat, he lived peacefully in his beloved Badaon for twenty-eight years. No ruler in any part of the whole subcontinent ever had such a pleasant, undisturbed life with friends and family round him as well as musicians and poets.

With Bahlul began the rule of the Lodi sultans. Bahlul buttressed his position by bringing in huge numbers of Afghans (his countrymen) whom he could trust. He then took on the other competing sultans of Jaunpur and Malwa. His son, Sikandar, founded the city of Agra, took over Bihar and finally destroyed the power of the Sharqis of Jaunpur. A patron of the arts, he was also an able administrator. Sikandar's son, Ibrahim, however, was a disaster. Both arrogant and inefficient, he made enemies even among his own Afghans. In desperation, his kinsman, Daulat Khan Lodi, governor of the Punjab, invited Babur, the king of Kabul, to invade India and occupy the throne of Delhi. The king was waiting for just such an invitation. The year was 1526.

While the Muslim sultans were warring with each other, the Rajput clans had recouped their losses and, under Rana Sangha, were the paramount military power in the north. In the Deccan and the south, however, there were powerful Hindu as well as Muslim kingdoms.

THE SULTANS AND VIJAYANAGAR

*In the 1443-44 campaign against Vijayanagar the Bahmani
sultan's chief ally was the ambitious Hindu king of Orissa.*

Muhammad bin Tughlak, it will be recalled, despatched many Turkish
nobles to south India since, in Delhi, they were prone to sedition. In
south India, therefore, the word 'Muslim' became synonymous with
'Turk' even though Muslim Arab traders had already settled in Kerala.
However, the man who established an almost 200 year long Muslim
dynasty in the south was Hasan Gangu. His earliest patron and guide
was a Brahmin named Gangu and in gratitude Hasan took his patron's
name. On seizing the throne of Daulatabad in 1347, he became, in honour
of his patron, Bahman Shah ('Bahman' being another form for 'Brahmin')
and named his realm the Bahmani kingdom. He ably consolidated his
possessions with wars against Gujarat, Malwa, Orissa and Vijayanagar.
    There were eighteen Bahmani sultans, and some of them were
involved with the murder of rival claimants to the throne. Two men, in
particular, demand attention. Firoz Shah, who reigned for twenty-five
years (1397-1422), was an intellectual who made his court a centre of
Islamic culture at a time when Delhi was culturally dead. He had several
Hindu wives, one of them being the daughter of the Vijayanagar king;
he also appointed Brahmins to some of the highest offices of state. The
second, Mahmud Gawan, was a loyal minister and brilliant administrator
who served three sultans. He rooted out corruption, reformed the revenue
collection and financial system, and disciplined the army. He aroused a
lot of jealousy and his enemies managed to convince a weak-willed sultan
that he was a traitor. Gawan was executed in 1481 and thenceforth the
kingdom went into decline.
    The Bahmani kingdom was beset with a problem similar to that which
affected the Delhi sultanate. The first wave of rulers, who came to be
known as *dakhinis* resented the newcomers, mainly Persians and Arabs,
who were called *afaqis*. There was constant friction between these two
groups of Muslims. The problem was further complicated by a nucleus
of Hindu converts to Islam as well as Hindus who held important positions
in the government. In addition, there was the old dispute with the
Vijayanagar kingdom over the Raichur *doab*, the fertile land lying

between the rivers Krishna and Tungabhadra. It is worth noting that in the 1443-44 campaign against Vijayanagar the Bahmani sultan's chief ally was the ambitious Hindu king of Orissa.

The break-up of the Bahmani sultanate eventually resulted in no less than five independent kingdoms jostling each other and cynically shifting loyalties and alliances. Bijapur, Golconda, and Ahmadnagar were ruled by Shias; Bidar and Berar by Sunnis. Vijayanagar, in the meantime, had become stronger and posed a constant threat to the sultanates. Often a Muslim sultan, in an effort to save his own position, would join Vijayanagar against another Muslim kingdom. It was not until 1565, at Talikota, that an alliance of the sultans destroyed the power of Vijayanagar and the question of the *doab* was finally settled. The chief beneficiary of the victory was the sultan of Bijapur.

Vijayanagar, the Hindu kingdom of south India, was founded by two outstanding brothers, Harihara and Bukka. Both occupied high posts in Kampili but when the state fell to the forces of Delhi they were taken captive. In Delhi they converted to Islam and, on account of their experience, were sent back to Kampili as governors. Soon, however, they renounced Islam and declared their independence. They defeated Ballala, raja of Dorasamudra, secured a strong base and, in 1336, sited their capital south of the Tungabhadra river. Bukka, based at Gatti, was the joint ruler.

The brothers now began to enlarge their territories by incorporating lands belonging to petty Hindu chiefs. On Harihara's death his brother became the sole ruler and almost the first act that Bukka performed was to conquer the southern Muslim sultanate of Madura. He also conducted wars against the Bahmani sultans. These were inconclusive; but he did manage to establish the Krishna river as the recognised frontier between Vijayanagar and the Bahmani kingdom.

Bukka wanted to centralise power and to that end started appointing his own direct descendants as governors, revenue collectors, administrators and generals. Distant nephews, uncles, cousins and in-laws were sacked and replaced by incompetent closer relatives and this caused alarm bells to ring. As soon as Bukka's son, Harihara II, ascended the throne there was a revolt in the Tamil areas instigated by disgruntled relatives who had lost their lucrative jobs. The problem was brought under control but was far from solved.

However, the assassination of a Bahmani sultan and the consequent confusion in the enemy camp came as a boon to Harihara II. He moved fast. His army marched north and occupied Goa and other ports on the western seaboard. Later, he achieved a diplomatic coup by concluding an alliance with the Muslim kingdoms of Malwa and Gujarat which lay to the north of the Bahmani domains. Malwa and Gujarat had always been uncomfortable with the ambitions of the Bahmanis and the alliance with Vijayanagar in the south meant that the Bahmani sultanate was, in effect, contained.

With ports both on the Bay of Bengal and on the Arabian Sea, Vijayanagar's trade flourished and the economy made enormous advances.

The three sons of Harihara II fought over the succession and Deva Raya eventually ascended the throne. He set about improving his army by importing horses from Arabia and Persia and employing Turkish artillery instructors. The confrontation with the Bahmanis flared up again over who should sit on the throne of the Reddi kingdom. Deva Raya and the Bahmanis backed rival claimants.

One of Deva Raya's successors, Deva Raya II, recruited large numbers of Muslims into his army and reclaimed lost territories. He incorporated areas of Kerala, took tribute from Sri Lanka and defended his frontiers from an incursion by the army of Orissa. After Deva Raya II's death in 1446, the Bahmanis repossessed large areas which they had lost to Vijayanagar but the main danger came from Kapilendra, king of Orissa. This powerful king and his son, Hamvira, advanced down the east coast taking Rajamundhry from the Reddis of Andhra, Kondavidu from Vijayanagar, and Warangal and Bidar from the Bahmanis. The invading army came right up to the Krishna river. Like other conquerors before and after him, Kapilendra made no religious distinctions when it came to war and the acquisition of treasure and territory.

The last king of the first Vijayanagar dynasty was Virupaksha who was murdered by one of his sons. After the murderer himself was done to death by his brother, a governor named Narasimha Saluva usurped the throne and headed the second dynasty. However, both the sons of Narasimha, left in the care of his chief minister, Narasa Nayaka, were murdered. Narasa Nayaka was the power in the land though he never took the throne. He preferred to call himself the regent. However, it was his son, Vira Narasimha, who decided to end the pretence. In 1505, he took the crown and ushered in Vijayanagar's third dynasty.

Vira Narasimha's brother and successor, Krishna Deva Raya, who ruled for twenty years (1509-1529) was, during his reign, the most celebrated monarch of the entire subcontinent. Vijayanagar became a glittering example of south India's high Hindu culture. Foreign visitors have written about the magnificence of the kingdom, the art and architecture, the temples, palaces, and the public works such as roads and reservoirs. Paes, already quoted elsewhere, compared Vijayanagar with Rome and described Krishna Deva Raya as a "perfect king". Barbosa, cousin of the celebrated navigator Magellan, was greatly impressed with the prosperity he saw and predicted that when the king died many women would willingly throw themselves on his funeral pyre.

The Vijayanagar army, now a force to be reckoned with, invaded Orissa and penetrated as far as Cuttack. The Gajapati raja of Orissa sued for peace and gave his daughter to Krishna Deva. Bijapur was next on his list and Krishna Deva installed his preferred claimant, a Bahmani, on the Gulbarga throne. With the Portuguese he maintained the best of trade relations for it was through them that he got his cavalry horses from the Middle East.

A scramble for power followed the death of the "perfect king". Rama Raya, an experienced administrator who had once been employed by the sultan of Golconda, came out on top. He cleverly played one Muslim king against the other and, on one occasion, even joined the hated enemy Bijapur against an alliance of Ahmadnagar and Golconda. The Vijayanagar army ravaged Ahmadnagar and atrocities on Muslims were widely reported. However, stories of the destruction of mosques, the burning of Qur'ans and the rape of Muslim women seem grossly exaggerated. It must be remembered that Rama Raya's army had thousands of Muslims in its ranks as well as many Muslim generals. He was, in fact, often accused by his Hindu advisers of appointing too many Muslims to top administrative positions.

The theory goes that because of the Vijayanagar soldiery's unspeakable behaviour in Ahmadnagar the sultans sank their differences and declared a *jihad*. The more likely reason for the 'holy war' is that they were frightened of Vijayanagar's might, especially since the Muslim-hating Portuguese (militant Christians with superior European artillery) were tilting in favour of the Hindu kingdom.

Ahmadnagar and Golconda, the sultanates that had suffered most at the hands of Vijayanagar, proposed the *jihad* and Bijapur and Bidar joined in. Berar's position was ambiguous. The armies battled it out at Talikota and two of Rama Raya's Muslim generals defected. Vijayanagar's fate was sealed. A hundred thousand were put to the sword, the city was sacked and the kingdom plundered. Rama Raya was captured and beheaded.

Remnants of the kingdom survived in bits and pieces for another century but the glories of Vijayanagar were well and truly past. The

Nayaks of Madura, Thanjavur and Jinja asserted their autonomy and local chiefs resorted to lawlessness and banditry. Sriranga, the last leader of Vijayanagar, was attacked by the combined forces of Bijapur and Golconda in 1645. In desperation he appealed to the Nayaks for assistance but they refused to lift a finger in his defence. He was decisively defeated.

Within the next few years the sultans, on the advice of the Mughal emperor Shah Jehan, had established their rule over the whole of the Carnatic.

MUGHALS, RAJPUTS
AND MARATHAS

*Akbar, to the delight of the Hindu population, sent the
disaffected mullahs, in the flowery Persian prose of the
historian Badauni, "to the closet of annihilation".*

Zahir-ud-Din Muhammad Babur was descended from Timur on his
father's side and from Chengiz Khan on his mother's side. When his
father died as the result of an accident in 1494, Babur ('Tiger') inherited
the central Asian province of Ferghana. He was then hardly twelve.
Confronted on every side by the sworn enemies of his family, the boy
king had to learn fast and this he did. The Uzbeks caused him many
problems as did the turbulent tribes of Afghanistan. His small army was
repeatedly beaten but he learnt from every defeat. Eventually he managed
to gain control of Kabul.

The dynasty that Babur established in India has come to be known as
'Mughal' and this requires explanation. They were certainly not pure
Mongol though they had some Mongol blood. Descended as he was from
Timur, on the paternal side, Babur was essentially a central Asian Turk.
His mother tongue was Turki though he had imbibed Persian culture.
Later Mughal emperors had Rajput Hindu blood; not only was Shah
Jehan's mother a Rajput but his father Jehangir's mother was also a
Rajput. Hence, Shah Jehan, the emperor best known for the Taj Mahal,
was more Rajput than Mughal.

Babur's personality was compounded of intoxicating ingredients:
great ambition, an insatiable curiosity and the soul of a poet. He knew
that his ancestor, Timur, had invaded parts of north India and had left
Khizr Khan Sayyad as his viceroy there. Later, the viceroy had declared
his independence and inaugurated the short-lived Sayyad dynasty. Babur,
therefore, had some sort of an excuse for invading India. When it came
to legalisms, Babur could argue that he was only doing what every man
should do; that is, reclaim his ancestor's dominions that were his by
right of conquest.

Soon came the answer to his most fervent desires. The disaffected
Lodi governor of the Punjab begged Babur to dislodge the Afghan tyrant,
Ibrahim Lodi, and occupy the throne of Delhi. Now Babur became,
almost, a pious do-gooder. His army, moving swiftly, crossed into India
and, in mid-April 1526, faced Ibrahim Lodi's army at Panipat, some

INDIA: DEFINITIONS AND CLARIFICATIONS

miles north of Delhi. The Mughal's generalship was superior as were his 700 heavy guns under his master gunners, Ustad Ali and Ustad Mustafa. Both Ibrahim Lodi and his Rajput ally, Bikramjit, raja of Gwalior, were slain. The total death toll was in the region of 40,000 men. Babur occupied Delhi and Agra and declared himself sultan. But the title 'Emperor of Hindustan' could not be his until he had vanquished the real power in the land, namely Rana Sanga of Chittor, now known as Udaipur.

The Rana's reputation as a brave general had spread far and wide; he sported eighty battle wounds on his body apart from having lost an eye and an arm. His allies consisted of no less than seven rajas of the highest rank, nine raos (heads of large states) and over a hundred chieftains. The Rajput cavalry numbered 80,000. Earlier, Rana Sanga had also written to Babur assuring him that the Rajputs would happily assist in the toppling of the hated Ibrahim Lodi. However, when the time came, Rana Sanga decided not to intervene at Panipat. Babur did not forget what he considered was a broken pledge.

The Mughal army became disheartened when rumours spread that the Rana was invincible and an astrologer in the Mughal camp predicted the worst. Morale was low. Babur thereupon decided on a piece of high drama. In full view of his army he took a solemn oath on the Qur'an that henceforth, like a good Muslim, he would abstain from all alcohol. Pitchers of wine were poured onto the ground and his gold goblets were smashed, melted down, and the gold distributed to the poor. He proclaimed a *jihad* and called on Allah to help him vanquish the *kaafirs.* He stopped shaving, for the wearing of a beard was a sign of sanctity. The officers and soldiers followed Babur's example. And then, before going into battle, he delivered a stirring speech not unlike Shakespeare's Henry V before Agincourt.

The Mughal army was filled with zeal and the will to die, should that be Allah's wish. The news of the oath-taking reached the enemy camp and caused not a little consternation. The armies met at Kanwaha and, as at Panipat, Babur's matchlocks and cannon balls caused havoc. To make matters worse, Raja Saladi of Raisina turned traitor. His cavalry joined the Mughals in attacking the very centre of the Rajput army. The flower of Rajput chivalry was cut down though Rana Sanga managed to escape.

At Panipat, the Afghan power had been broken and at Kanwaha the Rajputs met a similar fate. In both battles the victor's eldest son, Humayun, proved his mettle. And yet again, as at Panipat, it was not a clear-cut Hindu-Muslim conflict. Fighting alongside the Rana were Hassan Khan of Mewat and Mahmud Lodi. The latter, the brother of

Ibrahim Lodi, was a claimant to the sultan's throne and the Rajputs recognised him as the rightful ruler of Delhi. Mahmud Lodi fielded ten thousand men and Hassan Khan, who headed the Sharqi confederacy against the Mughals, commanded a force of twelve thousand. Hassan Khan was killed at Kanwaha.

Though the undisputed master of Hindustan, Babur was not enamoured of India. The heat and dust made him uncomfortable and he longed for Kabul and Ferghana, for musk melons and grapes. Moreover, he did not take to his new subjects. In his famous *Memoirs* he writes: "Hindustan has no pleasant things to offer. Its people are neither good looking nor good-natured. The beauties of social life are unknown to them. Intellectually, they are duds. Uncouth of manners, they are incapable of understanding the viewpoint of others. In handiwork, they have neither ingenuity nor a sense of planning. In building, they lack skill in designing. Neither good horses nor good dogs are to be found in Hindustan. Good grapes and melons are not to be found here anywhere... Good meats and breads are also rarities here... Not even a glass of cold water is to be had in the bazaars of its principal cities... Heat, dust and wind are the three curses of Hindustan."

He was highly critical of the clothes that both men and women wore but delighted in the country's "great quantities of gold and silver". He also appreciated the rainy season and the "numberless workmen of every category".

One of Babur's first acts was to design and construct a water-garden in Delhi. He was a keen observer with an insatiable curiosity. In the middle of describing the tactics he had adopted in a particular battle, he would break the blood-soaked narrative to record, "I have now seen twenty-four different kinds of tulips in India." And once, after having his kitchen servants crushed to death by elephants he calmly strolled into his private garden to contemplate the colours of the autumn leaves. Poet he was but, above all, a man of action. He swam the Ganges twice, "for amusement," he explained. This throw-away remark may have been intentional. Babur knew that the Ganges was the holiest river for the Hindus; they worshipped 'Mother Ganges' then as now. He, a mere human but a Muslim, had conquered the holiest river of the *kaafirs* not once but twice and he wished to record that fact for future generations. He was almost constantly on horseback. It was not uncommon for him to ride eighty miles a day.

Babur died at Agra aged 48 but he was buried in Kabul at a spot beside a cool stream that he himself had selected.

Humayan, the designated heir, ascended the throne of an empire that stretched from the Oxus in central Asia to Bihar in eastern India. But the empire was newly-won and, hence, shaky. Humayun had lived under the heavy shadow of his father and though he was successful on the battlefield whilst Babur ruled, he did not display conspicuous success as a king. He most probably lacked confidence or possibly was irresolute. His father's letters hardly helped to build his self-confidence. When Humayan was in distant Badakhshan, he wrote to his father complaining of the remoteness of the place. Promptly came the curt reply reminding him that there was no bondage like that which kings had to endure, and it was thus unbecoming of Humayun to whinge. "The world is his who exerts himself," admonished Babur.

A master of prose, Babur was highly critical of his son's style. He chides Humayun: "You certainly do not excel in letter-writing... you fail chiefly because you have too great a desire to show off your acquirements... write unaffectedly, clearly, and in plain words..."

In spite of his strictness, Babur loved his son dearly. It is recorded that when Humayun was very ill and there were fears that the prince might die, Babur prayed fervently for his son's life. He then walked round Humayun's bed three times and offered his own life in solemn sacrifice should his son recover. Humayun got better and his father's health deteriorated. Soon after Babur passed away.

Humayun had a troubled reign; it was divided into two parts.

Babur had expressly advised his son to treat his brothers with kindness and understanding, but in spite of Humayun's best efforts they were always a problem as were his numerous cousins. Soon Bahadur Shah, the king of Gujarat, revolted and then the extremely capable Sher Shah Suri made it his business to expel the Mughals and restore Afghan supremacy. Humayun was badly beaten at Chausa and while fleeing was nearly drowned in the flooded Ganges. A humble *bhisti* (water carrier) named Nizam managed to save the emperor's life by getting him to float on his inflated *mashak* (large leather bag usually sewn from buffalo hide). Landing safely on the other side of the river, Humayun promised the *bhisti* that as a mark of his gratitude he would let him sit on the imperial throne for half a day. Later, when Nizam presented himself at court, Humayun fulfilled his pledge. The *bhisti* was, with all due honour, made to sit on the throne of Hindustan for the promised period.

The *darbaris* (courtiers) as well as Humayun's brother, Kamran, ridiculed what they regarded as the emperor's unbecoming behaviour. But such was the way of all monarchs who wielded absolute power.

They were an odd composite of honour, arrogance, decency, sensitivity, and extreme cruelty.

Sher Shah Suri followed up his victory at Chausa by finally humiliating the Mughals at Bilgram. Humayun, his entourage and the remnants of his shattered army fled to the deserts of Sindh and Rajasthan. They wandered like refugees, as indeed they were, searching for sustenance. Many perished from the heat, the lack of food and, above all, from thirst. They were eventually given shelter by Rana Prasad, raja of Amarkot and a chief of the Sodha Rajputs. It was in the rana's fortress that Hamida, Humayun's favourite wife, gave birth to a son. The date was October 15, 1542, a Sunday. The boy was named Jalal-ud-Din Muhammad. The world, however, knows him as Akbar, one of history's greatest monarchs and a man who never forgot that he was born under the roof of a Rajput.

Four days earlier, Humayun had left Amarkot with Rana Prasad on an expedition to punish two local rulers, Jani Beg and Shah Hussain, who were a thorn in the raja's flesh. When a messenger brought news of the birth of his son, Humayun was expected to distribute gifts to his *amirs* (chiefs) as was the custom. But the fugitive emperor, who was in debt, had nothing to give. All that could be found was a small bag of musk. Humayun opened the bag on a china plate and distributed the musk to his nobles. "This event diffused its fragrance over the whole habitable world," writes Jouhar, the emperor's faithful ewer bearer, who witnessed the event.

Soon, however, Humayun's situation became so untenable in India that he was forced to flee to Iran and seek assistance from Shah Tahmasp. There are opposing accounts regarding Humayun's reception in Iran. He did receive help, but it was conditional. Tahmasp wanted the Mughal, a born Sunni, to become a Shia and Humayun did make some sort of a show that he had Shia leanings. He also employed many Shias, the most celebrated among them being Bairam Khan. On account of these concessions, made out of necessity rather than conviction, Humayun has always been reviled by orthodox Sunnis.

For nearly fifteen years, Humayun was without crown, throne or territory. In Afghanistan he was forced to fight his ambitious brothers, Askari and Kamran. From the latter he recovered Kabul and in an act of extreme cruelty had Kamran blinded.

In India, in the meantime, Sher Shah Suri (the Afghan who had dislodged the Mughals) was proving to be an efficient administrator. Revenue collection was reorganised as was the military and judicial system. Many roads were built and trade and commerce flourished. Unfortunately, the good times were not to last for long. Sher Shah Suri's short reign was followed by fierce civil war between the rival Afghan contenders for the crown. Humayun, therefore, thought that this was the opportune time to reclaim his lost Indian empire. He crossed the Indus on January 2, 1555 and occupied most of the Punjab without even having to fight a battle. At Machhiwara, on the Sutlej river, the army of Sikandar Suri (one of the claimants to the throne) was defeated and the road to Delhi lay open. By July, both Delhi and Agra were taken and Humayun was back on the throne. He was 48, the age at which his father had died, when fate intervened.

Humayun was a great lover of books and apart from composing poems in Persian, he was fascinated by mathematics, astronomy and astrology. One evening, while descending the staircase from his library in Delhi, he slipped and fell. A few days later he died of his head injuries.

Akbar, barely in his teens, was campaigning in the Punjab with his tutor and guardian, Bairam Khan, when riders brought the news from Delhi. Without delay, in a town called Kalanaur, Bairam Khan proclaimed Akbar emperor of India. The decisive guardian also declared himself the emperor's regent. And, thus, obscure Kalanaur in the Gurdaspur district of the Punjab, found its name in the history books.

Very wisely the Mughal court, headed by Tardi Beg, had decided to keep the death of Humayun a state secret for a fortnight. In those troubled times there had to be a reigning emperor securely *in situ* and, moreover, the Mughals now had a new and dangerous enemy at their door. His name was Hemu, the Hindu general of Adil Shah, another Afghan claimant to the Delhi throne.

History has always been seen through the eyes of the victors and it should, therefore, come as no surprise that Hemu and his king were vilified by Mughal historians. Adil Shah was described as a dissolute pleasure-seeker who was happier in the company of dancing girls than performing his royal duties. These he left to his prime minister and commander-in-chief, the crafty *bania* (shopkeeper) Hemu, who never carried a sword and had not even learnt to ride a horse. They held Hemu's caste against him; it was understandable for a Rajput to take up arms against the imperial armies, but what right had a mere low-born *bania* from Rewari to do so?

Adil Shah had learnt classical music from Miyan Tansen, the legendary saint musician, and had himself instructed Baz Bahadur, the king of Malwa who became a famous musician. Although accused of effeminacy, Adil

Shah died on the battlefield. Hemu, who ran the government, was possessed of tremendous talents and amazing courage; he won no less than twenty-two battles, one of them against the brilliant Mughal general Tardi Beg from whom he took both Delhi and Agra. He was no ordinary *bania.*

While in possession of Delhi, Hemu enthroned himself with the title of Maharaja Vikramaditya and, had his luck held, might well have established a Hindu ruling dynasty of his own. Certainly, he had the right qualifications. Many Afghans now threw in their lot with the new Hindu king since they considered him less of a threat to them than the Mughals whom they execrated.

Hemu's successes worried the new emperor's advisers and the majority counselled Akbar to abandon India, pull back across the Indus and retreat to Kabul. The only one to raise a voice of dissent was Bairam Khan and Akbar agreed with him. The army was, therefore, ordered to march east towards Delhi.

Hemu's heavy artillery, which he had imported from Turkey, was under the command of Afghan *topchees* (cannoneers). He knew that Babur's guns had won the first battle of Panipat. Hence now, in the second battle of Panipat, he wanted the artillery to dictate the result – but this time against the Mughals. Hemu's plan was that once the guns were favourably positioned on the battlefield he would bring up his infantry and cavalry fresh from the Delhi garrison and await Akbar's arrival. He had worked out a devastating reception for Babur's grandson, especially since he knew that the opposing army would be weary after its long forced marches.

Akbar, however, with remarkable sagacity had despatched ahead of the main army a division of 10,000 horsemen under Ali Quli Khan to raid and reconnoitre. Moving fast, they arrived at Panipat to see Hemu's prize artillery pieces being moved about without much support or protection. Ali Quli Khan couldn't believe his eyes. There, before him, was the ordnance that the Mughal army had been dreading. He swooped and captured the lot.

The loss of the cannon on which he had relied so much depressed Hemu but he was made of stern stuff. He worked out alternative tactics and immediately took the offensive. Leading 30,000 Rajputs and Afghans, his generals, Shadi Khan and Ramayya, smashed through both the left and right wings of the Mughal army. High on a leading elephant, Hemu directed operations. At the right moment he unleashed hundreds of armoured elephants against the enemy's centre. The Mughals reeled and were almost at breaking point when destiny, as always, decided the day.

An arrow struck Hemu in the eye and knocked him temporarily unconscious. His soldiers, presuming that he had been killed, panicked, broke ranks and fled the field. Bairam Khan ordered his cavalry to hunt them down without mercy.

Hemu was taken prisoner and brought before the young emperor. Bairam Khan told his protégé that he must execute the infidel with his own hands. To which Akbar replied, "He is now no better than a dead man. How can I strike him?" Whereupon the regent drew out his sword and cut down Hemu.

This is the version that has come to us from the pen of Abul Fazl, the historian at Akbar's court. Writers in the 16th century, like today's PR persons, always provided glorious and gracious accounts of their patrons and paymasters. However, another contemporary writer, Arif Qandhari, asserts that Akbar took his guardian's advice and beheaded Hemu himself.

Bairam Khan, it must be pointed out, was pitiless even towards his fellow generals. The hatred he harboured against Tardi Beg was well known. Much has been made of their ethnic and religious differences. Bairam Khan, a Persian, was a fervent Shia while Tardi Beg, a Turk, was a Sunni. Be that as it may, each wanted to influence the young Akbar to his own way of thinking. Hence the rivalry. Tardi Beg's defeat at the hands of Hemu had provided Bairam Khan with a very good excuse to get rid of him. He had Tardi Beg assassinated.

As a young man, Akbar spent most of his time pursuing his favourite passions: playing polo, hunting wild animals, and riding unruly elephants. The empire was administered by the regent. But the hot-blooded young man soon changed his ways. Firstly, he could not let Bairam Khan continue ruling in his stead particularly since instances of maladministration and injustice were being brought to his notice. Hence, after thanking the regent for the great services that he had rendered, Akbar suggested that he should make the mandatory pilgrimage to Mecca and even settle there. This was a courteous way of telling Bairam Khan that he had been honourably retired. While on his way to Mecca, however, the former regent was murdered by a group of disaffected Afghans.

Even though Akbar was illiterate he was a highly educated man. His huge library housed books in several languages on various subjects and he had them read, translated and explained to him by scholars. His memory was phenomenal and the scholars were astonished that the emperor could retain and understand so much. It was noted that he could accurately measure a man's character and weigh him up at a glance. His wisdom was immense as his glorious reign of nearly half a century was to prove.

Akbar was among the very few rulers in the whole of India's history, and certainly the first Muslim monarch, who understood that a whole subcontinent with its vast diversities could be successfully governed only when justice was impartially administered; when the various groups and factions were respectful of each other; when there was absolute religious freedom; when the ruler was prepared to serve the interests of every single person who recognised him as emperor. This meant, quite simply, that the majority of his subjects, who were Hindus, had to be convinced that they mattered. They were, therefore, treated decently, as equals of Muslims. Hindu personal law was respected. In short, Akbar became a just and benevolent father to all his people.

Chandragupta Maurya, Ashoka, Vikramaditya and Harsha were men of similar mould and stature but during their times the problems that confronted them did not have the magnitude or complexity of those of 16th century India. In any case, the population of India during Akbar's reign was very much larger than it was in former centuries.

Not only were the emperor's own relatives – the Mirzas – always plotting against him but there was discord between the Mughals, the Afghans, the Uzbeks and the Persians. There were, moreover, the old animosities between the Sunni and Shia factions. To neutralise these forces Akbar looked to those whom he respected most: the Rajputs. Their sense of honour, their intense loyalty, their courage, their innate respect for women, their fighting qualities, appealed to Akbar and struck a chord with him. When Bhar Mall, Raja of Amber (present day Jaipur) recognised Akbar as his overlord, he offered his daughter, Jodha Bai, to the emperor. Akbar, then twenty years old, graciously accepted the marriage alliance. It was the beginning of a rewarding relationship and the dawn of warm Hindu-Muslim harmony in several areas such as architecture, painting, music, dance, dress, cuisine, language, literature, culture and religion.

Valiant princes such as Bhagwan Das and Man Singh (the empire's most successful general) joined the Mughal army and the Rajputs became the emperor's staunchest allies. In fact, Akbar trusted only the Rajputs with his personal safety; they formed the imperial guard. It can be said, without exaggeration, that the massive structure of Akbar's empire rested firmly on its Rajput foundation. Today's secular India is, without doubt, a legacy of Akbar's India.

The emperor's power and dominions were greatly extended. He crushed rebellions in Afghanistan and appointed Man Singh governor of Kabul; the Rajput fort of Chittor was reduced and 30,000 brave defenders put to the sword; the Rajput states of Ranthambor, Kalinjar, Jodhpur, Bikaner, Jaisalmer, Dungarpur, Bundi, Pratapgarh and Banswara, like Amber (Jaipur), recognised Mughal suzerainty; Gujarat was taken from its ruler, Ibrahim Mirza; with the defeat of the nawabs (Muslim equivalent of rajas) Daud Khan and Munim Khan, Bengal and Bihar were incorporated into the empire; Kashmir was conquered and its ruler, Yusuf Shah, recruited to the imperial service; Sindh, Balochistan, Orissa, Qandahar, Khandesh, Berar, Ahmadnagar and Gondwana were also annexed.

In the Deccan, the emperor encountered the toughest opposition from a woman. She was Chand Bibi, sister of the sultan of Bijapur and regent of Ahmadnagar. It was only when she was murdered by one of her own officers that Akbar's army could take Ahmednagar. Another woman, Durgavati, queen mother of the ancient central Indian kingdom of Gondwana (also known as Graha-Katanga), fought the Mughals to the bitter end. The heroism of both these women has been praised by Akbar's historians.

Akbar abolished the *jizya*, the hated poll tax that was previously levied on non-Muslims, and promulgated humane laws that affected the betterment of both Hindus and Muslims. The civil service and the revenue collection system which were established by his able minister Raja Todar Mall became the models for British administrators during the era of the Raj.

The organisation of the empire from the remotest village upwards was carefully structured. The duties of government officials from the village *patwari*, who meticulously recorded the crops and revenue returns, to the *subahdar* (the provincial governor) were clearly specified. Akbar created the *mansabdari* system. Mansabdars (holders of rank) were graded from the lowest (commander of ten horsemen) to the highest (commander of 10,000 horsemen). They were appointed by the emperor on the basis of merit alone without regard to religion or race. Mansabdars were accountable to the emperor and could be posted to any station, in either a civil or military capacity, as and when required.

Great artists, writers and musicians (such as Miyan Tansen) graced Akbar's court as did savants and theologians of many faiths. In his *ibadat-khana* (house of worship) he listened for hours to religious debates which often became acrimonious. He could not understand why so-called 'holy men of religion' detested each other so vehemently.

The emperor was keen to learn and to imbibe goodness from whichever source it came. Narrow-minded Muslim clerics spread ugly rumours that Akbar was turning his back on Islam. When he performed *surya namaskar* (paid his respects to the sun), celebrated Diwali and Dussehra and was seen with a *tilak* (mark on the forehead) they said that he had become a Hindu. When he invited Jesuits from Goa to his court and knelt before paintings of Mary and the baby Jesus, they said that he had converted to Christianity. When he allowed the Jesuits to build churches in Lahore and Agra and permitted them to preach without let or hindrance, he was criticised by both the Hindu *pandits* and the Muslim *mullahs.*

Many Muslim clerics advocated open rebellion against the apostate emperor. Mullah Muhammad Yazdi issued a *fatwa* calling on all Muslims to take up arms against Akbar. The emperor, to the delight of the Hindu population, sent the disaffected *mullahs*, in the flowery Persian prose of the historian Badauni, "to the closet of annihilation".

The Brahmin priests, on the other hand, took to flattering the emperor. He was told that he was an avatar (a reincarnation) of the god Rama. Some put about a theory that in his last life Akbar was a saintly Hindu named Mukand and it was only in error that he came to be born a Muslim; nevertheless, the emperor's love for the Hindus proved that he was still a Hindu at heart. Many Hindus, because they believed in this tale, would not start their day or even breakfast without first having a *darshan* (viewing) of the emperor. Hence, every morning Akbar appeared at the palace window (*jharoka-é-darshan*) to oblige his adoring subjects. This ritual was observed without fail.

Many Hindus were more than ready to proclaim Akbar a living god-king such as the Dalai Lama is to Tibetan Buddhists.

Akbar did start what he called the Din-é-Ilahi (Religion of God or Divine Religion) which has been much written about but little understood. It was not a new religion. It was, in reality, a restricted order of high-minded men who believed in one all-pervading divinity, truth, toleration, universal love, human harmony and principled living. It was motivated by mysticism and the lofty precepts of all the major religions. Membership was carefully controlled and the emperor had to be satisfied as to the candidate's aims, intentions and objectives. It was, in today's terms, a type of freemasonry. The historian S.M. Burke postulates that Akbar was, in fact, a sort of sufi. The membership of the order was never more than a few thousand. On Akbar's death the order he founded also died.

The mysticism of both Hinduism (*bhakti*) and Islam (*sufism*) had a great influence on Akbar. He was also well acquainted with Jainism, Zoroastrianism, Christianity and Judaism. The universal appeal of the teachings of Kabir (1440-1518) and Nanak (1469-1539) were already having beneficial effects and Akbar's benevolent rule buttressed the socio-religious reforms.

Akbar's son, Salim, who succeeded him as Jehangir, was born in interesting circumstances. On a hill at Sikri, not far from Agra, lived a saint called Sheikh Salim Chishti and the emperor, who was praying for a son and heir, went barefooted to pay his respects to the saint and to ask for his blessings. The saint assured Akbar that his prayers would be answered. A little while later Jodha Bai was with child. The birth of his son gladdened the emperor's heart and he named the child Salim in honour of the saint of Sikri. Later, he built a beautiful new city on the hill and called it Fatehpur-Sikri (City of Victory at Sikri). It was his capital for a number of years. Unfortunately, a shortage of water due to a fall in the water-levels, forced Akbar to abandon the city. It still stands, deserted but beautiful. The hot winds whistling through the filigreed terraces sound like ghostly voices from a vanished age. However, the inscription on the central archway still proclaims to the world Akbar's message which will always be relevant and contemporary:

> Jesus son of Mary (on whom be peace) said:
> The world is a bridge; pass over it,
> But build no house upon it.

The Great Mughal died in 1605 and was buried at Sikandra, near Agra. At his graveside I have seen Hindus bowing with folded hands in respectful silence. Jehangir, who had at the time been in disgrace, ascended the throne. The new emperor, half Mughal and half Rajput, was wayward and spoilt and addicted to alcohol and opium. But he was fortunate in that he had loyal Mughal and Rajput relatives as well as a queen consort of exceptional talent. Nur Jehan was the *de facto* ruler and, in fairness to her, did encourage her husband to control his excesses. The result was that Jehangir, rather surprisingly, escaped being the failure that many, including Man Singh, had predicted.

Man Singh, for reasons of his own, wanted Khusraw, Jehangir's eldest son, to be Akbar's successor. Akbar himself had considered the prospect of nominating his grandson in preference to his son. Khusraw, young and good looking, was liked by the people at large. He was, moreover, three-quarters Rajput. His mother was Man Bai, Jehangir's Rajput wife; and Man Bai was Man Singh's sister. In other words, had Khusraw become emperor, Man Singh would be the emperor's *mama* (maternal uncle) and in India a *mama* has tremendous influence.

Jehangir, to his credit, did not victimise Man Singh but was never reconciled with Khusraw. The prince, very foolishly, raised an army to fight his father and went to Arjan Dev, the fifth guru of the Sikhs, and secured his blessing. Khusraw was defeated, put in chains and partially blinded. A fine was imposed on Arjan Dev; he refused to pay it, and the death sentence followed. Some years earlier Akbar himself had called on Arjan Dev to pay his respects but now, intoxicated with his newly-acquired status, Jehangir committed this act of arrant stupidity and earned the Mughals the abiding hatred of the Sikhs.

The emperor was more successful with the Sisodia Rajputs of Chittor; they recognised his overlordship and he, with certain conditions, restored their rights and lands. In the north, the hill state of Kangra in which the Jwalamukhi temple is situated, was annexed and, in the Deccan, Malik Ambar of Ahmednagar was made to cede large tracts to the empire. However, Shah Abbas I of Persia, taking advantage of the problems Jehangir was having with his son Khurram, attacked Qandahar and occupied it. There was also Mahabat Khan, an ambitious general, who had to be curbed.

Nur Jehan, though much celebrated in folklore and fiction, must be seen for what she was. Daughter of a Persian adventurer, she was an arch adventuress herself. Possessing great personal magnetism, she exercised more power than Jehangir and soon raised her relatives to the highest positions. The way in which she insinuated herself and her kinsfolk into the royal family would do credit to Machiavelli himself. Starting as an employee, a lady-in-waiting, she dazzled Jehangir with her beauty, intelligence and wit. He couldn't wait to marry her though he knew she had been married before and that her husband had died in suspicious circumstances. He became her willing slave and appointed her father, Ghyas Beg, prime minister. Nur Jehan then contrived a double coup: her brother Asaf Khan's daughter was married to her stepson, Khurram, and her own daughter, from her previous marriage, was married to another stepson, Shahriyar. No matter who succeeded Jehangir, the future prospects for her and her family were now secure.

As it happened, Khurram, whose mother was also a Rajput princess, took the throne on his father's death in 1627. He assumed the title Shah Jehan. The very first order that he gave his father-in-law, now also his prime minister, was to get rid of all the princes who could be claimants to the crown. Asaf Khan carried out his instructions with alacrity. Shah Jehan had already ensured that his elder brother, Khusraw, was out of the way by having him strangled.

Ruthlessness was an essential quality of kingship; there was also the matter of self-preservation. Those who were tortured, blinded, or murdered would have done exactly the same, perhaps worse, had they had the opportunity. Men who craved power had to have strong stomachs, for the stench of death was everywhere. The Mughal emperors, especially, waded through blood to get to their thrones. Yet a calculating killer like Shah Jehan was so moved by love that he created the Taj Mahal, regarded as the most beautiful building in the world, to house the body of his wife who died while giving birth to their fourteenth child. It took 20,000 workers twenty-two years to complete the work. The woman he cherished was Mumtaz, none other than his stepmother Nur Jehan's niece.

Shah Jehan's reputation as a builder on the grand scale is well deserved; Delhi's Jama Masjid and Red Fort were also his creations as was the Peacock Throne. He proved to be a just and able ruler and a patron of the arts. Sanskrit, Persian and Hindi literature were equally encouraged as was miniature painting, a passion which the emperor had inherited from his father.

The thirty-year reign of Shah Jehan was marked by peace and economic prosperity. In the Deccan, the Marathas were beginning to flex their muscles but presented, as yet, no serious problem to the Mughals. In the north, the rebellious raja of Orchha, Jujhar Singh, was defeated when one of his kinsmen, Bharat Singh, went over to the Mughals. However, there were failures in central Asia. Shah Jehan wished dearly to retake Qandahar which his father had lost to the Persians and he relished the romantic idea of raising his imperial standard in Samarkand and the regions from which his ancestor, Babur, had come. The Mughal military expeditions failed mainly on account of the alliance between the Shah of Persia and the Uzbeks. Indeed, relations between India and Persia deteriorated greatly during Shah Jehan's time on the throne.

When Shah Jehan was seriously ill in 1657, he made a will in favour of his eldest son, Dara Shikoh, who was an educated, outgoing, liberal-minded prince much influenced by sufi and vedantic thought. He was equally at ease with Sanskrit, Arabic and Persian; he might possibly have surpassed Akbar. Many scholars are of the opinion that had Dara Shikoh become emperor the history of India would have been radically different. But the other three sons also bid for the throne and civil war followed. In the end, Aurangzeb triumphed after he had got rid of his brothers and imprisoned his father in the Agra fort. For eight long years Shah Jehan languished there, attended by his faithful daughter, Jehan

Ara. With his eyesight failing he would sit by his balcony for hours on end gazing wistfully at the Taj Mahal. On his death he was entombed next to Mumtaz.

During his reign, which lasted nearly half a century, Aurangzeb extended the empire to its greatest extent. However, his misplaced Islamic (specifically Sunni) zeal wrecked the very foundations of Mughal might. Though intelligent and hardworking, he failed to see the obvious: no government, no matter how powerful, can function in a country where the majority of the inhabitants are made to suffer discrimination and humiliation. Aurangzeb dreamt of making the whole of India a Sunni Muslim state. He, therefore, conducted a concerted campaign against Hindus, Sikhs and Shia Muslims as well as the Sufis whom he regarded as heretics. He reimposed the *jizya* (tax on non-Muslims), destroyed temples, and started forcible conversions to Islam.

The rebellions that ensued were caused solely by Aurangzeb's uncompromising, autocratic policy. The Sikhs, the Jats and even the Rajputs – for long the supporters of Mughal rule – rose in revolt. The Sikh saint-soldier, Guru Gobind Singh, created the martial Khalsa Brotherhood (from *khalis*, meaning pure) and thenceforth the Sikhs were to be a constant problem for the Mughals. But it was the Marathas who became the standard-bearers of Hindu nationalism.

Aurangzeb thought that his armies – larger and better armed – could easily exterminate the forces of Shivaji, the inspired Maratha leader and guerrilla commander, whom the emperor once scornfully dismissed as "that mountain rat". However, it was Shivaji who gnawed at the very roots of the Mughal empire. Aurangzeb spent twenty-five fruitless years in the Deccan but failed to subdue the Marathas. His only successes were the annexation of the Shia Muslim kingdoms of Bijapur and Golconda.

Aurangzeb suspected even his own children of treason and imprisoned them. One of his sons, Akbar, first sought refuge with the Rajputs and then with the Marathas. With Aurangzeb's death in 1707, the Mughal empire went into slow and painful decline. There were wars of succession and both internal and external threats. No emperor possessed the will or the ability to establish his authority. In theory, however, the empire lasted for another 150 years.

The Marathas, descendants of the Rashtrakutas who in earlier times had welcomed Muslim missionaries, now emerged as the greatest threat to Muslim rule in India. There were two reasons for this. Firstly, despotic Muslim rulers, through their tyrannical behaviour, had succeeded in stoking up Maratha hatred. Secondly, the poet-saints of Maharashtra, such as Ramdas, Namdev, Eknath and Tukaram, had awakened the consciousness of lower caste Hindus and instilled in them a sense of dignity which refused to accept humiliation, either on account of the religious hegemony of the Brahmins or the unjust dictates of Muslim rule. The *dalit* poets of Maharashtra are, even today, in the forefront of social revolution.

Shivaji, born in 1627, harnessed his people to a common cause and led them to nationhood. His exploits became the stuff of folklore. He, himself, assassinated the Bijapur general Afzal Khan by tricking him; he then led an audacious raid on the residence of the Mughal governor Shayistah Khan. His horsemen harassed and looted the cumbersome imperial armies. He captured and successfully held a string of hill fortresses. In desperation the emperor commissioned his tactful Rajput general Jai Singh to bring Shivaji to heel. With great patience Jai Singh managed to broker a deal with the Maratha leader and arranged an important meeting with Aurangzeb.

Shivaji duly presented himself at Aurangzeb's court at Agra but felt insulted when he was not treated with the respect which, he believed, was due to him. He pretended to faint and was ceremonially carried off. He was confined in the Agra fort but soon made good his escape in a basket of fruit. In 1674, Shivaji had himself accepted as *Chhatrapati* (royal title signifying supreme leadership) of the Maratha nation. Though uncompromising in the matter of his basic principles, such as the overthrow of Muslim rule, Shivaji was scrupulously fair in the dispensation of justice. Being a realist, however, he was well aware of the might of the Mughal empire and hence made efforts to establish a secure Maratha power base in southern India. He died in 1680, aged 53.

The charismatic leader's successors were unworthy of him. His son, Sambhaji, first colluded with the Mughals and then fell out with them. After defeating him, Aurangzeb humiliated Sambhaji by making him march in the garb of a common buffoon before the general populace and then had him hacked to death. His wife, Yesubai, and son, Shahu, were kept in Mughal custody for eighteen years. Though they were, in effect, prisoners they were treated like guests. The aged emperor, oddly for a man of his stern, unbending character, looked upon Shahu as a son and bestowed upon him the rank of *saat-hazari* (a general in command of seven thousand men).

So mean, greedy and low had many Maratha *sardars* (leaders) become that at one time there were as many Marathas fighting for Aurangzeb as were those who opposed him. Even two of Shivaji's own relatives, Achalji and Madhaji Narayan, went over to the Mughals. The list of the *sardars* who sold their souls for Aurangzeb's gold and imperial honours is long and is headed by grandees such as Satva Dafle, Suryaji Pisal, Nagoji Mane, Kanhoji Shirke and the Jadhavs of Sindkhed.

Bahadur Shah, who seized the throne after his father Aurangzeb's death, released Shahu. Whether this was a conciliatory move or a clever piece of statecraft is open to question. The new emperor's policy was prone to compromises (he made important concessions to the Rajputs) and so it is quite likely that he wanted to adopt a similar policy towards the Marathas.

Whatever might have been the motive of the Mughals, Shahu's return to his people caused a near civil war because not every Maratha was happy with this turn of events. Rumours abounded that this man was a Mughal stooge and not the real grandson of the great Shivaji. His chief enemy and prime instigator of the rumours was Tarabai, widow of his father Sambhaji's half-brother, Rajaram. During the long years of Shahu's absence whilst he was a 'guest' at the Mughal court, Tarabai had taken over the government and had declared herself regent. In 1701, she had her son, Shivaji, crowned king and at the same time got her co-wife Rajasbai and her son, Sambhaji, thrown into prison.

The Marathas were thus divided into three factions: those for Shahu, those for Tarabai and her son, Shivaji, and those for Rajasbai and her son, Sambhaji. At one time, Kama, an illegitimate son of Rajaram, was also in the running for the crown. There were intrigues and counter intrigues and in 1712, Rajasbai, through bribes and promises of preferment, had her chief opponents, Tarabai and her son, Shivaji, overthrown. Sambhaji was crowned king and set up his capital at Kolhapur.

Shahu now quickly came to an arrangement with Rajasbai whereby her son, Sambhaji, would rule the lands south of the Krishna river while he, Shahu, with his capital at Satara, would rule the region north of the Krishna. However, the new Mughal viceroy of the Deccan who had the title of Nizam, decided to upset the Maratha applecart. He backed Sambhaji against Shahu and soon the latter's nobles began drifting away to support Sambhaji. To make matters worse, the hereditary admiral of the Maratha fleet, Kanhoji Angre, also threw in his lot with Sambhaji.

Shahu's situation was desperate. Any day he expected a concerted attack from the Nizam, his cousin Sambhaji, and the admiral. Searching for a saviour, the king discovered a capable Chitpavan Brahmin named

Balaji Vishwanath who turned his fortunes, chiefly through the use of brilliant diplomacy. Shahu appointed Balaji Vishwanath his Peshwa (a Persian word meaning prime minister or chief executive) and thus ushered in an unusual phenomenon – a dynasty of hereditary Brahmin prime ministers. Baji Rao, who succeeded his father as Peshwa when he was only twenty, far outstripped his father's achievements. He extended the power and territories of his sovereign and in the process made the position of the Peshwa more important than that of the king.

Baji Rao's life, though short, was exciting and eventful. His passionate love for Mastani, the intelligent and beautiful Muslim girl who bore him a son whom they named Shamsher Bahadur, has become legendary. To quote the historian, K.M. Panikkar: "The Nawabs of Banda, the descendants of Baji Rao and Mastani, never forgot their origin and on the last occasion when the flag of the Peshwa flew over the battlefield of Kalpi in 1858, the Nawab of Banda was there with the Rani of Jhansi." The Rani was the heroic warrior who led her army in the uprising against British rule.

In time, the Peshwas made Pune their capital and became the political leaders and arbiters of the Maratha confederacy. The other chief components of the confederacy were the Bhonsles of Nagpur, the Sindhias of Gwalior, the Gaekwads of Baroda and the Holkars of Indore. Only the Peshwas were Brahmins and thus Hindu nationalism, yet again, assumed a Brahminical mentality, form and outlook. Even the troublesome Tarabai saw what had happened and raised the slogan of 'Brahmins versus Marathas'. This was her way of savaging Balaji Vishwanath and his son Bajirao, the two Brahmins who had foiled her ambitions.

While recognising the later Mughal rulers as emperors of India, the Marathas made sure that succeeding emperors were amenable to their demands. There was, however, a flaw in the Maratha system. Even local chiefs eagerly asserted their independence and encouraged freelance horsemen to ride far and wide in search of booty. Mounted Maratha marauders and Pathan horsemen – known as Pindaris – pillaged the country because there was no effective central administration; and, in the absence of imperial authority, India now also lay open to foreign predators.

Nadir Shah, an adventurer who had made himself king of Persia, famously took advantage of the weakness of the Mughals. In 1739, he defeated the emperor Muhammad Shah at Karnal and proceeded to loot Delhi. After putting 30,000 men, women and children to the sword, he carried away vast treasure including Shah Jehan's Peacock Throne and the *Koh-e-Noor* ('Mountain of Light') diamond. He also detached the province of Kabul from India and made it a part of Persia.

The Persian king had planned to attack the Marathas as well but did not do so. Instead, he sent a message to the Marathas telling them to serve the Mughal emperor honestly. It is probable, and it is the only logical explanation, that Nadir Shah was reminding the Marathas of a promise of fealty that the young Shahu had once made to Aurangzeb.

Muhammad Shah is popularly known as Muhammad Shah Rangila (*Rangila* being one who is colourful and pleasure loving). It is said that he was watching a musical drama when news of Nadir Shah's invasion arrived. No one dared interrupt the emperor's enjoyment. But danger was imminent and something had to be done. The producer did some quick improvisation. He got one of the performers to sing the news on the stage as part of the play. And thus the emperor was made aware of the Persian tiger at the gate.

It was during Rangila's reign that the Nizam, viceroy of the Deccan, became an independent ruler. The Shia governor of Avadh (Lucknow) also virtually broke away from Delhi. The eastern provinces (Orissa, Bihar and Bengal) became independent in all but name. Rohilkhand was taken over by a Pathan adventurer and the Marathas, with their fast-moving light cavalry, began ravaging Mughal territory in north India. As a desperate measure to stem the rot, Rangila made the Peshwa the governor of Malwa.

After Nadir Shah's assassination in Persia, a member of his bodyguard, Ahmad Shah Abdali, made himself king of Afghanistan and avidly took over his former master's role as the pillager of India. The country offered little or no resistance till Abdali's fifth invasion. Abdali had been invited in by the Rohillas and the Bangashes who were being harassed by the Marathas. Moreover, a holy man named Shah Wali Allah implored Abdali to come and save India from falling under the rule of the *kaafir* Marathas and Jats.

Both Shah Jehan III, whom the Marathas soon deposed, and Shah Alam II, whom the Marathas proclaimed as the new emperor, were powerless. The Mughal empire, or what was left of it, now looked to the Marathas for assistance. Bloated with their recent successes the Marathas boasted that their power extended from Attock to Cuttack and from Kashmir to Kanya Kumari. They believed that they were invincible. A large army under Sadashiv Rao Bhao, the Peshwa's cousin, was therefore despatched to north India to destroy Abdali. But the Marathas were on their own. The Hindu rajas of the north, the Sikhs, and the Rajputs who had suffered at the hands of the Marathas, refused to help Bhao as did Shuja-ud-Doulah of Avadh. Even Suraj Mull, the Jat ruler of Bharatpur, withdrew from the contest.

For two months at Panipat, the Afghan and Maratha armies faced each other. Daily there were probing skirmishes and the Afghans managed to disrupt the supply of food and other provisions to the enemy. In short, the Marathas were being slowly starved out. Then, on January 14, 1761, in an almost suicidal act of desperation, 13,000 Marathas took their ceremonial baths, said their prayers, armed themselves, and mounting their horses charged the enemy chanting their battle cry "Har, Har, Mahadeo!"

The Afghan artillerymen had a field day and Abdali must have thanked Allah for delivering the enemy to him in neatly packed phalanxes. Nevertheless, the Maratha cavalry nearly broke through; but the Afghans held the line and counter attacked furiously. It was then that the butchery began to the cries of "Allah-ho-Akbar!"

Men have often invoked their gods when slaughtering their fellow men. The saffron flags and standards of the Marathas were stained with blood; mingled with the severed bodies and mangled limbs they littered the landscape in tattered strips. Panipat, it is said, looked like a field of tulips, newly mown.

The Maratha army was wiped out. Most of the Maratha nobility including Bhao and the Peshwa's son, Vishwas Rao, were slain. The artillery commander, Ibrahim Gardi, a Muslim, who had displayed conspicuous gallantry, was also killed. Sindhia of Gwalior survived only because he fled the field after he was wounded. In Pune the Peshwa died of grief. The grand plan for an India-wide Maratha empire collapsed. Abdali shattered India and left it divided ready for the British to move in.

Was the Third Battle of Panipat really a 'national disaster' as some later Hindu historians have lamented? It certainly resulted in the humiliation of the Marathas, but how many other Indians were involved? And had Abdali been defeated and sent packing back to Afghanistan, could the Marathas have stemmed the inexorable advance of the British?

What went wrong?

Firstly, it must be said that though the Marathas were past masters at swift guerrilla warfare, a pitched battle on the scale of Panipat was not their forte. Secondly, there was indecision and bickering; the titular generalissimo of the army was Vishwas Rao, his main qualification being that he was the Peshwa's son. Sadashiv Rao Bhao was the commander of the Peshwa's forces but other experienced veterans, such as Sindhia, who led their own armies, were often overruled. Significantly, the reason that Suraj Mull (the Jat ruler of Bharatpur) gave for pulling out of the battle was his discord with the other commanders over tactical operations. Thirdly, the Marathas squandered valuable time at Panipat itself. They were there first and had set up camp; they were thus at an advantage. The Afghans arrived three days later. The Marathas should have attacked the Afghans immediately, while they were still tired after their march. Even if such pre-emptive action had not resulted in absolute victory, it would at least have fragmented and dispersed Abdali's forces. Later, it would have been an easy matter for the efficient Maratha cavalry to mop up the remnants of the Afghan army.

But mere victory is not what the Maratha high command wanted. What they were looking for was spectacular glory on the historic battlefield of Panipat so as to demonstrate to the world that it was the Maratha nation led by Brahmins which had reclaimed the glory and honour of Hinduism.

While they got busy discussing plans and drawing up schemes, Abdali dug in and made himself secure and comfortable. If too many cooks spoil the broth then too many generals lose the battle. And thus it was at the third and last Battle of Panipat.

For over a decade, from 1760 onwards, the throne of Delhi was vacant because the emperor Shah Alam II was domiciled in Bihar. After the battle of Buxar in 1764, when the British defeated the combined forces of the emperor, the Nawab of Avadh and Mir Qasim, the deposed Nawab of Bengal, the emperor was at his wit's end. He took the easy way out and, as S.M. Burke, mentioned earlier, picturesquely describes it, "pitched his camp beside that of the British and sought their protection". The very next year, the emperor assigned to the company the right to collect taxes in Bengal, Bihar and Orissa in return for which he was to get a 'tribute' of somewhat over two and a half million rupees annually.

After their Panipat defeat and the departure of Abdali, the Marathas regrouped. They decided to legitimise their India-wide position by bringing back the Mughal emperor to Delhi. He was to be the acceptable face of the power they would wield from behind the throne. In short, they would 'protect' him and he would thus become their puppet. An invitation, suitably couched in the humblest terms, was delivered in Persian (the language of diplomatic discourse) by the Peshwa's representatives. The Mughal emperor gracefully accepted the Peshwa's proposals.

In 1771, Shah Alam II was installed on the throne of his ancestors and simultaneously appointed the Peshwa of Pune as the regent of the empire – more an honour than an appointment. The Sindhia of Gwalior was made deputy regent and exercised actual control of Delhi. Gwalior was closer to the capital and Sindhia was regarded as more reliable than most Indian princes of his day.

However, Sindhia somewhat rashly went to war with the Rajputs who, before Aurangzeb's reign, had upheld the Mughal state in the service of three emperors. Sindhia was beaten and had to withdraw his forces from Delhi. In his absence, the Afghan Rohillas occupied the capital and treated the royal family abominably. The emperor was blinded. When Sindhia fought his way back to Delhi the following year he, to his credit, fulfilled his oath of loyalty to the Mughal emperor. He captured Ghulam Qadir, the Rohilla chief who had blinded Shah Alam II, and had him torn to death.

The formidable Tipu Sultan had been killed in 1799 while defending his capital, Seringapatnam, and thus at the dawn of the 19th century there were effectively only two contending powers in India – the British and the Marathas. The former were organised and well led, the latter were in disarray. In 1802, the Holkar of Indore attacked the Peshwa of Pune and put him to flight. The British immediately took advantage of Maratha disunity. Lord Lake took the field against the Sindhia of Gwalior and the Bhonsle of Nagpur and defeated them. Parts of their states were annexed to the Company's territories. In 1803, Lake entered the old Mughal city of Delhi after decisively defeating a combined force of Mughals and Marathas at Patparganj, now an integral part of Delhi.

Once again, the Mughal emperor had to accept British protection since his protectors – the Marathas – had been vanquished. After the Peshwa (the head of the Maratha confederacy) had given himself up to the British in 1818, his territories, which included the city of Pune (then called Poona), were annexed and his office, privileges and title were abolished. The British gave him a decent pension (from revenues raised in India) and persuaded him to leave Maharashtra. He gracefully retired to a town on the banks of the holy river Ganges. The British believed that this was a suitable location for a Brahmin to end his days on earth.

The later Mughal rulers present an interesting psychological phenomenon. They liked to believe that they were still the emperors of India but, in truth, they had become mere figurehead kings of a very depleted and dangerous Delhi. The British, with their superior guns, their dynamic leadership and their talent for organisation, were now the paramount power in the entire subcontinent. The Mughals, in these circumstances, fought shy of asserting their authority lest it be proved to the world – and, more significantly, to themselves – that they had little or no means of exercising that authority. They seem, therefore, to have retreated from political affairs and responsibilities in the hope that something fortuitous would turn up in their favour. Much of their time was spent in artistic pursuits as a form of emotional compensation for the loss of power and empire. Their courts were crowded with poets, painters, musicians, dancers and flatterers.

Some of the kings were themselves quite competent poets and musicians. Bahadur Shah II, who wrote under the pen name *Zafar*, was unprepared for the dire moment of truth when the anti-British uprising of 1857 – of which he was the proclaimed figurehead – collapsed miserably. The British exiled him to Burma where he died in 1862. This was the official end of the Mughal empire with *Zafar* lamenting his miserable fate in memorable poetry.

On the promptings of Benjamin Disraeli, a Jewish Prime Minister of Great Britain, Victoria (a full- blooded German married to a full-blooded German) was soon to be proclaimed Empress of India.

India had come a long way from Chandragupta Maurya, Ashoka and Jalal-ud-Din Muhammad Akbar.

THE EUROPEANS

*"They make a disturbance all over my country, plunder
the people, injure and disgrace my servants… oppress
the peasants, merchants and other people…"
(Mir Qasim, Nawab of Bengal)*

The senior civilisations of Europe – the Greek and Roman – were late developers in comparison with Babylon, Egypt, China and India. When Rome declined, the whole of Europe plunged into what western historians call the Dark Ages. However, the half millennium (500 AD – 1000 AD) was dark only for Europe; in other parts of the planet the light of learning flourished brightly. Only very recently has it been acknowledged that during Europe's dark period the Islamic states of west Asia and Spain became not only the custodians of Greek learning but also served as cultural and commercial conduits for China and India.

The Europeans, ever-keen to trade with China and India, had either to traverse Muslim lands or deal through Muslim middle-men. When the Byzantine empire – the last bastion of Christianity in west Asia – fell to the Turks in 1453, there began, by an ironic twist of history, a new era for the Christian countries of Europe. The scholars, monks and teachers of Byzantium packed their books, scrolls and manuscripts and fled westwards. It was these men from west Asia (many of Greek origin) who engineered the Renaissance – the rebirth of learning in Europe. The continent was gripped by a spirit of adventure, exploration and expansion.

Also, since the Muslim powers now strictly supervised and controlled all land routes to the east, the Europeans were forced to find alternative sea routes and because of this it became necessary for them to improve navigation techniques and ship design. It was the bigger, better-armed, ocean-going vessels of Europe that founded empires and created untold wealth for countries which, at the time, were comparatively poor. Europe had, moreover, stolen a march over the rest of the world in the technology of war, particularly in artillery. Armies with bows and arrows or even matchlocks did not stand a chance when bombarded with heavy cannon. Personal valour was not as crucial as organised and disciplined manoeuvres backed by field guns that could mow down both infantry and cavalry. There is no question about it; the age of Europe had arrived and no eastern empire, no matter how rich or powerful, could withstand the outward expansion and exploitation of Europe.

During the last years of the 15th century, two Italians in the service of Spain sailed westwards in search of India but, by chance, landed upon the northern and southern continents of the New World. The first was Christopher Columbus; the second was Amerigo Vespucci who gave his name to the New World – hence 'America'. Thenceforth, the Spaniards concentrated on looting the 'Indians' of the New World. Gold and silver was ferried back to Spain by the shipload. The Portuguese, not to be outdone, despatched Vasco da Gama to find the real India. He managed to negotiate the Cape of Good Hope and later, with the assistance of a pilot who was most probably a Muslim from Gujarat, arrived at Calicut on the south-west coast of India on August 26, 1498. It was a Sunday; an auspicious day for the Portuguese and Da Gama had made no secret of his intentions: he was seeking not only spices but also Christians. From that day onwards Europeans have loved, hated, exploited, ruled, used and on occasion even benefited India.

Later, Alfonso d'Albuquerque was raised to the mighty sounding rank of 'Viceroy of the Indies' and the admiral, with his big ships and heavy cannon, conquered Ceylon (Sri Lanka), Hormuz (an island off southern Persia which controlled entry to the Persian Gulf), Malacca and the Sunda Islands (Indonesia). In 1510, he took Goa, on India's western coast, from the sultan of Bijapur and made it his capital. For over four and a half centuries, the Portuguese ruled Goa. They had come to the subcontinent before the Mughals and the British, and outlasted both the Mughal empire and the British Raj, thus establishing a record of colonial rule.

There wasn't any gold or silver to ship back to Portugal but there were spices, perfumes, silks, cottons, handicrafts and hard woods. Pepper and spices were rare and extremely expensive in Europe and the country that had the monopoly of these commodities had a tremendous trading advantage.

There is no honour among thieves and, by extension, there is little honour to be found when rival nations indulge in a mad scramble for wealth. The Dutch, the English, the French and even the Danes rushed eastwards. It was a free-for-all and each grabbed what was going. Europe, after the Renaissance, was bursting with energy and a sense of adventure and thus the whole earth became Europe's oyster. Crucially, the banking families in Europe funded merchant adventurers who were, in effect, no better than economic pirates.

It has often been remarked, and with some justification, that the British acquired their Indian empire as an afterthought. Indeed, the break up of the Mughal empire and the ensuing muddle left them only two choices: they could either leave the country to its fate and to the French, or take over the country themselves. They decided on the second option not least because of their rivalry with France.

The English East India Company, which was chartered by Queen Elizabeth I on the last day of the 16th century, was quite a modest affair. The object was purely and simply trade, not empire building. The Company's employees had to grovel, bribe and suitably humble themselves before the Mughal officials and only then were they granted trade licences and permission to construct warehouses, offices and living quarters. In time, these Company compounds were protected by walls, ditches and earth embankments and were dignified with the term 'fort'. Hence, Fort Saint George at Madras and Fort William at Calcutta. The cities and ports of Madras, Bombay and Calcutta were planned and constructed by the British in order to facilitate their trade with India. Calcutta became the premier city from where the Company's governor general administered commercial and political policies on behalf of the directors in London. However, he exercised his initiative very widely since, in the age of sail, instructions from London took a long time to get to Calcutta. Often, no directives came at all on account of ships going down in storms or being captured by the French who, after the Portuguese and Dutch had faded from the Indian scene, were Britain's chief rivals.

When the Company started raising armies and acquiring territory it became, in fact, a state in its own right. In India it was called 'The Company Bahadur' ('The Brave and Valiant Company') and started annexing lands and collecting taxes.

Even those who know India fairly well are often unaware that it was a commercial company that purloined an entire subcontinent and it was much later that the British government and the British crown came into the picture. So that, in time, Britain's imperial and economic policies worked hand in glove.

The Mughals had a landlocked mentality. It never occurred to them that a large empire such as theirs with its long coastline ought to have a navy. Even Akbar was powerless in the face of the Portuguese navy which dominated the Arabian Sea. The Portuguese had to be appeased since, with their naval bases at Socotra and Hormuz, they were in a position to intercept vessels that carried India's Muslim pilgrims to Mecca. In fact, the Portuguese imposed a tax on all non-Portuguese ships in the Arabian Sea. In his own words, the emperor was fully aware that the Portuguese had "stretched out the hand of aggression upon the pilgrims". But the greatest of the Mughals could do nothing since he did not have the warships to carry his writ on the high seas.

In his best known book *The Discovery of India*, Nehru noted with dismay a certain mental blockage that afflicted the 16th century Indian mind. Akbar, for instance, greatly admired the clocks and printed books that were presented to him by the Portuguese priests from Goa. And yet, comments Nehru, for some inexplicable reason it never occurred to the emperor or to any of his courtiers that Indian craftsmen were perfectly capable of making clocks and printing books. All they would have needed was a short period of training.

Before the Mughals, however, the Hindu rulers of Calicut (the Zamorins) were conscious of sea power and therefore helped and maintained the Kunjalis – the hereditary Muslim Moplah admirals – who had opposed the Portuguese relentlessly since the days of Vasco da Gama. Unfortunately, during the closing years of the 16th century there was a rift between the Zamorin of the day and the fourth Moplah admiral. For the Portuguese this was a golden opportunity to seal forever the fate of the Kunjalis whom they detested. They supported the Zamorin and their combined forces destroyed the Kunjalis. Deprived of their navy, the Zamorins, too, soon declined.

In the 17th century, the influence of the Marathas rested to a large extent on the prowess of the Angres – the Hindu admirals who commanded an efficient fighting fleet on India's western seaboard. Shivaji was perhaps the only ruler in the whole of south Asia who understood the importance of sea power. In a pathetic and belated counter measure the Mughals had to depend on the Sidis of Janjira who were, in effect, pirates. The Sidis, interestingly, were Black Muslims from Africa who had been brought to western India as slaves by various Muslim rulers. To this day, the descendants of the Sidis live in Gujarat.

European nations often indulged in state-sponsored piracy and Elizabeth I made no secret of her pacts and arrangements with men such as Drake and Hawkins. The Spanish Armada (1588) was defeated mainly by pirates who were hailed as national heroes. England emerged as a major world power when no Indian or Asian potentate possessed anything approaching a navy in the European sense.

In 1608, the first British ship arrived at the port of Surat but received a cautious reception since the Portuguese claimed a monopoly on all trade with India. The Mughal authorities were careful not to offend the Portuguese. Hawkins, the vessel's captain, went to intercede with Jehangir himself but failed. Only four years later, after the British had demonstrated their naval strength by defeating a Portuguese squadron off Gujarat, were trading rights granted. The man who issued the licence was none other than the emperor's son, Khurram (later Shah Jehan) who was then viceroy of Gujarat.

There can be little doubt that the Mughal empire as well as the various other Indian kingdoms and chiefdoms preferred the British to the Portuguese. The Portuguese not only traded but were also fervent Roman Catholic missionaries. The British, quite simply, came to make money. That was their sole mission and preaching the message of Christ was certainly not on their list of priorities.

However, one footloose Englishman, Thomas Coryate by name, who managed to get to Agra during Jehangir's reign, thought it a capital idea to proclaim the verities of the Christian Gospel to the people of India and so ascended the minaret of a mosque and began preaching in English. No one understood a word and many were convinced that the white man was certainly mad. Why else would he be shouting gibberish? The sun, they thought, had touched his senses.

Muslims, always considerate towards those with mental maladies, got Coryate down from the minaret in case, in his agitated state, he fell down and killed himself. After feeding him they put him on his way. Coryate headed for Surat, sure that there he would meet up with some of his fellow countrymen. He did get to Surat but died there. The intrepid traveller had come to India by the overland route via Turkey, Persia and Afghanistan. He was the ultimate eccentric who had left Oxford without a degree and thenceforth devoted his life to travelling on foot. Nobody invited him, no one sent him and certainly no one financed him. He is recorded as the first Englishman to have preached the message of Christ in India. The fact that no one understood a word of his famous exhortation in Agra is irrelevant.

The Portuguese had arrived in India before the British imperialists with not only a king-granted right to trade but a God-given mission to spread true Christianity which, they fervently and piously believed, was submission to the Pope of Rome who was Christ's representative on earth. They converted as many Indians as they could, often forcibly at the point of a sword. Temples and mosques were destroyed and supplanted with churches. They also brought with them the terrors of the Inquisition and persecuted India's old established Christians who were not Roman Catholics. These ancient Christians were, in Portuguese estimation, heretics and hence to be punished.

Though the Portuguese despised the Hindus (whom they called Gentoos or Gentiles) they harboured a special hatred for all Muslims (whom they called Moors). Ever since the Crusades there was animosity between Christians (Roman Catholics) and Muslims and, moreover, it must be remembered that Muslims had conquered and lorded it over huge chunks of the Iberian peninsula. This the Portuguese remembered only too well. Thus, when they encountered Muslims in India the age-old animosity was mutually rekindled.

In 1500, long before the Mughal conquest of India, the Portuguese monarch, Don Manoel, despatched a fleet of thirteen ships under Pedro Cabral to overawe the Muslims who were trading very profitably with western India. The Zamorin of Calicut, who had permitted the Muslims to settle and trade in his territory, was unable to protect himself or the Muslims. Cabral bombarded Calicut and sank several merchant vessels belonging to the Muslim merchants.

Cabral was, it is recorded, welcomed by the rulers of Cochin, Cannanore and Quilon – the Zamorin of Calicut's sworn enemies. Two years later, when Vasco da Gama came, this time with twenty ships, he spread fear amongst the Indian rulers, including the mighty king of Vijayanagar, with a massive show of force. Calicut was attacked, pilgrim and merchant ships were taken and the Zamorin's emissary (a Nambudiri Brahmin) was sent back to Calicut with his ears and lips cut off and a pair of dog's ears attached to his head.

Da Gama's lust for blood came to the fore when he captured a ship returning from the Middle East. It was laden with treasures, merchandise, and many homecoming pilgrims. It also carried the sultan of Egypt's ambassador to Calicut. The gold, silver and merchandise were taken off and then the ship was set alight. It is estimated that over 400 men, women and children perished in the inferno.

In an important naval battle the Calicut fleet, under the Moplah commanders Kassim and Ambar, was defeated and Vasco da Gama claimed the Indian seas for Portugal. Thus, India's trade with Persia, Arabia, Egypt and the Middle East was instantly cut off. A Portuguese writer, Joao De Barroes, justified his country's usurpation of the high seas in the following terms: "For although by common right the seas are common and open to all navigators ... yet this law has force only in Europe among Christian folk". He goes on to state that since Moors and Gentoos did not recognise Christ as their saviour, they fell foul of Christian law and ethics. Hence they "cannot be privileged with the benefits of our laws".

James I was prevailed upon by the East India Company to send an ambassador, at the company's expense, to the Mughal court and so, in 1615, Sir Thomas Roe presented himself before Jehangir. Roe, greatly impressed by the splendours and pageants that surrounded him, had an interesting time in India but achieved little apart from managing to get an extension on the trading licence. The British, however, had broken the Portuguese stranglehold and took Hormuz in 1622 after setting up the Persian king, Shah Abbas, against the common enemy. Trading posts were set up at Masulipatnam and Madras. Later, when Charles II married the Portuguese princess Catherine of Braganza, she brought with her as part of her dowry the Portuguese possession of Bombay. Charles, chronically short of cash, was happy to let the Company have Bombay for £10 a year so long as they agreed to give him a loan. The Company advanced the loan and set up shop in Bombay.

The richest part of India at the time was Bengal and the Portuguese had already established a trading station at Hooghly. The British, too, got permission to trade at Hooghly, and between 1686 and 1690 – under Job Charnock's inspiration and instructions – built their own fortified township (Fort William) which grew into the sprawling city of Calcutta. Profits soared and being made aware of the imminent break-up of the Mughal empire, the Company's chairman, Sir Josiah Child, began thinking of bigger ventures. However, nothing could be done while the unbending autocrat, imperialist and Sunni fundamentalist, Aurangzeb, the last of the Great Mughals, was still alive.

The curtain now rises on the careers of Robert Clive and Warren Hastings, the two men who firmly planted the British presence in India. Both came from what might be called good families that had seen better days. Neither went to university though the former had been to Merchant Taylors' and the latter to Westminster – both then, and even today, leading schools. As India was the place to acquire wealth and thus reclaim one's family fortunes, they were sent out in their teens with that goal firmly planted in their minds.

Arriving at Madras in 1744, Clive instantly took an intense dislike to India, its people and, significantly, his fellow Englishmen who exhibited the worst forms of social snobbery. As a junior clerk his status was low, his pay meagre, and the work drudgery. The heat caused him untold suffering. He became something of a loner and suffered bouts of extreme depression. He attempted suicide. Fortunately for him, and unfortunately for India, the pistol failed to fire – not once but twice. It was a sure sign, he convinced himself, that he was, to use his own words, "destined for something".

At the time, France and Britain were at war in Europe over the question of the Austrian succession. Simultaneously, rival Indian princes in the

Carnatic – the region on the eastern side of the Indian peninsula – were fighting each other. Dupleix, the governor of the French colony of Pondicherry, got involved. The British, naturally, backed the faction that the French opposed. It was in this local war that Clive, who had no military training, first attracted notice. His intelligence and audacity paid off when, instead of going to bail out the beleaguered British ally at Trichinopoly, he marched on Arcot, the capital of the Carnatic, with a force of 200 white troops and 600 sepoys. Then, in spite of a gruelling siege that lasted fifty days, he held on to Arcot. So impressed were Clive's sepoys by their young commander's nerve, that they called him *Sabit Jung* ('steadfast in battle').

Muhammad Ali, the claimant backed by Britain, was installed on the Carnatic throne; the claimant backed by France was beheaded. This success sent the following signal to the Indian princes: "The British are invincible".

The princes also noticed that sepoys performed much better when trained and led by European officers. Thenceforth, it became common practice to employ Europeans and India became a favourite area of operation for freebooters of all kinds who came to be called 'soldiers of fortune'.

The Indian ruling class – both Hindu and Muslim – had become so degenerate and effete that people of Clive's ilk soon discovered ways of exploiting them. There were, of course, exceptions but they were extremely rare. Robert Orme, who was in India during Clive's time, observed that the Indian rulers possessed "no idea of national honour in the conduct of their affairs". Dupleix, who had been foiled by Clive and who was sent back to France in disgrace, held similar views. Another Frenchman – Bussy – recommended to one and all that to succeed in India one had to be even more duplicitous than the natives. Clive seems to have taken Bussy's advice to heart for he succeeded admirably. When he left India in 1753, he took back £40,000 which gave him an *entrée* into the highest circles in London. He bought a fine house in the capital and cleared the mortgage on his parents' property. Two years later he hurried back to India.

There was, it is perfectly true, "no idea of national honour" amongst the people of India in the 18th century. This is simply because they never regarded themselves as belonging to one unified nation. You might certainly have heard loud and earnest declarations such as: "I am a Tamil", "I am a Sindhi", "I am a Maratha", "I am a Bengali", "I am a Pathan", "I am a Brahmin", "I am a Sikh", "I am a Shia", "I am a Bania", "I am a Rajput", "I am a Punjabi", "I am a Kashmiri", etc., etc. No man would have said: "I am an Indian" because the term was meaningless. The term took on meaning only after British education made an impression on a particular section – a tiny minority – of the population. The consciousness of being Indian and, indeed, the idea of Indian nationalism itself is a direct consequence of British imperial rule.

On his return to India, Clive continued his depredations but this time in Bengal. The situation in the province lent itself to exploitation. The nawab, a hot-headed but cowardly young man named Siraj-ud-Doula, was keen to assert his authority not only over the East India Company but also over the rich Hindu families which controlled trade and banking in Bengal. The Company had, in 1717, obtained from the Mughal emperor, Farrukhsiyar, several licences and permits in the matter of taxes and trading rights. The nawabs of Bengal, who by the mid-18th century were independent in all but name, believed that they were not bound by Farrukhsiyar's rash and ill-considered concessions.

In a show of force, Siraj-ud-Doula took Calcutta. A number of Europeans were locked up in a small room and many were suffocated. The deaths in the 'Black Hole of Calcutta' have been the cause of passionate debate over the years. The atrocity did occur; that is undeniable. But there is wide variance as to how many were shut in the room, how many died and how many survived. The figures, for example, for those who died vary from twenty-three to 140. Even if one accepts the lower figure – which most Indians prefer – the crime was heinous, and whether the nawab was personally responsible or not is neither here nor there.

The memory of massacres often serve to keep alive racial animosities. The British used to hark back to the 'Black Hole' to illustrate the bloodthirsty treachery of Indians.

The number who claimed to have had some connection with a victim or an escapee must have run into thousands. If the claims of even half had substance, one would have to marvel at the perpetrators of the crime who were able to pack a thousand or more into a tiny room. One has heard of the Indian rope trick; were the dissolute nawab's hired henchmen experts in the Indian packing trick?

The Company sought revenge and the moment found the man. Clive sailed to Bengal, in a squadron under Admiral Watson's command, and easily retook Calcutta. In order to buy time he made peace with Siraj-ud-Doula and then immediately started working out a scheme to get rid of him. Apart from the Company and himself, the other participants in the plot were Mir Jafar, the nawab's kinsman and commander-in-chief, a Hindu banker named Omi Chand and the heads of the Jagat Seth banking family who were well-known financiers. Clive had forged Watson's signature on the agreement in order to convince Omi Chand who, being a money-lender, was a cautious man.

On June 23, 1757, there was fought what has often been called the Battle of Plassey. It was little more than an exchange of cannon fire and a brief skirmish. Siraj-ud-Doula had 50,000 men, Clive 3,000 out of which 2,000 were sepoys. The nawab's elephants and bullocks took fright and bolted and Mir Jafar switched sides. Siraj-ud-Doula lost heart and tried to get away on the fastest camel he could find. But he was hunted down and done to death by his own sepoys who only a few hours before had bowed before him as their king and master.

Clive – 'Clive of India' – on being ennobled, took the title 'Baron Clive of Plassey'. A ruthless operator, he had the power to make or break any ruler in the entire subcontinent. He made Mir Jafar the nawab of Bengal and in return exacted vast rewards in cash, treasure and land grants. The Company also did extremely well. When Mir Jafar proved difficult he was quickly replaced and the next nawab, Mir Qasim, was made to lavish similar rewards. The new nawab, however, seems to have had more of a conscience than his predecessors because he complained to the governor of Fort William in the following terms: "... and this is the way your countrymen behave. They make a disturbance all over my country, plunder the people, injure and disgrace my servants ... oppress the peasants, merchants and other people ... They forcibly take away the goods of the peasants, merchants, etcetera, for a fourth of their real value and, by way of violence and oppression, they oblige the peasants to buy goods for five rupees which happen to be worth only one rupee ... and for the sake of five rupees they bind and disgrace a man who pays a hundred rupees inland tax ..."

The Company and its employees had gone to India to trade. They were now looting on a massive scale. Mir Qasim, who had the temerity to complain, was deposed and the more pliable Mir Jafar brought back. Thus, within the span of a few years, there were four nawabs. Bengal was bled because, in order to pay their British overlords the nawabs, who were no nationalists or lovers of the poor whether Hindu or Muslim, imposed heavier and heavier taxes on the people. Macaulay, much later perhaps in a confessional mood on behalf of his countrymen, wrote: "Thirty million human beings were reduced to the last extremity of wretchedness. They were accustomed to live under tyranny, but never tyranny like this."

What emerged in Bengal set the pattern for the rest of the subcontinent. The British never ruled or exploited directly. The dirty work was done by pliant princes in what came to be called the 'Princely States'. In the provinces of 'British India' the administrative head was the governor who had a hard core of white officials to assist him. The day-to-day running of the Raj was in the hands of a huge army of 'native' civil servants whilst the economic exploitation was carried out effectively by *zamindars* (hereditary feudal landlords) and merchants and traders who knew well how to keep the white sahibs happy.

In short, therefore, the British Raj is a history of collaboration. The British could never have ruled and exploited the subcontinent without the willing and active collaboration of a very sizeable and powerful section of Indian society. This client class was pampered by the imperial authorities and honoured with titles such as 'Rai Bahadur', 'Khan Bahadur' and 'Sardar Bahadur' and even, on rare occasions, a Knighthood of the Indian Empire. However, the vast majority – the Indian masses – endured grinding poverty, disease and the long-term effects of recurrent famines.

The Hindus of Bengal and particularly the merchant castes were happy that the British had humiliated their Muslim masters. There had for many years been conversions to Islam from the lower sections of the Bengali population and this had caused a deep division in society. Also, upper caste Hindus were always afraid of getting on the wrong side of the Muslim rulers. Their lives and property were never wholly secure. Siraj-ud-Doula, for instance, once threatened a family of Hindu bankers that they would be forcibly converted to Islam and that the men would therefore have to be circumcised. The wayward prince did not carry out the threat and so it can be presumed that he was given what he wanted, which usually meant money, property or women. The Hindus knew that the British would get their way by war or other means although not with such painful prescriptions.

After consulting their charts and almanacs, Hindu sages and astrologers now discovered that 1757 was an important year for the 'Hindu nation'. It was the year that signalled the end of Muslim domination and the establishment of British power. In other words, an era of lesser evil. But, they calculated, British rule would last only a century. In 1857, they predicted, the Hindus would regain their independence.

The Company, meanwhile, continued to expand and grow more powerful. Clive's final, and perhaps greatest, stroke in India was executed in 1765 when he obtained from Shah Alam II (still the titular emperor of India) the *diwani* of Bengal, Bihar and Orissa. This meant that the Company became the sole collector of taxes in those provinces. This momentous event is graphically recorded in a large painting by Benjamin West.

The Company's employees now accumulated huge fortunes through naked corruption and private trading on their own account. In 1769-70, they engineered an artificial famine by buying up all the rice production and holding on to it till people were starving to death in their hundreds of thousands. The grain was then sold at vastly inflated prices making several of the Company's employees millionaires in a matter of months. This was capitalism at its ugliest. Walpole wrote: "The groans of India have mounted to heaven ... What think you of the famine in Bengal in which three millions perished, being caused by a monopoly of the provisions, by the servants of the East India Company?"

Some of the most influential families in Britain, even today, owe their status, wealth and country estates to fortunes looted in India. At first, those who returned to Britain laden with wealth were despised and envied in equal measure by the nobility who labelled them 'nabobs' (newly rich upstarts). But in Britain, as elsewhere, money manages to overcome prejudice. The 'nabobs' bought titles and made convenient matrimonial alliances with many aristocratic and proud, though often impoverished, families.

Clive was an extremely wealthy man when he finally left India's shores. He personally delivered extravagant presents to the King and Queen. Walpole observed: "Lord Clive is arrived, has brought a million for himself, two diamond drops worth twelve thousand pounds for the Queen, a scimitar, dagger and other matters covered with brilliants for the King worth twenty thousand pounds more." He bought prestigious property including Claremont, the Surrey estate of the Duke of Newcastle. Baron Clive of Plassey had certainly arrived; but he had made enemies in London. His detractors vilified him and branded him as avaricious and lacking in principle. John Burgoyne, general, playwright and politician, and Charles James Fox attacked him mercilessly. The latter accused Clive of being "the origin of all plunders, the source of all robbery". In November 1774, Clive of India attempted suicide once again. This time he was successful.

Clive reveals himself in the statement he made to a parliamentary committee when he was accused of extortion and malpractice in India: "A great prince was dependent on my pleasure; an opulent city lay at my mercy; its richest bankers bid against each other for my smiles; I walked through vaults which were thrown open to me alone; piled on either hand with gold and jewels! Mr Chairman, at this moment I stand astonished at my own moderation."

Since the Company's servants in India were preoccupied with their private money-making interests, it follows that the volume of trade and the profits of their employer – the Company – plummeted. In 1773, the directors in London were obliged to seek a £1.5 million loan from the British government. He who pays the piper calls the tune and Parliament, therefore, passed two Acts which aimed to regulate the Company's functioning in India. A supreme court was set up in Calcutta and the governor general, headquartered in the same city, was to be advised by a supreme council.

The Whigs, particularly Fox and Burke, wanted the British government to take over and govern all the Indian territories that the East India Company had annexed. Motivated by what they considered the highest principles of justice, they advocated a type of Magna Carta for India. It is surprising that even though they were well aware that the provinces in India had been purloined through deceit and chicanery, no parliamentarian or jurist ever suggested that the British had no right to be there in the first place. Pitt, the prime minister, whose own family owed its eminence to a fortune made in Madras by Thomas Pitt (of Pitt Diamond fame), cleverly piloted through his India Act of 1784 which gave the British government greater authority in India's affairs. But the Company was not nationalised and this placated the influential directors and shareholders. The net result was that the paramount power in India was still the Company Bahadur but it now also had the full backing of the British government.

Warren Hastings, very different from Clive in temperament, was a complex man. Some claim that he was a true imperialist, a man of vision; others that he lacked integrity. He was made governor general in 1773 and immediately encountered animosity from the majority of his council. Matters came to a head when he and Philip Francis, his fiercest enemy, fought a duel. Francis was wounded and carried his hatred for Hastings back to London where the Whig opposition MPs were glad to listen to his accounts of mismanagement and corruption and, especially, his views concerning the character of the governor general.

Unusual for a man of his times, Hastings had the highest regard for the achievements of Indian culture. He helped Sir William Jones to found the Asiatic Society of Bengal, encouraged Sanskrit and Arabic studies and had the *Ain-é-Akbari* (an account of the life and achievements of Akbar) translated into English. He thought of Hindus as "gentle and benevolent" and believed that among the natives of India could be found men of "strong intellect" and "sound integrity".

Hastings, however, was no sentimentalist when it came to dealing with Indians. Seeing that Shah Alam II had moved to Delhi and had accepted the goodwill and mercy of the Marathas, Hastings quickly discontinued the annual payment that the company had agreed to send him. His reasoning was: If you go over and accept the hospitality of our enemies, why should we pay you even though we had agreed to do so? Since neither the emperor nor his Maratha protectors had the power to enter Calcutta and take the payment by force, Hastings was not in the least concerned by the fact that a solemn signed treaty had been violated.

Although he established an efficient system of revenue collection, the wars against Hyderabad, Mysore and the Marathas, were financially disastrous. These wars, it must be said, were not of Hastings' making – it was the governors of Bombay and Madras who had embarked upon these adventures. Hastings, however, was responsible and money had to be raised. This he did by hiring out the Company's army to the nawab of Avadh, who was waging a campaign against the Rohillas; by exacting a fine from the raja of Benares for not helping out against the Marathas; and by confiscating much of the property of the princesses of Avadh. His probity was also questioned when a Hindu merchant named Nand Kumar (a prime witness in a corruption case against Hastings) was hanged on a forgery charge.

Hastings and his second wife (the divorcee of a German baron) certainly harboured grand ambitions. Their lifestyle was splendidly aristocratic; the family seat in Worcestershire was repossessed – a dream Hastings had cherished since he was a boy; fine jewellery and a big diamond were acquired; Reynolds was commissioned to paint a portrait of the empire-builder in a pose befitting his superior status. None of this was designed to please envious politicians in London and, in 1788, Hastings was impeached.

Edmund Burke's famous oration on the evils perpetrated by Hastings is an outstanding example of political and character assassination. But Burke did not prevail. Hastings was acquitted after a long and painful trial which left him financially ruined. The Company, however, made funds available to him and he spent his time quietly as a country squire. In his last years, he was partially rehabilitated when he was made a Privy Councillor in 1814.

George III ('Mad George') and the various cabinets that served him were only marginally concerned with India. They had two main worries: firstly, the grim possibility that dangerous French revolutionary ideas might seep across the Channel and, secondly, the seething unrest in Britain's North American colonies. The problem with the colonies, which revolved on unjust taxation, was grossly mishandled and the colonists were literally forced to rise in revolt.

The French, ever ready to aid and abet England's enemies, eagerly handed out assistance to the colonists who were, it must be borne in mind, mostly of English stock. They were, in fact, Englishmen who happened to be living in North America. George Washington, their hero, was a typical English gentleman; upright, paternal and fond of hunting and hunt balls. His Black slaves toiled on his vast estates in Virginia. He was extremely reluctant to get involved in an uprising against his king even though he knew that George III did not possess a drop of English blood. It was the stupidity of the British government that forced Washington to the conclusion that war was the only option open to the American colonists. Whereupon, he assumed command of the colonial army.

French assistance started crossing the Atlantic. Rochambeau sailed with a force of 6000 to aid Washington's army and the French intervention was important at Yorktown (1781) which ended the American War of Independence. Ironically, the British general, Cornwallis, who surrendered his sword to Washington had many German soldiers from Hanover in his army. In 1786, Cornwallis was despatched to India as governor general and commander-in-chief and very soon arrived at the following conclusion: "Every native of Hindustan, I verily believe is corrupt."

The memory of military defeat in North America and the resulting humiliation had to be wiped out. The ideal area where this could be achieved fairly easily was India and it is to this part of the world that Britain's leaders turned their attention. The playground bully, worsted by boys who can take his bullying no longer, often vents his anger on some lone weakling wending his way home.

In India, with Pitt's fullest backing, Cornwallis got to work with a will. Even before he landed in the country, the French had been making overtures to Hyder Ali, the brilliant Muslim mercenary who had made himself ruler of Mysore. French officers had been hired by Indian princes all over India and some had attained such power and influence that they were in a position to topple their own employers. Tipu, Hyder Ali's son who was known as the Tiger of Mysore, sent an arms purchasing mission to Paris, planted a Tree of Liberty in his capital, Seringapatnam, and started calling himself 'Citizen Tipu'. A dedicated Muslim, Tipu began planning an alliance with Napoleon with a view to expelling the British infidels from India. Napoleon had pleased the Muslim world immensely by making the notorious statement, "I am a Mussalman".

Bonaparte's army, however, was stranded in Egypt after Nelson wrecked the French fleet in the battle of the Nile (1798) and 'Citizen General' soon made a hasty and unceremonious retreat to France.

Tipu, an expansionist, had embarked on a policy in south India which alienated not only the Hindu Marathas but the Muslim Nizam of Hyderabad as well. Cornwallis, calculating that this was an opportunity to deal with Tipu, attacked Tipu with the aid of the Marathas and the Nizam. Mysore had to cede territory to the Marathas, the Nizam and the Company Bahadur. Thus, with very little effort, no less than 20,000 square miles came under British jurisdiction. Also, as an insurance of good behaviour, the governor general took with him two of Tipu's small sons as hostages. In a well known painting, Robert Home has recorded this event from a most unusual standpoint. Cornwallis appears like a favourite uncle and the princes are far from sad; it's almost as if the boys were being taken out for a weekend holiday by the sea. This humiliation, however, fuelled Tipu's hatred even more.

In Bengal, Cornwallis undermined the very foundations of India's agricultural economy by imposing what he called the Permanent Settlement. By this he created, somewhat on the English model, a permanent class of land-owning gentry, the *zamindars*, with absolute land rights. Hitherto, under Hindu and Muslim rulers, the tillers of the soil were regarded as landholders who could not be evicted; but under the new arrangement their position had been reduced to that of mere tenants who could, therefore, be evicted. The *zamindars* had indisputable rights. In Bengal, surmised Cornwallis, the *zamindars* would become the pillars of the establishment and the upholders of Pax Britannica.

The Bengali Hindus were happy to see the end of Muslim rule. The Muslims had lost out and therefore execrated the British. The relationship between the Muslims and the British was one of mutual distrust. In economic terms this resulted in the Hindus (more correctly, the upper sections of Hindu society) getting preferential treatment from the Company Bahadur. Hindu merchants and bankers did business with the company and many Hindus, such as the ancestors of the poet Tagore who were not originally Bengalis, were installed as *zamindars*. A number of favourite *zamindars* were granted the titles of 'Prince' and 'Raja'. The Tagores were such title holders.

Hindus learnt English and populated the company's offices as clerks and even, in some cases, as head clerks. These were the people who spawned what came to be known later as the *bhadra-lok* (the elite of Bengal). It was from this social class of Hindu Bengalis, conversant with English literature and European thought, that what is called the Indian Renaissance eventually emerged.

The Muslims, on the other hand, moped and licked their wounds. Drawing down the shutters they became psychologically withdrawn and introverted. The language and culture of the *firanghis* (a term meaning "foreigners" and previously used to describe foreign Muslims, but now applied to all Europeans) was declared *haram* (unclean) and hence forbidden by many mullahs. The majority of Muslims cut away from all things European and consoled themselves with the past glories of Islamic history. Education in the *madrassas* (Muslim schools) was confined to learning the Qur'an by rote. Thus, over a period of time, India's Muslim population lost out educationally, economically, culturally and socially. The women, in particular, were educationally deprived. This situation persisted for generations with the inevitable result that Muslims lagged behind Hindus who, from the very beginning, had eagerly accepted British education, science, technology and liberal social values. There emerged an educated Hindu middle class which produced doctors, lawyers, professors and engineers and so gained economic power. The Muslims, who had once dominated the country, became second class citizens through nobody's fault but their own.

Richard Wellesley, who became the Marquis of Wellesley, was of Anglo-Irish extraction. On being appointed the next governor general, he worked out a cheap and practical method of extending British power. It was called the System of Subsidiary Alliances. A prince who signed up was guaranteed British assistance should he be attacked by any other prince and he was also free to rule his state as he wished. This, in effect, gave him *carte blanche* for tyranny. In return he had to agree to the following: he was to have no dealings with foreign powers; he had to pay the full cost of maintaining the Company's regiments in his state; if he could not afford to pay in cash or kind he was to hand over part of his territory. The territories thus ceded became part of 'British India'. In addition, a British Resident was stationed in the state. These Residents, usually military intelligence officers, kept a discreet though sharp eye on what was happening. Their spies kept them informed of the ruler's movements, his friends and enemies, his weaknesses in the matter of women and drink, his liaisons, his bastards and all the palace intrigues.

The subsidiary alliance device only succeeded because the Indian states were constantly warring with each other. Baji Rao II, the Peshwa of Pune, concluded an alliance with the company after he was defeated by the Holkar of Indore; later, the combined forces of the Sindhia of Gwalior and the Bhonsle of Nagpur were defeated and they too accepted subsidiary alliances after surrendering large territories; Delhi, then under the control of Sindhia's French general, Perron, was also taken and once again the Mughal emperor came under the 'protection' of the Company Bahadur. Wellesley instructed Lake, the victorious general, to treat the emperor with the respect and reverence due to him so that he might "immediately experience the benefit" of British protection as opposed to that which the Marathas had offered. Lake accordingly assured Shah Alam II of his "loyalty and attachment" and how it would be an honour for him to execute imperial commands. The benefit, such as it was, did not include the resumption of the annual payment (the actual term was "tribute") that Hastings had summarily stopped.

Wellesley, who had ordered the statue of Cornwallis in Calcutta to be removed and his own placed on its plinth, knew that words cost nothing. They had little worth when guns spoke louder and more effectively. His younger brother Arthur (then a colonel and later to become the Duke of Wellington) had also furthered his career prospects in India. In 1799, he participated in the final assault on Seringapatnam where Tipu died fighting. Because of his successes in India, principally against the Marathas whose power he broke at Assaye and Argaum, his enemies laboured under the impression that he was only good enough to command native troops and win campaigns against Indian adversaries. Napoleon disdainfully called him a "sepoy general" and a Prussian general before Waterloo warned his compatriots not to place too much trust in Wellington for he had been schooled in duplicity in India.

Clive's elder son, Edward, was governor of Madras when Tipu was vanquished and his palace stripped. Colonel Wellesley, who was given command of Seringapatnam, recorded, "Scarcely a house in the town was left unplundered ... the property of everyone is gone". The prize agents of the company and the generals busied themselves dividing the spoils. Edward Clive was created Earl of Powis because his wife, Henrietta Herbert, was the sister of the Earl of Powis who had died a bachelor. It thus happened that the Indian collections of the Clives (father and son) came to be housed in Powis Castle which is in Welshpool in

Mid Wales. The exhibits connected with Tipu are of particular interest though 'Tipu's Tiger', a large mechanical device showing a tiger mauling a British soldier, is in London's Victoria & Albert Museum.

India was the ideal hunting ground for British generals intent on making a quick fortune. This was because of the big prize money that came their way after a successful campaign. The vanquished princes were forced to pay fines and reparations and the commanders, quite naturally, got the lion's share. Prompted, therefore, by the prospect of monetary gain, field commanders in India invariably took an aggressive stance. They wanted wars and, if necessary, provoked them. As a rule they were successful but there was one notable adventure that went awry.

Both London and Calcutta were apprehensive about Russia's intentions in central Asia especially after it was widely reported that the Czar's agents were busy in Persia and Afghanistan bribing the local *amirs* with guns, grain and gold. This was the beginning of what Kipling called the 'Great Game'. The Russian Bear, it was believed, wanted a warm water port and had, therefore, set its greedy eyes on India.

Afghanistan was in an unsettled state and Dost Mohammad, who had seized the throne of Kabul, was parleying with the Russians. The deposed king Shah Shuja was, meanwhile, in exile in India under the protection of the Sikh ruler Ranjit Singh, known as the Lion of the Punjab. It would be an excellent move, thought Auckland, the then governor general, if Shah Shuja were reinstalled in Kabul as a British puppet. The British position in India would then be secure, with a grateful king thwarting Russian ambitions in central Asia.

Apart from being ignorant of the Afghan character, Auckland was poorly advised by his officials. Moreover, the idea that a British military expedition in Asia could possibly fail did not occur to him. He might have learnt from the experience of Ranjit Singh whose army, under Hari Singh Nalwa, had notoriously sacked Kabul. Incidentally, it was the clever Ranjit Singh who had taken possession of the *Koh-e-Noor* diamond from the Afghan royal family by a judicious mix of diplomacy and subtle blackmail.

Ranjit Singh was short and dark with a pockmarked face. He had only one eye. Though illiterate, he possessed tremendous intelligence and commonsense. Above all, he was valiant in battle. Emily Eden, Auckland's sister, has left a vivid account of him. She describes him as "a very drunken old profligate" but concedes that "he has made himself a great king; he has conquered a great many powerful enemies; he is remarkably just in his government; he has disciplined a large army; he hardly ever takes life, which is wonderful in a despot; and he is excessively beloved by his people".

At a conference convened at Simla in the Himalayan foothills, the governor general was outflanked by the Sikh king. Though it was decided that Shah Shuja should be reinstated in Kabul, the Sikhs declined to assist in any way apart from, of course, providing moral assistance. In fact, the British expeditionary force was not even allowed to traverse Sikh-controlled territory although it stretched right up to the Afghan border. Ranjit Singh knew something that Auckland did not: Kabul might be easy to take but it was difficult to hold. It was a lesson that Soviet Russia learnt to its cost in the following century. Currently, the Americans and their allies, among them the British, are also learning a few bitter lessons in turbulent Afghanistan.

In 1838, the British moved a whole army through the Sindh desert and invaded Afghanistan via the Bolan Pass; Qandahar, Ghazni and Kabul were taken and Shah Shuja was proclaimed king. But the man himself was corrupt and incompetent. The population despised him and there were bloody revolts all over the country. What the Afghans refused to accept was a ruler who had been imposed on them by the hated infidels. Many British officers were assassinated, chief among them Macnaghten, who had masterminded the sorry enterprise. There were murders, ambushes and guerrilla attacks every day and the morale of the troops, who were by now short of ammunition and supplies, fell to an extreme low. A retreat was ordered and the Afghan snipers picked off, with deadly accuracy, the stragglers in the narrow defiles. Anyone taken alive was mercilessly tortured; hundreds were enslaved. The withdrawal became a rout. Only one man, a doctor named Brydon, managed to escape. The British government has yet again sent troops into Afghanistan. Perhaps the government and today's British generals have forgotton the events of the 1838 'invasion'.

The proconsuls in Calcutta and the government in London could not believe what had happened in the Afghan mountains. For the first time in well over two hundred years, a well-trained, disciplined British army had been annihilated on the soil of Asia. Wellington deplored the disaster; the British had lost face because now every native of India knew that the British could be beaten. Moreover, said the victor of Waterloo, Muslims from Peking to Constantinople would be rejoicing in the knowledge that "European women had been surrendered to the mercies of a lusty Afghan chieftain".

Auckland was in disgrace and unceremoniously sent home. Something had to be done immediately to restore British prestige. The hawkish Ellenborough replaced Auckland. He ordered revenge. Fast moving columns were despatched into Afghanistan on retribution raids. Villages and crops were burnt; men, women and children were massacred. After conducting their bloody business the columns were pulled back. Some 'honour' was retrieved by this despicable conduct even though Dost Mohammad was back on the throne after Shah Shuja had been done to death.

It was Ellenborough who discontinued a small courtesy that the Company had extended to the Mughal emperor. A present, called *nazar*, used to be offered to the emperor. In 1843, this practise was stopped.

British officers in the Afghan debacle had noticed that their Muslim sepoys were unhappy to confront the tribesmen who were their co-religionists. The sepoys were conscious of the fact that the British had usurped the Muslim hegemony of India. From being the rulers the Muslims had been reduced to the level of the Hindus; in fact they were worse off since the British clearly preferred the Hindus. It thus became necessary to remind the Muslims of India of British military might in case they thought that they, too, like the Afghans, could easily eject the British.

The region that presented itself as ideal for such a demonstration was Sindh. It was largely Muslim and was ruled by feudal Muslim *amirs* who owed some sort of an allegiance to Afghanistan. The man chosen for the job was Charles Napier, a fanatic who believed that he had been sent to Sindh on a sacred mission. He was there to prove to the Muslim infidel that the Christian God was infinitely superior to his Allah.

With a force composed almost entirely of sepoys, Napier marched into the desert with a couple of support ships sailing up the Indus. The *amir*, whose army was made up largely of ill-disciplined Balochis, was conciliatory and prepared to talk peace. Napier, who branded the *amir* and his advisers as untrustworthy scallywags, was rude and dismissive; a showdown was what he wanted. At Miani, a few miles from the Sindh city of Hyderabad, powerful cannon fire proved, thought Napier, the superiority of his God.

Napier's model was Wellington and from him he had learnt that in India a British commander never retreated no matter what the odds. It was, they believed, a question of face. Also, men like them took it as gospel that in India revenge was respected. And so, remembering that European women had been left behind in Kabul, Napier allowed British officers and the men of his only white regiment (Irish, as it happened) to violate and carry off Muslim women, many of them of the highest rank.

In 1843, Sindh was incorporated into British India with Napier as its governor.

There was a terrible hue and cry in India and in Britain. Outram, whom Napier despised, wrote and spoke about the general's unprovoked invasion. As happens even today, righteous voices were raised but nothing happened. Napier was hailed as the Conqueror of Sindh and later promoted commander-in-chief in India. In fact, he is still with us – his bronze figure gazes at tourists and pigeons in London's Trafalgar Square.

Victorian schoolboys were brought up to hero-worship the likes of Napier. The Latin word "peccavi" ("I have sinned") became associated with his name. It was put about that after his victory at Miani, he had despatched a rider carrying a single scribbled word to Ellenborough. It was "Peccavi" ("I have sinned / Sindh") – a pun perpetrated by a phlegmatic soldier-saint.

All this was, of course, pure mythology. *Punch*, hitting at Napier's religiosity, had satirised him with sending the "peccavi" message. It was an unknown cartoonist who had punned.

Meanwhile, the Sikh state of the Punjab, with Lahore as its splendid capital, had attained considerable military muscle. Punjab, 'Land of the Five Rivers' (from *punj*, five, and *ab*, water), had always been an area of racial diversity. It is only in the Punjab that one can, even today, see a unique blend of Hindu-Muslim culture. The Sikhs – a minority community – had established their dominance over a Muslim majority region and the man who achieved this was Ranjit Singh already mentioned above.

Ranjit Singh's civil and military administration was largely secular. There were trusted Muslim ministers and the *tope-khana* (artillery) was mostly Muslim. The army was trained by about two hundred Italian, French, American and Anglo-Indian officers to a high standard and the ordnance, manufactured in Lahore by a family of Muslim gunsmiths, compared favourably with its European counterparts. The Sikh kingdom now presented the only obstacle to Hardinge, an experienced soldier, who had succeeded his brother-in-law, Ellenborough. Hardinge whose wounded left arm had been amputated two days before the Battle of Waterloo, came to be known in the Punjab as 'Toonda Laat', the governor with the stump.

When Ranjit Singh died in 1839, he left several heirs but none of them was worthy or competent. Heavy drinking and whoring had sapped the character of the Sikh aristocracy. The army's pay was in arrears and the generals were in sullen mood. To make matters worse the dead king's junior wife, Jindan, whose minor son, Dalip Singh, became the nominated heir, was a selfish schemer who played one faction against another. An attractive woman, a little over thirty years old, she bestowed her sexual favours indiscriminately. 'Toonda Laat' noted that she was "handsome" though "debauched". Many expressed their suspicions about Dalip Singh's paternity since it was believed that Ranjit Singh was too ill and frail in his last years to have produced a child. The chief proponent of this theory was none other than Lord Dalhousie, the new governor general, who spread it about that the old and impotent king had got perverse pleasure from seeing the sexual activity between his passionate young wife and a lustful *bhisti* (water carrier). The child of this carnality, said Dalhousie, was Dalip Singh.

The atmosphere of confused distrust at the Sikh court suited the British admirably. A large force was moved up to the Sutlej river and after four battles (at Mudki, Ferozeshehr, Aliwal and Sobraon) Lahore was occupied. A treaty was drawn up whereby some districts of the Punjab were taken over and what remained was recognised as independent with Dalip Singh as the ruler. Since he was a minor, Jindan became the queen regent. A British resident was, however, posted in Lahore to monitor the day-to-day situation.

The Sikh *sirdars*, who had lost their estates and the power that went with the ownership of land, were seething with discontent and so, too, were the Muslims, but for a different reason. The behaviour of the British in Afghanistan and Sindh had convinced the Muslims of the Punjab, as elsewhere, that the *firanghi* was implacably anti-Muslim. And so, unusually, but as a matter of political convenience, Sikhs and Muslims made common cause. There was insurgency all over the Punjab and, in an outbreak of violence, two British officials were murdered in Multan.

Here, again, was a heaven-sent excuse for military intervention. Dalhousie worked up a holy rage. The Sikh nation wanted war, he declared. Hence: "War they shall have and with a vengeance!" A vengeful army descended on the Punjab.

Mul Raj, an honest and trusted leader, defended Multan bravely but was vanquished by the overwhelming forces pitched against him. The Company's soldiery – whites and sepoys alike – looted and raped without mercy. Mosques and Sikh temples were burnt down. The final battles were fought at Chillianwala and Gujrat. The Sikhs were beaten. On March 29, 1849, Dalhousie proclaimed the annexation of the Punjab.

The British became the owners of the *Koh-e-Noor* which is still a part of the British crown jewels. The young Dalip Singh was packed off to England to be brought up properly; in other words, to be remoulded as an English gentleman. Later, Jindan, too, followed him. Mother and son lived pathetic though far from poverty-stricken lives in England. Their story has all the ingredients of an absorbing film script.

Jindan, who liked to call herself 'Dowager Queen of the Punjab', took to sporting European dress and promenading in Kensington Gardens. Dalip Singh had converted to Christianity while a boy in India. In England he regularly attended Anglican services. He married a part-German, part-Ethiopian girl named Bamba Muller. She, now called Maharani Dalip Singh, spoke only Arabic. They lived on his country estate in Suffolk and his good works for the poor and the afflicted became well known. The generous pay-off that he received for the privilege of being a decent chap, afforded him a comfortable and gracious lifestyle. He cultivated Queen Victoria, the rich, the famous and the landed aristocracy and indulged his passion for hunting and shooting. He often went on hunting trips with the Prince of Wales and was one of the best shots in England.

Unfortunately, with the passage of time, Dalip Singh became an embarrassment to his English friends. This was because of his preoccupation with the Punjab. He made it a habit of reminding his hosts that the Punjab belonged to him by right and that he hoped one day to be enthroned as its sovereign ruler. The British did not take him seriously until Dalip Singh opened talks with the Czar of Russia about his plans to regain his lost kingdom.

Dalip Singh's best friends began avoiding him; invitations to garden parties and the theatre became fewer and fewer; ministers discovered prior commitments when he asked them over for the weekend. In a word, Dalip Singh had been dropped. He was furious; in high dudgeon he ditched Christianity and reverted to the faith of his fathers. He died in Paris, an extremely embittered man.

The fall of the Sikh kingdom was due, in no small measure, to the treasonable conduct of three Indian rulers and to the hatred that other Indian nationalities harboured against the Sikhs. The Muslim ruler of Bahawalpur actively assisted the British and the raja of Patiala (a Sikh himself) was bought off by Hardinge; Gulab Singh, the Dogra raja of Jammu who was Ranjit Singh's vassal, colluded with the governor general. As a reward, Kashmir, a Muslim majority state, was given to Gulab Singh for a cash consideration of a million pounds. This is how Kashmir, once an independent Muslim kingdom, was saddled with Hindu Dogra rule. Thus, the seeds of today's Kashmir problem were sown by the British in the 19th century.

Afghans, Pathans, Gurkhas, Hindus and Muslims from central and eastern India, as well as Marathas and Rajputs, served in the Company's British officered regiments. They were all happy to see the Sikhs humiliated as was depicted on the infamous medal which was distributed to the army. Sikh warriors were shown surrendering their arms in abject defeat. The Raj was the result of shabby and craven collaboration from which the Sikhs, as we will see later, were not exempt.

Dalhousie was convinced that the British were a godsend for the natives of India who were, he believed, sunk in ignorance and degradation. He wanted India to benefit from the fruits of Britain's administrative and inventive genius. Roads, railways, colleges and hospitals were built; a postal and telegraph service was started; and irrigation canals and bridges were constructed. In his zeal Dalhousie invented a useful device which he termed the Doctrine of Lapse. According to this doctrine, an Indian state would automatically be incorporated into British India if the ruler died without leaving a direct and legitimate heir. He thus justified the annexation of Nagpur, Satara and Jhansi, and when the Peshwa died, denied to Nana Sahib the pension his adoptive father had received.

The British, being paramount, could not only create titles but also abolish them. The rulers whose states had been absorbed into British India continued to use their titles such as 'Raja' or 'Nawab' with British permission. Although they were meaningless, Indians, like their rulers, loved titles. Dalhousie, however, gave notice that these honorifics were to be discontinued. All these stern measures, enforced with imperial indifference, created a huge ground swell of antagonism to British rule.

It could be argued that the feudal India of Oriental despotism was being dragged unwillingly, shrieking and kicking, into the modern age. Hindu widows could now remarry and the children from such marriages were legitimate. *Sati* had been banned, the Thugs had been liquidated, and Persian had been replaced by English. Macaulay's famous Minute on Education (1835) became official policy. The poet-historian laid down that those who know the English language have "ready access to all the vast intellectual wealth which all the wisest nations of the earth have created and hoarded in the course of ninety generations". He was also convinced that "a single shelf of a good European library was worth the whole native literature of India and Arabia." The author of the *Lays of Ancient Rome*, the staple poetic diet of Victorian schoolboys did, however, confess that he was unacquainted with any of the ancient or modern languages of Asia.

Macaulay's aim in imparting a working knowledge of English to a section of Indians was "to form a class who may be interpreters between us and the millions whom we govern". Educational institutions on English models were founded and Indians such as Ram Mohan Roy, who liked the title 'Raja' which the powerless Mughal emperor of the day had conferred on him, supported the policy wholeheartedly. In fact, when the government proposed setting up a Sanskrit School in Calcutta, Roy opposed the idea on the grounds that the money would be better spent on an English medium school teaching science and other useful subjects.

During the previous two centuries, the Company had kept Christian missionaries at bay. The Company was in India to make money; it was not in the business of spreading Christianity. However, pressure from Evangelical crusaders in Britain such as Wilberforce – best known for his campaign to emancipate the slaves – forced a change of policy. Missionaries representing the various Christian denominations started hospitals, schools and colleges. It was, after all, the age of Victoria and militant Christianity went hand-in-hand with empire building. "Onward! Christian Soldiers" became the battle hymn of the imperialists.

Macaulay himself believed that once the natives of India had been exposed to the Christian religion and its values, their belief in idol worship and superstition would disappear. Exposing the sepoys to Christian virtues and piety was one thing, but blatantly luring them to change their religion for material profit and promotion was quite another. An officer named Wheeler, who commanded a sepoy regiment at Barrackpur, took upon his shoulders the task of converting his men and there were others like Wheeler all over India.

Missionaries, such as Martyn and Carey, mastered many Indian languages and their scripts and translated the Christian gospels with the idea of spreading the good news to the natives who, they believed, were living in stygian darkness. Printing presses, owned and operated by Christian missionary societies, brought out books and tracts extolling Christianity at the expense of the two main religions of India. These publications, in English and the several regional languages, upset Hindus and Muslims alike not least because they, the Hindus and Muslims, did not possess presses or the know-how to counter the aggressive Christian proselytising. The British, it seemed to many Indians, had not only requisitioned Mammon but also God.

There was a spirit of desperation and disgust abroad and many recalled the prognostication made after Plassey in 1757. By the time Dalhousie, described as the "greatest of Indian proconsuls", left in 1856, there was a time bomb ticking in India. The very next year the incendiary exploded.

1857 AND ALL THAT

Armed uprisings need finance, either from within the country or from abroad. The 1857 uprising in India had no financiers.

'The Great Indian Mutiny', 'The Sepoy Mutiny', 'The Great Indian Rebellion' and even 'India's War of Independence' are some of the labels used to describe the events of 1857. None of them is correct because each presupposes a particular point of view. What there is no doubt about is that the 'mutiny' was a disorganised shambles. Unfortunately, it also served to confirm the low opinion that the whites in general, and particularly those living in India, had of all Indians irrespective of rank, religion or status. "Blackie can't get anything right"; "The sepoy is OK – so long as he's led by whites"; "Niggers can't rule themselves"; "They'll kill their own mothers for money". These were commonly and openly expressed statements. In these times of political correctness not many know – or prefer not to recall – that Indians were called 'Blacks', 'Niggers', 'Wogs' and 'Darkies' not too long ago.

In 1857, the rebellious sepoys had no strategy, no clear cut plans, no command structure, no military leader with the requisite training or education, not even the semblance of concerted action. The various disparate malcontents went on a binge of burning and pillaging and committed the most heinous crimes. It was not a vast and marvellous uprising of the Indian masses. Far from it. The majority of India's 'martial races' stayed steadfastly loyal to their white masters.

When Hardinge was busy liquidating the Sikhs, he observed that if every "black man" (his own words) had thrown a handful of sand in unison the British in India would have been buried without trace. United action, of course, is what Indians have always notoriously lacked. This is evident even today. After Hardinge, another Englishman made the following statement which is revealing: "One Englishman, a simpleton; two Englishman, a club; three Englishman, a nation. One Indian, a philosopher; two Indians, an argument; three Indians, chaos."

The British East India Company had acquired vast Indian territories chiefly through the use of sepoys (Indian mercenaries) trained and led by British officers. There were, as well, all white British regiments but these were few and widely dispersed. The generals often used their privileged white regiments to lead an attack and to "show the sepoys how to do it". In this way the sepoys were goaded into proving that they were as good as, if not better than, the white soldiers. And they proved their valour by killing more of the enemy than the British soldiers did. The 'enemy' were, needless to say, always their fellow Indians.

The English – past masters in the game of 'divide and rule' – were adept at using mercenaries from subjugated races. This they learnt from the Romans. The number of Scottish, Irish and Welsh regiments that were deployed in India is not surprising. Hence, after Nepal was trounced in 1814-16, Gurkha regiments were raised. The Gurkhas were then used to subjugate the Sikhs and, soon after, Sikh regiments were recruited. Marathas, Rajputs, Dogras, Pathans, Balochis, Punjabi Mussulmans and Garhwalis all flocked to serve the British for they were, after all, the winners of battles. Mercenary soldiers love and respect officers who lead them to victory and the spoils of war.

The British did not create the notion of 'martial races' in India as they have often being accused of doing. The notion of 'martial races' was well established in India well before the white man arrived on the subcontinental scene. Hinduism always accepted that Kshatriyas and Rajputs were born for war and Vaishyas were not. Muslim princes preferred Afghan and Uzbek soldiers to Indian Muslims. And in South India the Hindu kings paid their Arab and Afghan mercenaries much more than they paid their own Hindu soldiery.

The British did, however, organise the whole system. Official government publications carefully detailed the districts and regions from which recruiting officers might enlist their sepoys. They also specified the castes and sub-castes that were 'martial'. It will shock many to learn that even today's Indian army follows this practise in large measure. Hence, in the modern Indian Army there is no Gujarat Regiment or Bengal Regiment though there is a Bihar Regiment and even a Madras Regiment. Based on caste lines, for example, there is a Dogra Regiment, a Jat Regiment and a Mahar Regiment (the Mahars are Untouchables, now called Dalits); but no Kayasth Regiment, Patel Regiment or Bania Regiment.

There were, however, rumblings in the ranks well before 1857 (see *Caste and Colour*). The question of money was also pertinent. The Indus was regarded by the sepoys as the natural boundary of their native land; therefore, when a sepoy was ordered to cross the Indus he expected, and was paid, an extra allowance. After 'Peccavi' Napier's conquest of Sindh, however, the trans-Indus territories became part of British India and the allowance was discontinued. To add insult to injury, a new army regulation stipulated that sepoys, on joining up, had to agree to serve overseas if so ordered. For Hindus, 'crossing the sea' was tantamount to losing caste and Muslims were always suspicious that they could be called upon to fight England's enemies who might well be Muslims. A number of sepoys demonstrated vociferously against the new regulation and half a dozen were executed on the orders of their colonel. Later, a whole regiment was disbanded.

There was what would now be called a crisis of management. Regimental officers, so used to laying down the law and knowing that their sepoys would never question an order, thought that exemplary punishment was the answer to every problem. Thus, a Brahmin sepoy named Mangal Pandey was promptly executed when he called on his fellows not to use the army's newly-issued cartridges because they were waterproofed with a mixture of cow and pig fat (see *Caste and Colour*). Two regiments that refused the cartridges were disbanded with dishonour. This meant that hundreds of sepoys were in disgrace and on the scrap heap with no means of providing for their families.

In their arrogance the commander-in-chief and his advisers, who had moved to the cool heights of Simla for the summer, thought that the matter had been resolved. Firm action, they believed, is what Indians understood. For well over a month the top brass did nothing other than prepare for the gymkhanas, dances, dinners and picnic parties so essential to the Simla season. Meanwhile, news of Pandey's execution and the disbanding of the native regiments spread to the other garrison towns with amazing speed.

On May 10, in Meerut (some miles from Delhi) the bomb burst. The sepoys murdered their officers as well as any white women and children that they could find. Rowdy elements, (*goondas*) joined in the carnage. The rag tag army marched on Delhi and, after killing and torturing the white residents, bullied the octogenarian emperor Bahadur Shah II into becoming their supreme leader and issued a stirring call to expel the British from Indian soil in the emperor's name. South India, however, was unaffected and the sepoys there stayed loyal to the British.

There were murders and mass looting in Jhansi, Kanpur, Allahabad, Lucknow and many outlying district towns. North India was in turmoil and unspeakable atrocities were perpetrated on anyone who had a white face. There were several deeds of amazing heroism as well, with servants shielding their masters and escorting them to safety. Heady with initial success and too busy blasting their way into government treasuries, the insurgents failed to cut the telegraph lines. The high command in Calcutta was thus kept well informed of what was happening and British regiments were ordered to danger points or to relieve beleaguered pockets of white civilians. Perhaps the most celebrated and stirring action was Campbell's relief of Lucknow (with kilted Scotsmen marching to the music of their bagpipes) which has become part of British military folklore.

What had begun as an effort to throw off the yoke of the *firanghi* quickly degenerated into blood-soaked chaos and almost into civil war with, yet again, Indians killing Indians. This was to be repeated, tragically, on a much larger scale in 1947, exactly ninety years later.

In 1857, the Sikhs, the Punjabi Muslims and the Gurkhas were the main 'martial races' that stayed loyal to the British. Fighting shoulder to shoulder with British troops they settled old scores with the sepoys from the United Provinces – known today as Uttar Pradesh. The Sikhs and other northerners despised all Purbias (men from the east). It was, therefore, galling for them to have been defeated in the Sikh wars by mainly Purbia regiments. Now it was the Purbias who were fighting the British and this gave the Punjabis an opportunity to get even.

Not a single Indian prince of any importance lifted a finger against the British; many actively sided with them. Among these were all the Sikh rulers, notably the raja of Jind; the Rajput raja of Jodhpur; the Muslim nawab of Rampur; the Dogra ruler of Kashmir; and the two leading Maratha princes, the Sindhia of Gwalior and the Holkar of Indore. Commenting on the role of the princes Nehru wrote, "Many played the part of quislings." With reference to the people at large, he lamented, "It is clear, however, that there was a lack of nationalist feeling which might have bound the people of India together."

There were three main characters in the anti-British upheaval and each of them – two women and a man – had personal rather than nationalist reasons for resorting to arms. There was no man to measure up to the slave Spartacus who, decades before the Christian era, shook the very foundations of the Roman empire by defeating well trained armies in pitched battles and capturing no less than five legionary eagles and twenty-six standards. There was, however, one woman who could be compared to Boudicca of the ancient British Iceni tribe who fought the Romans relentlessly. This was the young Lakshmi Bai.

Both women – one British and the other Indian – were local queens who had lost their rights on the deaths of their husbands. In their dealings with both widows, the imperial power (in Boudicca's case, the Romans; in Lakshmi Bai's case, the British) had been arrogant and unjust.

Jhansi had been incorporated into British India by Dalhousie, the governor general, because there was no direct heir. Lakshmi Bai, rani of Jhansi, contended that her late husband's adopted son had the right of succession. Her case was rejected. Hence, when the chance came, she raised the standard of revolt. A fearless woman, she fought valiantly and was killed in battle. Rose, the general who defeated her, greatly admired her and she is held up as an exemplary Indian heroine. Village bards recite poems to her memory even today.

The last nawab of Avadh, Wajid Ali Shah, was a pleasure-loving patron of the arts who had made his capital Lucknow renowned as a centre of high culture. He was himself a poet, musician and dancer. Affairs of state were neglected and, giving misgovernment as the reason, it was easy for the British to annex Avadh. The nawab was exiled to Calcutta where a close watch could be kept on him. The estates of many of his favourites and vassals were also seized. The Muslim aristocracy of Avadh, the majority of whom were Shias, were, therefore, very anti-British. The nawab's wife, a woman of resolve, and the nawab's diehard adviser, Ahmad Ullah, declared her minor son the new nawab and spearheaded an uprising which was composed mainly of dispossessed gentry who lived beyond their means. Having led lives of decadence and self-indulgence, they were hardly the stuff of which freedom fighters are made. They were soundly beaten and the queen of Avadh had to take refuge in the *terai*, the jungles that straddle the Indo-Nepalese border.

Nana Sahib, adopted son of the deposed Peshwa of Poona, whose pension had been discontinued by Dalhousie, also jumped onto the bandwagon. First, he sent a British-hating Muslim named Azim-ullah Khan to London to make representations against Dalhousie's decision. Khan returned sullen and empty handed. Nana Sahib then proclaimed himself Peshwa and, promising future rewards to his followers, since he had no ready assets, managed to raise a small force. At Kanpur he perpetrated a dastardly deed. British families had been promised safe passage to Allahabad by boat but he had them gunned down in cold blood. Those who did not die were shut up in a small house which was once occupied by the Indian mistress of a British officer. It was called the *bibi-ghar*, 'the lady's house'. Later, on Nana Sahib's orders, those in the *bibi-ghar* were slaughtered and the corpses thrown into a well.

After being deserted by his followers, Nana Sahib took flight and made for the Nepalese border. His lieutenant, Tantia Tope, a born guerrilla leader, continued the struggle for some time together with Lakshmi Bai – but British generalship and gold prevailed. One of his inner circle, a man named Man Singh, took a bribe from a Company agent and betrayed his master. Tantia Tope was hanged.

Two others who stood up to be counted were Feroz Shah, a Mughal prince, and the Nawab of Banda, a descendant of Peshwa Baji Rao I, whose forces joined up with those of Jhansi. Both paid heavily for joining the insurrection.

Seeing that neither the Mughal emperor nor the British exercised meaningful power, a number of petty chiefs made a bid for independence. Most of these chiefs and their relatives were in debt to the local banking families and so, on declaring their independence, they cancelled their obligations by the simple expedient of having all records of the loans destroyed. This caused panic amongst the moneylenders who were Hindus and Jains of the *bania* caste. The anti-British revolt was, so far as the *banias* were concerned, a money loser and so they refused to extend credit to anyone who was against the British. The *banias* were used to doing business with the Mughals and the British and had done well out of both; they were not prepared to put their money into unsafe hands with no collateral. Armed uprisings need finance, either from within the country or from abroad. The 1857 uprising in India had no financiers.

The Company, on the other hand, could raise as much money as it needed. The governor general in Calcutta had tremendous powers of patronage. He could create rajas and *zamindars* and award lucrative contracts at his pleasure. He had only to drop the slightest hint and the heads of the leading Hindu banking families would line up before him, hands folded, ready to advance credit facilities for the supply of guns, grain, horses, mules, provisions, uniforms, meat, liquor and prostitutes for the Company's armies. Napoleon memorably said that an army marched on its belly. In India, the British marched on the money provided by Indians.

It was hard cash that enabled Company agents to recruit a network of spies – all Indians – to report on events throughout the northern provinces. Men such as Nahar Singh and Jehan Khan, who had sold their souls for lucre, worked as the willing tools of their British masters. After 1859, when the pockets of resistance had been mopped up, hundreds of Rajas, Nawabs, Khan Bahadurs, Rai Bahadurs, and Sardar Bahadurs, as well as a motley class of lesser title-holders, were created. These honours were bestowed on those who had been loyal to the British and disloyal to their fellow Indians. Some of today's leading families in India, Pakistan and Bangladesh were founded by an enterprising adventurer, faithful retainer, informer or clever moneylender who had served the British during 1857-59.

For the uprising of 1857, and the atrocities perpetrated, the British exacted revenge with a bloodthirsty ferocity difficult to imagine. The scale was far out of proportion to the crimes that were committed. Before being blown from the mouths of cannon, for example, Hindus had beef stuffed down their throats and Muslims pork. Anyone suspected of anti-British activity was strung up; the countryside was festooned with decomposed, crow-picked corpses hanging from the trees. Shooting down fleeing sepoys became a field sport. It would take pages to list the grisly methods of retribution. Even those who, out of fear, had remained neutral were punished because, to the vultures of vengeance, they were guilty by association.

Among the leading avengers was Havelock who, like Napier, saw himself as a soldier-saint. Both stand honoured in Trafalgar Square, open to the elements. There are plans afoot to redesign the crowded Trafalgar Square complex and it is an appropriate time to consider the relocation of the two statues. It might be an idea to remove the two generals to the quieter and less frequented precincts of the Imperial War Museum. They'll certainly be happier there south of the Thames amidst the mementoes of war.

Delhi, after it had been occupied by the sepoys from Meerut, attracted mutineers from other cantonments together with a sizeable assortment of freebooters. Because of age and infirmity, Bahadur Shah II was in no condition to handle affairs of state and his much younger wife, Zeenat Mahal, began wheeling and dealing. She was, according to R.V. Smith, a Delhi historian, "beautiful and ambitious". And many believe that it was she who poisoned Thomas Metcalfe who had succeeded his brother Charles as British Resident. The morally lax queen, reports Smith, "had her eye on him". However, the hardworking and fastidious Thomas was, unlike his profligate brother, not interested in women or heavy drinking though he did love poetry and music. Ghalib, the greatest poet of the Urdu language, was often at the *mushairas* (poetry readings) at Metcalfe House.

Several princes of the blood eyed the throne and looked for backers to press their claims as and when the opportunity presented itself. In the meantime, a strong force under Nicholson (he who famously ordered his officers to lead their sepoys from the front) seized the high ridge outside the city. Within Delhi itself there was confusion and a notable lack of leadership. Kashmiri Gate and Lahori Gate were breached and Delhi was taken. Hundreds of innocent citizens were executed. The wounded Nicholson was tended during his last few days by a faithful servant, a

Punjabi Mussalman, who was later generously rewarded. The sepoys, it must be said, literally worshipped Nicholson.

On being taken prisoner, the emperor was treated shamefully. He became an object of derision and contempt with British families going to see him as if he were a strange animal in a zoo. They would laugh in his face and call him names. While the old man dozed, small boys would steal up to 'The Great Mughal' and pull his beard. At his trial, the chief charge was treason although he was not, and never had been, a British subject. Pathetically, he pleaded for clemency saying that he was forced to side with the sepoys or else be killed together with his whole family. His pleas fell on deaf ears. Stripped of every shred of respect, Bahadur Shah II was found guilty and exiled to Rangoon where he died and was buried.

Many Europeans at the time had raised irregular light cavalry units which were hired out to the highest bidder. One such 'soldier of fortune' was the villainous Hodson. At the emperor Humayun's tomb he promised three captured princes (two were Bahadur Shah's sons and one a grandson) a safe passage to the Red Fort where, he said, they were to be tried. On the way, however, he ordered them to strip and collected their personal effects. He then shot them dead and boasted that he had made "the last of the House of Timur eat dirt". Among the jewels that he pocketed and presented to his wife were "the turquoise armlet and signet-rings of the rascally princes whom I shot".

The murderer was hailed as a hero in England; the British in India wished that they had bred more men like him. He received messages such as: "I hope you will bag many more." Hodson's regiment, with others such as a similar one raised by Skinner, was later incorporated into the Indian Army. Even after India attained independence in 1947, the regiment was officially designated Hodson's Horse. It would appear that none of the Indian generals who had taken over from their white mentors had read much Indian history.

This year (2007) is the 150th anniversary of the uprising and in early May there were marches in the Indian capital. Patriotic songs were sung with fervour and tableaux were staged. Politicians made impassioned speeches about the dedication and "great sacrifices of the freedom fighters". Some, like Mangal Pandey, were certainly brave men and ought to be honoured as such, but the freedom of India was hardly his priority. He refused to use the new cartridges because he believed that the cow fat which waterproofed them would pollute him and he'd lose his Brahmin caste.

Most of the sepoys were motivated by hatred and revenge and assassinated their British officers on account of the indignities they had suffered at the hands of men who were arrogant and racist. But why did innocent women and children have to be killed as well? In the euphoria of the celebrations no one asked that obvious question.

What if the British had been evicted from the subcontinent? What would have been the alternative? The aged, half-senile Mughal was hardly capable of ruling India. In any case, the Mughal court had by 1857-58 become decadent and thoroughly corrupt. Delhi would not have been able to control Agra and Avadh let alone Bengal, the Rajput principalities, the Marathas, the Nizam and the many states in southern India. There can be no doubt that the subcontinent would have split up into several Hindu and Muslim states which would constantly have been at war with each other. The ruling dynasties all over the subcontinent were uncompromisingly despotic. They would have dragged India back into the Middle Ages and the emergence of the 'world's largest democracy' might never have happened. It is, therefore, to the British that we owe a political system based on 'one man, one vote'. India's democracy is full of flaws; but a corrupt, creaking democracy is better than no democracy.

The government of India was taken over by the Crown in 1858 and the governor general was invested with the additional and superior title of Viceroy of India. Victoria issued a proclamation promising just rule and gave a solemn assurance that she had no desire to impose her religion on the people of India.

In the mid-19th century, most Muslims and Hindus considered the Mughal – rudely ousted from Delhi and languishing in Rangoon – as the rightful emperor of India. It would have offended them and even, perhaps, raised questions as to the legitimacy of such an action, if the British queen had taken the imperial title while Bahadur Shah was still alive. He died, most conveniently in 1862, only a year after Albert, the Prince Consort. In 1877, Victoria was invested with the title of Empress of India after her son and heir, Edward, the Prince of Wales, had toured the country accompanied by his wife. Bertie and Alex, as they were known, were well received in India. The British government then decided that the time was ripe for Victoria to assume the imperial mantle.

After Albert's death, the queen had taken to widow's weeds and had gone into mournful seclusion. This struck a sympathetic chord with all Hindus; over the centuries they had been conditioned to believe that great royal ladies never remarried and always conducted themselves with dignity. Also, Victoria's womb was rich; she had produced four sons and five daughters. She qualified as a mother figure. Stories proliferated that Victoria took a personal interest in the welfare of all Indians and this was confirmed by the fact that she had started to learn Hindustani and had a number of Indians on her personal staff. The dashing Rajput prince, Sir Partab Singh, who had saved many British women and children in 1857, was appointed ADC to the Prince of Wales and became one of the queen's favourites. The 'Great White Mother' who dearly loved her brown children across the seas was an appealing idea.

At Osborne, on the Isle of Wight, evidence can be seen of the queen's interest in India. The Durbar Room, designed by Bhai Ram Singh of Lahore, is crammed with Indian art objects that were presented to the queen by her beloved Indian princes. In the adjacent corridor hang nearly fifty paintings of her favourites; the most impressive is one of Dalip Singh, the deposed king of the Punjab, which was executed by Winterhalter, the German artist who was the court painter. Rajas and nawabs bearing gifts visited her regularly and she treated them like she would her own her sons and godsons. She even gave them names such as 'George' which she could easily pronounce. On her acceptance into the Christian faith the young Coorg princess, Gouramma, was named 'Victoria' after her royal sponsor.

The princely order took to Victoria enthusiastically for they believed that in her hands their possessions and interests were safe. She had, after all, stated categorically: "We shall respect the rights, dignity, and honour of native princes as our own."

If only those princes had read Shakespeare or British history they would not have been so trusting of the promises of monarchs. A mere 46 years after Victoria had died, her German descendant, Louis Battenberg (better known by his anglicised name Mountbatten) conveniently swept aside her oath to the princes of India. In a prime example of British pragmatism the princes were deserted.

It must be said that Victoria had created a sense of goodwill in India in spite of the following little known fact: between 1857 and 1900 about 30 million Indians perished from famines. Never before, not even under the most bloodthirsty and tyrannical freebooters from central Asia, did the people of India suffer so greatly.

When the British empire was at its mightiest – with pink the predominant colour on the world map – the majority of the British people (the working class) lived in penury and degradation. The few Indians who visited Britain in those days were shocked to see the number of prostitutes, many hardly in their teens, who solicited in the streets. It was remarked, even then, that the poor in Britain had all their dignity ground out of them. So moved was a prince of Jodhpur after he had seen living conditions in the East End of London that he offered the unemployed the opportunity of emigrating to his state where they might restart their lives in comparative decency.

Who, therefore, were the beneficiaries of empire?

In Britain, the mill-owners, mine-owners, ship-owners, bankers, capitalists, and international traders were the ones who benefited. In India, it was the trading class and the princely order who did well out of the Raj. The former were the agents of British capitalism; the latter the lapdogs of British imperialism.

However, it was entirely due to British rule and the introduction of western education that there emerged a small but significant class which was intellectually aware and politically active. Seeing that this class consisted mainly of upper caste Hindus, Syed Ahmed Khan resolved to create a Muslim intelligentsia, and to this end founded an educational institution that was later to become the Aligarh Muslim University. A scholar with a vision for the future of his community, his role can loosely be compared to that of Ram Mohan Roy.

Canning, the first British viceroy, tried to heal the wounds caused by the events of 1857. His efforts were mocked by the British in India who called him 'Clemency Canning' even though Indians were given only a very limited role in the running of their country. Soon, they were asking for a bigger role but none uttered the dreaded word "independence". The Indian National Congress, after its first session in Bombay (held on Christmas day 1885) ended with three rousing cheers for Queen Victoria. "The founders of the Congress were proud to describe it as an offspring of British rule," wrote the Indian historian Masani. The speeches of loyalty to both Queen Victoria and Britain were, by today's standards, embarrassing.

Allan Octavian Hume, a former member of the civil service who had supervised the government monopoly on salt in India, founded the Congress as a platform for airing complaints in a proper attitude of submission. Amongst its earliest members were gentlemen such as Bonnerjee, an anglicised Bengali Brahmin. They had no intention of upsetting the imperial apple cart. Most Indians, in fact, would have been more than happy if India had been granted self-governing Dominion Status like Canada and Australia. But for the British government that would have meant accepting Indians as equal to whites. With a very few notable exceptions, no white person in Victoria's reign was prepared to go that far. The 'wogs' (westernised oriental gentlemen) played cricket and were well mannered enough; but they weren't fit to take over and rule a subcontinent. That was the prerogative of whites. The problem, therefore, was one of race and the colour question that goes with it, and, of course, religion.

RACE AND RELIGION

"Of this foolish, surly, national pride, I see too many instances
daily, and I am convinced it does us much harm in this country."
(Bishop Heber)

Discussions on the subject of race are always heated. This is because
even those who declare, "I'm not a racist" or, "Race doesn't matter",
hold definite views on the subject. Therefore, in the sense that everyone
has strong views on race, everyone is a racist.

In Europe, the rise of militant Christianity, coupled with empire
building, fixed three ideas in the minds of all Europeans: firstly, white
people were superior to everyone else; secondly, their religion,
Christianity, was God's complete revelation and hence no other creed
had any validity; thirdly, it was the sacred duty of Europeans to spread
civilisation to all the earth's inferior races who were living, it was truly
thought, in ignorance and darkness. Many educated people in Europe
genuinely believed that 'Negroes' (Black people) had no souls and, hence,
enslaving them and treating them like animals was in no way a
contravention of God's laws. When this belief was buried, due to the
efforts of Christians of conscience, the scientists got to work and many
'proved' that non-whites and particularly 'Negroes' were genetically and
morally inferior beings. Later, the Nazi's justified their mass exterminations
on 'scientific evidence' that made 'non-Aryans' expendable.

Some years ago, a teacher in a London school told me, in all
seriousness, that her Black pupils were poor swimmers because "in their
brains there is a cell that doesn't function and so they can't float". If I
had accused her of being a racist she would have asserted that she was
not at all a racist but only stating facts.

The people of the Indian subcontinent are as racist as anyone else;
they are certainly more colour conscious than white people. On the streets
of London are to be seen Black girls with white boys and white girls
with Black boys; I can honestly say that in well over forty years I've not
seen an Asian girl with a Black boy or an Asian boy with a Black girl.
Youth being what it is, I'm quite sure that there must be some around;
but if there are, they are few.

Every group, social class, caste, professional association, club or
fraternity has an idea of its exclusivity and 'specialness'. However, when

a dominant ruling group happens to be of a particular colour and the majority that is ruled happens to be of a different hue, it follows that the colour of the ruling group is equated with superiority. The British in India were not the only ones who believed that they were superior; many Indians also thought so.

The notion of racial superiority and inferiority was not new to India. It had taken root in the country several centuries before the British arrived. It first came with the white Aryans who conquered the non-white peoples of the Indian subcontinent. Why, then, did the racial arrogance of the British cause so much disquiet and raise so many problems? Was the British brand of racism particularly obnoxious? The observations of the hymnist Bishop Heber who toured India during 1824-25 might throw some light on the question: "Of this foolish, surly, national pride, I see too many instances daily, and I am convinced it does us much harm in this country ... we shut out the natives from our society, and a bullying, insolent manner is continually assumed in speaking to them." He accused the English, particularly, of possessing an "exclusive and intolerant spirit".

India was never colonised by large numbers of British people and most had no intention of settling there. Therefore, they never felt any need to become part of the landscape. They were always foreign, always the masters, the sahibs. Once they became the rulers they had to prove that they were not only different but better than the 'natives'. Hence the impelling desire of the Victorian to maintain a distance, to keep his nose and finger nails clean, and the fetish about starched shirts, neckties in the scorching heat and polished boots. These were the 'standards' that marked out the ruling race.

Typically, a young man, possibly thirty years old, posted as Collector of a district almost half the size of Wales was not only the chief magistrate with powers of life and death but also the officer responsible for the collection of land revenue. To the common peasant, (the *ryot*) he was the *mai-baap* (the 'mother-father' figure). He would have hundreds of Indian functionaries and clerks, some as old as his father, working under him as well as a score or more of personal servants to minister to his every need. He would be living in a vast rambling residence and, being the only white man for miles, the eyes of the entire district would be watching his every move. He was always being scrutinized. Therefore, he had not only to be scrupulously just but to be seen to be so. His was an intensely lonely life; he bore, in Kipling's telling phrase, 'the white man's burden'. It was at his level of administration that the British Empire, if it had any claims to legitimacy, had to be judged.

After a long day's administration or court sitting, at the end of which he might have sentenced a man to the gallows, he would go riding for an hour or two and then, after a bath, dress formally for dinner in stiff collar and bow tie. At the precisely appointed time he would be in the dining room and ring the bell. His butler, correctly attired, would appear and dinner would be served by the 'bearers' (waiters). The sahib, living in isolated splendour, would eat in silence casting a glance or two in the direction of his dog when a feeling of tenderness got the better of him.

After one of his 'back to Blighty' trips, on what was called 'home leave', the sahib would return with a delicately rose complexioned memsahib and the servants of his household would dutifully line up to pay their respects. She would then, as her skin turned progressively more lined and leathery, rule the roost with an increasingly heavy rod of iron. Kipling, poet of Empire, knew what he was talking about when he said that the female of the species is deadlier than the male.

The servants, no doubt, carried tales of the Collector's personal life to the shopkeepers and traders in the town and from there the news spread far and wide. Very soon, a pervading mythology surrounded those who ruled and, in India, mythology is far more potent than mere fact. Never before had such men held sway in India; the people they ruled were not allowed to approach them. They did not indulge in orgies, they did not take bribes, they did not keep Indian concubines, they seemed to have no sex life, not even with their *memsahibs*. They were not driven by power, money or sex. The white administrator class convinced the average Indian that they were, indeed, a very superior breed.

The members of the 'heaven born' Indian Civil Service were a caste unto themselves. They were the super-Brahmins of India and almost approached the concept of the ideal philosopher king, an ideal cherished by both the Greeks and the ancient Indians. It has to be admitted that members of the ICS (wholly British, but with an Indian component later on) performed their duties fearlessly, judiciously and extremely honestly. Perhaps never in history, before or since, has there been a civil service quite like it. Nevertheless, the ICS buttressed the belief in British racial superiority because, so far as India was concerned, not even the Mughals, who had an efficient administration, could boast a better civil service.

In earlier times, however, things were very different. The sahib was a happier man. Without a wife to watch over him and stifle him and his servants, his life was relaxed. In the 18th century, and into the 19th, a number of Europeans adopted a life of opulence and eastern ease. If white women had not appeared on the scene with the advent of easier travel on account of the steamship, it is quite probable that European men in India would have followed the example set centuries ago by Christian knights and their retainers during the Crusades. Many settled in the warmer climes of the Middle East with women who were culturally conditioned to keeping their husbands happy and satisfied in every way. There would have been no moods, no nagging, no answering back and no objection to co-wives, junior wives and concubines. The arthritis-inducing cold and damp of Europe and the insipid food would soon and happily have been forgotten.

Even the most dedicated and committed civil servant needed the comfort of a woman. The ever-serious Shore, who succeeded Cornwallis as governor general, kept a mistress. Shore, elevated to the peerage as Lord Teignmouth, was the first president of the British and Foreign Bible Society which did sterling work in taking the Gospel to non-Christian lands.

Wellesley, elder brother of the Duke of Wellington, had left his wife in England and wrote to her pleading for permission to take a mistress. Sensible woman that she was, she gave it on the understanding that he undertook the sexual act "with all the honour, prudence and tenderness you have shown me". Lady Wellesley's concern for the feelings of her husband's future mistress in Calcutta was most touching.

Over the centuries, Europe had been stamped with feelings of intense guilt where sex was concerned. Celibacy was prized, as was virginity. Later, Protestantism considered the sex act as necessary for procreation but little more; it was a duty for the furtherance of God's grand design. In India, on the other hand, sexual intercourse for Hindus was a matter of pleasure. That is why the Europeans could not believe their eyes when they saw the celebration of sex on Hindu temples. Apart from straightforward lovemaking there was oral and anal sex and, what they considered, lewd and perverted practises. They jumped to the obvious Christian conclusion: all Indians, especially 'the idol worshipping Hindus', were thoroughly immoral. They had, it was concluded, no sense of decency or decorum; the sort of decency that Lady Wellesley possessed in such abundance.

Before the arrival of white women, many European men had discovered pleasure in India. There was a breaching of racial barriers and several taboos were flouted. The leisure hours of many white sahibs were no different from those of wealthy Indians. Wine, women, poetry and music were enjoyed and dancing girls were patronised. Composing verse was regarded as a mark of culture and many Europeans were competent poets in the Urdu language.

Some sahibs took Indian wives. Indian mistresses were "sadly common" with elderly army officers, according to the fervent Heber whose observant eye missed little. The bishop, who did his best to understand the ways of India, deplored the manner in which some of his countrymen of the better class had made it a habit of living 'in sin'. Many, he had not failed to notice, were positively revelling in it. Most were, he wrote, "the greatest profligates the sun ever saw". It was bad enough seeing the white soldiery frequenting native brothels; but they were, after all, base, uneducated men unable to control their lusts. They had to be pitied and prayed for; but the educated white man had a responsibility, a higher calling. It was his Christian duty to be a beacon, an example, to the people of India and especially to the decadent native princes.

The celebrated Charles Metcalfe was known to have an unusually unattractive face. However, this was no hindrance to his sexual conquests. When Resident at Delhi and its virtual king, he fathered three sons by an Indian woman; whether she was his wife or concubine was never ascertained. There is good reason to believe that she hailed from a Sikh family of some standing and may even have been related to Ranjit Singh, king of the Punjab. Metcalfe obviously met her in Lahore when he was the British representative there. She certainly brought him good fortune because Metcalfe went on to become governor general of India for a time and was later elevated to the peerage and appointed governor general of Canada.

William Fraser, who eventually became Resident, had "six or seven legitimate wives". All lived together, presumably very happily. His several offspring were "Moslems or Hindus according to the religion and caste of their mammas". Fraser, incidentally, was a well known big game hunter; it was said that he had killed over eighty lions. His luck with the ladies ran out when he was murdered at the instigation of a Muslim nobleman upon whose sister Fraser had set his predatory eyes.

The first Resident at the Mughal court was David Ochterlony. There is a memorable painting in which he is seen sitting cross-legged on cushions smoking a *hukkah* (hubble-bubble) watching a performance of Kathak dance. He is dressed in the fashion of an Indian aristocrat with an ornate necklace. He is surrounded by his obsequious acolytes and servants.

Ochterlony, who was created a baronet, had thirteen wives. He maintained a *zenana* (an establishment of women composed of wives and concubines). Members of the *zenana* were kept well away from the envious gaze of other men. His *zenana* moved with him when he travelled either on official duties or for pleasure, such as hunting expeditions or visits to friendly Indian princes. The general's penchant for an Oriental lifestyle is all the more remarkable for the fact that he was born in Boston, Massachusetts. It was largely due to his campaigns that the Gurkhas of Nepal were brought to heel and have ever since served loyally in the British army.

The Mughal emperor bestowed on Ochterlony the title of *Nasir-ud-Daulah*, 'Defender of the State'. However, since Indians could not pronounce the Resident's odd foreign name he was called 'Akhtar Loony', an unintended pun. 'Akhtar' in Urdu means 'star' or 'good fortune' and 'loony' of course is the English slang for a lunatic. Ochterlony was no lunatic but his star in India did shine brightly.

A military adventurer named Hearsey married a daughter of the exiled Nawab of Cambay. Known as Hyder Jung Hearsey, he too adopted the life of an Indian aristocrat. His descendants owned the beautiful Dehra Dun valley, which the British in India came to call the Doon Valley.

Prudery, hypocrisy and Victorian values came with the arrival of British women. The missionary type was quite often a middle aged spinster who, after being 'left on the shelf' in Britain, had heard the call to serve God in a heathen country inhabited by an assortment of swarthy peoples. Sometimes, she was the devoted spouse of a padre and invariably a keener Christian than her husband. These women, usually the daughters of schoolmasters and vicars, meant well, each in her own way. But they all had a propensity to be judgmental. Wilberforce had told them that Indian beliefs were an "abomination". Before leaving England's shores they had read the most horrifying accounts of India, many undoubtedly true; and so, considering themselves crusaders for change, they descended on the benighted natives.

They could not see anything good or uplifting in any of the religions of India and said so. They trumpeted the view that the way women in India were treated was degrading not only to Indian women but to women everywhere. Child marriage, the caste system, polygamy, dowry, the veiling of women, idols in temples, the worship of the *lingam* (the god Shiva's phallus), the display of lawless licentiousness during the Holi festival, the self-flagellations of Muharram; all were condemned out of hand, loudly and harshly. The people who indulged in these 'degrading practises' were black and their behaviour was proof of their inferiority.

The missionary woman, thoroughly scrubbed, was seemingly harmless with hair neatly pinned in a bun, strictly no make up and very sensible shoes. However, she did a great deal of harm in the area that is known today as race relations. Do-gooders have often caused disruption. It is no wonder, then, that many of the Raj officials politely kept these women well away from their offices and homes.

The senior administrators and officers of British regiments would go on 'home leave' and while in Britain would acquire suitable brides from among families of their own respective backgrounds. On the whole, they belonged to the professional upper middle class. When such women went out to India they had several servants at their beck and call but in Britain, also, they had had domestic help. Consequently, they were used to handling servants. Moreover, having had a modicum of education, they did not flaunt their superiority. Convinced as they were of their superiority to all Indians, they felt no need to rub it in. Some of them wrote the most interesting accounts and diaries of what they observed in the country, others wrote novels set in India, still others painted scenes from Indian life and studied the flora and fauna. Plants and seeds were ordered from England and the *malis* (gardeners) were set to work under the strict supervision of the lady of the house.

The majority of British males in India, however, procured their white wives in India. The brides came to them on what were jokingly called the 'fishing fleets'. Shiploads of young women disembarked at Indian ports with little more than a letter of introduction, usually from a friend to a friend. The 'boat bride' or husband hunter knew what she had come for and pursued her prey relentlessly. The man she would set her sights on might be a lower rung official, an officer in an Indian regiment, a police officer, a company employee, a tea, coffee, or indigo planter. These women were usually lower middle class and even working class; but in India they were white women and hence had the superior status of the *memsahib*.

Once she had seduced and led her besotted captive to the altar, the new *memsahib* settled down to rule him, his home, his servants and, indeed, the whole country. She displayed her racial prejudice openly. She treated her servants like slaves and all Indians as subhuman monsters. In Britain, women like her had next to nothing; in India she was a member of a whites only club, hardly entered the kitchen, had *ayahs* (nursemaids) to see to her children, and spent a life of leisure with rounds of parties. Yet nothing in India was good enough for her. It was always "This damn country!", "Can't stand the heat!", "Why do Indians stink?", "God, I can't wait for the day when I'll leave this bloody country", "M'dear, never trust the Indians!", "My servants are such bloody thieves!", etc, etc, etc.

In summer, it was usual for women to repair to the 'hill stations'; towns like Simla, Ootacamund, Darjeeling, Naini Tal, Mussoorie,

Dalhousie and several other smaller ones which the British had established. There, largely discreetly but sometimes blatantly, adultery was quite common. The shocking behaviour, particularly of the white women, led many Indians to believe that all European women were of loose character. This made them feel morally superior to the whites. Which Indian man, they argued, would allow his wife to dance with another man with his arm round her? A race and religion that permitted such conduct had to be debased and intrinsically inferior. It was this loose behaviour which contributed towards giving Christianity a bad name among most Indians, particularly the Muslims.

Ballroom dancing was held up as an example of the sinful nature of the white races. Morarji Desai, who, after independence, held important cabinet posts and later became prime minister, was a strict vegetarian, prohibitionist and upholder of what he considered to be Indian virtues and values. He once exclaimed to a friend of mine: "I really can't understand how any man can allow another man not only to touch his wife but actually to hold her closely!"

Desai gained fame – or rather notoriety – as a man who drank his own urine regularly. He called it "urine therapy". In fact, he was a propagandist of the practise and many followed his example. Some leading people in India today, among them a famous film star, are practitioners of urine therapy.

Apart from ballroom dancing there were many other things about the British that made most Indians feel extremely superior. However, since they were ruled by the British they could not openly give voice to their feelings; but the more they kept quiet the more confirmed they became in their sense of racial, moral, religious and social superiority. Defeated and humiliated peoples throughout history have resorted to self-righteousness; it became the opiate of the underdog. The American poet Robert Frost touched on the truth when he wrote that inside every underdog there is an overdog trying to get out.

Dogs, incidentally, were the cause of severe cultural conflicts. All Europeans, and especially the English, love dogs; it's a perfectly natural impulse. In cold climates, dogs can be kept healthy and hygienic. In India, a country of sweltering heat and steamy monsoon weather, dogs have always been regarded as unclean animals. The Europeans in India kept dogs as a matter of course and actually let them into the house. Even the most faithful of the sahib's retainers would retch when he saw his master, while dining at table, feeding his dog with his own hand, and then letting the animal lick his hand in appreciation.

Then, of course, there was the matter concerning toilet hygiene. Indians washed; Europeans wiped. Indians, hundreds of millions of them to this day, cannot accept toilet paper as hygienic. Bathtubs were abhorrent to Indians; they could not understand how soaking in one's own dirty water was considered an enjoyable experience. There was also the use of the right hand and the left hand. In India, the right hand is used for 'clean' purposes such as conveying food to the mouth; only the left hand is used for 'unclean' purposes such as washing oneself after using the lavatory. And so, when Indians saw their masters using the left hand for 'clean' purposes, they took it as a sign of barbarity.

The Hindu took a bath before visiting his temple; the Muslim had an elaborately prescribed washing ritual before entering his mosque. Both left their shoes outside. The Europeans went to church most probably after having had a bath, the heat saw to that, but it was not a religious requirement. However, they never removed their shoes before entering the church. Also, during their worship, men and women sipped wine at the altar rails from the same vessel. This practise was sickening to both Hindus and Muslims. It was on all these counts that the British, though the rulers, were regarded as Untouchables and earned the unhappy reputation of being an unclean people.

The European ate the Hindu's holy cow as well as the pig which, to the Muslim, was the most unclean animal imaginable. The question, therefore, of Europeans and Indians eating together or meeting socially did not arise. Eating together brings people together and this did not happen in India. Indeed, food became another area of conflict and racial tension. Very few Europeans in India ate Indian food; this may come as a great surprise to those in the west who today take Indian food for granted. It was not always thus, especially when the Raj was at its zenith.

After the mutual massacres of 1857 there was mutual distrust. The British ruled but at the same time erected safety barriers around themselves. They became exclusive; no perverse oriental pleasures such as opium or the *hukkah*, certainly no social contacts with Indians, and no Indian food. The *memsahibs*, armed with their cookery books from England, had disciplined the *khansamahs,* cooks, into the mysteries of roast beef, boiled vegetables, stews, puddings and sponge cakes. In any case, it was taken as a fact that Indian food made you decadent, oversexed, lazy and destroyed your moral fibre.

White faces were extremely rare within the old city walls and no European ever went shopping in the dangerous native bazaars, which were, it was widely believed, infested with pickpockets and grasping shopkeepers. The civilian sahibs lived in what were called the Civil Lines. These were conurbations of mansions and bungalow-type constructions with huge gardens and wide, tree-lined roads. The military sahibs lived in the spacious cantonments.

In the front would be a huge lawn and behind each house, tucked away out of sight and screened by fruit trees, were rows of servants' quarters where the armies of retainers were housed. The roads, named after viceroys, governors and generals, were clean and diligently patrolled by the police even though every house had *chowkidars* (watchmen) to guard against intruders. The only Indians in the Civil Lines and the officers' bungalows in the cantonments, were the servants.

The sahibs worked in the secretariats and courts which were also situated outside the old city precincts. In the big cities, social life was hectic and membership of a prestigious club, such as Calcutta's Tollygunge or the Imperial Delhi Gymkhana, was *de rigueur*. In Bombay, there was the Cricket Club of India and the toffee-nosed Royal Bombay Yacht Club. In the south, was the well known Madras Gymkhana but the Ooty Club of Ootacamund was perhaps the country's most coveted. The game of snooker was invented there and Churchill was once a member. Not for nothing was the town called "Snooty Ooty".

A few years ago I was invited to the Ooty Club and caused no small embarrassment. I noticed that one of the clubrooms was named after Winston Churchill. "It's a shame that after so many years as an independent country no one has thought of changing the name plate on this room!" I remarked rather loudly. There was an audible silence. A throat was cleared gently and I was ushered into another room to be shown the several stuffed animal heads adorning the walls. From there I was whisked away to be shown another local landmark. Even under the Brown Sahibs, Ooty is still snooty. Possibly snootier.

In the rural areas, the clubs were usually named after the towns in which they were situated. The Mirzapur Club, situated by the banks of the Ganges in the carpet weaving district of Uttar Pradesh, flourishes today as never before, though, with one exception – all the members are brown. The most senior member is the exuberant Edward Oakley, carpet king and last white grandee. There were some exceptions. In Ambala, for instance, the club was the Sirhind; and Simla had several clubs which included the Simla Club, though the most exclusive was the Green Room which encompassed the Amateur Dramatic Club and the famous Gaiety Theatre. It was here that perennials such as *The Mikado* were performed. The British in India loved amateur dramatics.

During the Raj, Indians who were Oxbridge men and members of the senior civil service were invariably black-balled when they applied for membership to these clubs. They were, of course, proposed and seconded by British members which proves that at least two members of the club were not racist or colour conscious. There were, however, other phobias and these had to do with sex. Two beliefs current at the time and very widely held were: firstly, Indian men were highly sexed on account of the hot foods and spices that they consumed, and secondly, they all lusted after white women. It followed that no white woman would be safe if an Indian were to be let into a club. Keeping Indians out was only a measure to safeguard 'our women'. Forster's *A Passage to India* analyses the dangers that lay in Indo-British social intercourse.

There was another, more understandable, reason for the black-balling of Indians. The Indian officer was anglicised, perhaps more English than the English; but his wife most certainly was not. Because she hardly spoke any English and wore only Indian clothes and jewellery, she'd be out of place. Not only would she, herself, be embarrassed but she would cause embarrassment to the other club wives as well. So the Indian gentleman, if elected to membership, would come to the club on his own. He would socialise with white women, dance with them and drink with them. Such a situation was fraught with the utmost danger.

While in Britain, some Indians married white girls, and this somewhat eased them into a social relationship with their British departmental heads and colleagues. However, these girls were very often lower middle class and even working class. In India, especially in the context of club life, these unfortunate beings were always treated badly. It was quite often their accent that gave away their background and brought down on their heads the disapproval of the *memsahibs*.

Discrimination is discrimination whether arising from race, colour, class, gender, caste or creed. Discrimination in India was rife amongst both the rulers and the ruled.

Indian students who were fortunate enough to come to Britain, always wrote home to their parents and friends assuring them that the British in Britain were very different from their rude and overbearing compatriots in India. Nehru (Harrow, Cambridge and the Inner Temple) became painfully conscious of this fact when he returned to Allahabad, his home city. He who was once the darling of the Mayfair drawing rooms now encountered social barriers; he could not mix with Englishmen on an equal footing.

Freemasonry flourished in India and one of the reasons might have been the sahibs' need for respite from their wives. Because of the secret rituals, the lodges came to be called *jadu-ghars* (houses where magic is practised). Since membership was restricted to men, and as freemasonry itself claimed universal principles of brotherhood, Indians of the right education and status came to be initiated. Thus, oddly enough, it was only as members of a secret society that whites met browns on the level and on the square.

When Kipling joined the masons in Lahore he might have been surprised to see Indian faces in the lodge but he was not, because one of the Masonic brothers who initiated him was an Indian. So, in a well known poem, it was not difficult for Kipling to concede that, in spite of his skin, Gunga Din was a far better man than him.

Freemasonry, however, did not touch the lives of ordinary Indians. Personal humiliations had to be endured every day. A man such as Raja Ram Mohan Roy was not immune. Even Roy was publicly abused by an English officer for not alighting from his palanquin and saluting. Roy stepped down from his palanquin and, saluting the white official, apologised profusely saying that he had not seen the sahib's palanquin coming towards him. The question that must be asked is: Whose behaviour was the more reprehensible?

Beating up 'wogs' and 'niggers' was a common event in and around the cantonments where British regiments were stationed. Even brutal killings of Indians went unpunished. The police rarely took notice or registered complaints, and even if a complaint were lodged at a police station, nothing ever happened. No Indian policeman was permitted to lay a hand on a white man and no Indian magistrate or judge had the power to try, let alone sentence, a white person. Beveridge, the ICS officer whose son, Lord Beveridge, wrote the socio-economic report which laid the foundations of Britain's welfare state, observed that racial tensions in India had never been worse than during the final quarter of the 19th century.

Anti-Indian feelings were at their highest in 1883 when a low caste Indian servant was accused of raping Alice Hume, the wife of a British lawyer in Calcutta. The Indian was sentenced to life imprisonment. It was a cover-up. The fact was that the bored woman had seduced the young man and they had been lovers for several months. One day, the husband, returning early from the office, discovered his wife and the servant in embarrassing circumstances. He set about his wife and injured her badly. In court, however, she claimed that it was the servant who had caused the cuts and bruises. Even then, there were doubts about her evidence. Most of the wounds were on her back, caused by her husband's walking stick. This was ignored by both judge and prosecuting counsel.

The Indian had touched a white woman and that was a criminal offence which merited the fullest punishment.

Annette Beveridge, the scholar-linguist mother of the great economist, could not be accused of racial prejudice. As Miss Akroyd before her marriage, she had been invited to Calcutta by the reformist Brahmo Samaj sect to set up a school for Indian girls from good families. Yet she too made the point that since Indian men had done little to help their own women, it was expecting too much of Indian judges to dispense justice to any woman, let alone to women of an alien race. She argued that her concerns were for women in general which, of course, included white women. These views, coming as they did from a woman of integrity and a self-confessed friend of India, carried tremendous weight. It was, after all, well known that she had married her husband in a Registry Office in Calcutta and the presiding official was an Indian. Her husband explained that this was an exercise in schooling themselves "into seeing Bengalis in office and yielding to them the submission due to their office".

Ripon, the viceroy who took office in 1880, was a former grand master of English freemasonry who had converted to the Roman Church. He was appalled to see the blatant state-sponsored racism in the administration of justice and put forward a bill to amend matters. It was named after Ilbert, the member of his council who held the law portfolio. The whites in India rose in revolt. How could an Indian, they argued, no matter how qualified or impartial, be allowed to sit in judgement on a white man? Ripon, they claimed, was undermining the majesty of British law which was, by its very nature, white. Petitions were sent to Parliament and to the Queen herself; one of the main thrusts being that no white woman could expect justice from an Indian judge. She would most probably be enticed or forced into his *zenana*, it was claimed.

Ripon was booed in Calcutta and a plot was hatched to kidnap him. The English language papers in India, which were owned by British interests, published vituperative articles on race and colour. A communication to the viceroy reminded him that since the natives of India were certainly not the peers of Englishmen it would make a mockery of English law if an Indian were given the power to try and sentence an Englishman. A suggestion was even mooted that if the British government and Parliament did not care for their kith and kin in India, the British in India had the right to sever connections with the Crown. In a word: secession. Much later, the same situation arose in Rhodesia.

Ripon, the English liberal, was defeated by the Anglo-Indian racists. His fiercest opponents were the planters who were described by Curzon, a later viceroy, in these words: "These managers are drawn from the most inferior class of Englishmen and Scotsmen ... they have a profound contempt for the natives ..." This was a rich statement, coming as it did from an individual who believed that Englishmen "partly by heredity, partly by upbringing" and on account of their "habits of mind" must, as a general rule, occupy the highest positions in India.

But Curzon was a special case; without a hint of embarrassment even while at Eton he considered himself a "most superior person". He was, of course, at the time comparing himself to other Etonians. Since he believed that he was far above other Englishmen it is not surprising that when dealing with Indians his hauteur was unbounded. He had no doubt that the British were in India by "a decree of Providence". Insofar as British rule was concerned he wrote, "I do firmly believe that there is no Government in the world (and I have seen most) that rests on so secure a moral basis ..."

In order to proclaim that moral basis, Curzon organised a grand imperial pageant in Delhi in 1903, ostensibly to celebrate the coronation of Edward VII as Emperor of India. Edward did not grace the occasion but sent his brother, the Duke of Connaught, accompanied by a German cousin, the Grand Duke of Hesse. Curzon recreated the splendour of a Mughal *durbar* (royal court) with the Indian princes and other notables lining up, bowing and paying homage.

Typically, he had *Onward! Christian Soldiers* deleted from the programme since he objected to Indians hearing a hymn that had the following forbidding and unimperial words:

> Crowns and Thrones may perish,
> Kingdoms rise and wane.

Curzon could not permit subversive Christian views on the transitory nature of great empires to filter down to the subject race. However, the 'natives' were already restless and the stirrings were not only loud but deep. Ghosh, the president of the Indian National Congress, accused Curzon of wasting "vast sums of money on an empty pageant" when the country was in the grip of a famine. The famine provoked Dutt, the senior-most Indian in the civil service, into a bitter controversy with the viceroy over the vexed question of land revenues. Dutt later became president of the Indian National Congress. Even an influential group of British ICS officers, who had served the Crown steadfastly, voiced their disquiet at the state of affairs in India.

In an effort to make the administration of the unwieldy province of Bengal more efficient, Curzon had partitioned the province in his characteristically highhanded fashion. This incensed the Hindus. In a united Bengal they were in the majority; now they were a minority in East Bengal which was the larger and the more important of the two Bengals. There were strikes, riots and the public burning of textiles imported from Britain.

Allan Octavian Hume, Theosophist and founding father of the Indian National Congress, issued the following challenge to the young graduates of Calcutta University: "There are aliens, like myself, who love India ... but the real work must be done by the people of the country themselves ... If fifty men cannot be found ... then there is no hope for India." William Wedderburn, whose excellent scheme for the setting up of rural banks in India had been turned down, threw in his lot with the Congress and presided over its fourth session. Back in London he entered Parliament and became the Congress representative in Britain. He declared that he had eaten of the salt of India and had thus a sacred obligation to serve India. The metaphor was a very Indian one and roused many young Indian radicals.

Men such as Henry Cotton wrote and spoke out against discrimination. There were, he pointed out, many Indians of culture and education who had studied abroad and it was wrong to expect them to kow-tow to every white man they encountered in the street. It was these Indians who were now qualified to share the white man's burden. This argument ignited other kinds of racist reaction: "As soon as you educate the wogs they get too big for their boots", "It's all Macaulay's fault; it was he who wanted them to be taught English", "You hand this country over to brown Englishmen and see what happens!", and "I'll never take orders from a Darkie!". A strong feeling also took root that the poor people of India were safe only under the protection of the white sahibs; if the brown sahibs ever took over, the poor would be exploited mercilessly. Thus, in the interests of the vast majority of India's inhabitants, British rule became a moral imperative.

Though the Anglo-Indians (those British who had lived in India for generations) detested educated Indians, they execrated English liberals who, in their opinion, represented the greater threat to them.

An Indian did not have to go to Oxford to learn that an Indian railway carriage marked 'Europeans Only' was an affront to him in his own country; he might never have heard of Shakespeare's *Othello* but he knew his place where the sahibs and memsahibs were concerned; he felt the pinch when, for doing the same job, he was paid a fraction of a white man's salary.

The Eurasians, however, were recipients of racism from both their progenitors. Both the British and the Indians discriminated against their in-betweens, the people they themselves had created. A study of the Eurasians' plight starkly illustrates the racism of the rulers – the British – and the ruled – the Indians.

Though most Indians in the north are the result of miscegenation due to wave after wave of foreign invasion and settlement, the Laws of Manu came down heavily on mixed marriages and the resulting 'half-castes'. Most Eurasians sprang from the loins of white soldiers and sailors who had fornicated with low caste, often pariah, women. The stigma stayed with them. Even those who were born within wedlock were tarred with the same brush. Indians despised the 'half-castes' and coined the derogatory term *dougla* to describe them. A British soldier who returned to Britain had to leave behind his native wife and children. The wretched woman had a very difficult time even though boarding schools for the children had been set up by the government. Indians started calling these establishments "schools for *haramis* (bastards)".

In British times, the boys from these schools became police sergeants, engine drivers, health and customs inspectors, railway guards, clerks, mechanics, factory foremen and the like. The girls became nurses, primary school teachers, typists, receptionists and secretaries. Very few aspired to a university education and so the higher professions were beyond their reach. For generations the Eurasians were the lower middle class functionaries of empire. While they looked down on all Indians, they admired the whites and tried to model themselves on their masters. The British, nonetheless, kept them at arm's length and referred to them as *chee-chee*, filth or human excrement.

In earlier times, Eurasians had been tolerated, to a limited extent, by both Indians and whites. Their fathers were either French, Portuguese, Dutch or British; many were flamboyant and adventurous. Since they could not join white regiments, even in the ranks, and were turned down for commissions in sepoy regiments, they did the next best thing; they hired out their services to the native princes. The well known James Skinner was one such. This son of a Scots father and a Rajput mother had a dark complexion and spoke only rudimentary English. His Persian, however, was superb and he wrote his memoirs in that language. His military career started under De Boigne, the Sindhia of Gwalior's general, who became his mentor.

Skinner then raised his own cavalry regiment, composed of horsemen known as *sawars*, and hired it out to the British. He acquired large estates; built a church near Kashmiri Gate in Delhi for himself and a mosque opposite for his Muslim wives. The British, eventually recognising his worth, made him a member of the Order of the Bath. There is a small portrait of him in the Indian Army Memorial Room at Sandhurst. Skinner revelled in Oriental splendour and his parties, picnics and hunts became legendary. His descendants – Christian and Muslim – still live in Hansi and Meerut. His regiment – Skinner's Horse – also survives as an armoured unit of the Indian Army.

A writer of the post-1857 period records that there was a lively Eurasian aristocracy in and around the Delhi territory. It declined, however, through pressure from two diametrically opposed forces: British racial arrogance and the inexorable rise of an educated Indian elite which was composed largely of upper caste Hindus.

At the beginning of the 20th century it was taken as a military fact that no non-white nation could stand up to a white nation. This fact was shattered in 1904-5 when Japan, a mere offshore country of Asia, humiliated the gigantic Russian empire in a modern 20th century war. The psychological implications of this were enormous and Curzon ominously noted that the reverberations of Russia's defeat had "gone like a thunderclap through the whispering galleries of the East". Curzon was right; many Indians had got the message. But Metcalfe, the uncrowned king of Delhi, had already written almost a century earlier, "We have ceased to be the wonder that we were for the natives; the charm that once accompanied us has been dissolved ..."

The reasoned arguments of men like the moderate nationalist Gokhale carried little weight with hot-blooded Indian youth, particularly from Bengal, Maharashtra and the Punjab. A number of them resorted to the gun and the bomb. Attempts were made on the lives of the two viceroys (Minto and Hardinge, grandson of 'Toonda Laat' Hardinge) who succeeded Curzon. And then, in 1909, Sir Curzon Wyllie, who held an important post in the India Office, was shot dead in London by a Punjabi student named Madan Lal Dhingra. Dhingra was hanged in Pentonville prison but not before he made the following declaration: "I am proud to have the honour to lay down my humble life for my country ... I believe that a nation held down by foreign bayonets is in a perpetual state of war."

Though the assassination was condemned by the Indian National Congress, the Radicals and revolutionaries hailed Dhingra and others like him as martyrs. Another who backed and assisted Dhingra was Savarkar whom the benchers of Gray's Inn had refused to admit to the bar; they claimed they had evidence that he was involved in sedition. Savarkar, a Maharashtrian Brahmin, later became president of the right wing Hindu Mahasabha, the party that advocated a Hindu India. Many years later, a few months after independence in 1947, his protégé, Godse, assassinated Gandhi, and Savarkar was arrested on a charge of conspiracy. Godse was hanged but Savarkar was acquitted. To this day, Savarkar is known as Veer Savarkar. 'Veer' means 'strong and brave hero'.

The Indians who took to assassination and bomb throwing were mostly Hindus who drew inspiration from the Gita. Aravinda Akroyd Ghosh, an early advocate of violence, set down the following: "Under certain circumstances a civil struggle becomes in reality a battle and the morality of war is different from the morality of peace. To shrink from bloodshed and violence in such circumstances is a weakness deserving as severe a rebuke as Sri Krishna addressed to Arjuna when he shrank from the colossal civil slaughter on the field of Kurukshetra ... Where, as in Russia the denial of liberty is enforced by legalised murder and outrage, or, as in Ireland formerly, by brutal coercion, the answer of violence to violence is justified and inevitable."

The writer of those words was the son of an anglophile Bengali doctor of the *kayasth* (scribe) caste. His middle name, Akroyd, was in honour of Annette Akroyd who became Mrs Beveridge. According to Ghosh's prescription, which he claimed he took from the Gita, the actions of terrorists, against what they regard as oppression, are justified.

Ghosh was himself implicated in a bombing incident in Bengal, notorious as the Alipore Conspiracy Case, which had resulted in the deaths of an innocent white woman and her daughter. After a lengthy trial, Ghosh was acquitted. The British trial judge, Beachcroft, was his contemporary at Cambridge where in an examination in classical Greek he had been beaten into second place by Ghosh. Ghosh was, without doubt, an outstanding classical scholar, yet in Bengali, his mother tongue, he was always shaky.

During his year-long period of detention as a prisoner under trial, Ghosh underwent what he believed was a spiritual experience. He claimed that the god Krishna had appeared to him. In 1910, he left British jurisdiction and settled in Pondicherry, then a French colony in south India. For the next forty years he wrote and meditated and concerned himself with yoga and philosophy rather than with politics. He also composed long and somewhat tedious poems in English. He had a preference for classical metrical forms. His work has been published in several volumes by the in-house Aurobindo Ashram press. To his devoted followers he was known respectfully as 'Sri Aurobindo' ('Sri' being a respectful honorific as in 'Sri Krishna' and 'Sri Rama'). His chief collaborator and spokesperson was Blanche Rachel Mirra Alfassa, the twice-married Frenchwoman of Turkish-Egyptian-Jewish descent who was hailed as 'The Mother'. Auroville, the centre named after the founder and financed mainly with French money, is still active in Pondicherry, which is now an Indian Union Territory situated south of Chennai.

The racial tension exacerbated by the presence of European women in India has already been mentioned. The Hindu holy men of India, however, attracted white women followers in the past and continue to do so even today. Vivekananda's faithful devotee, Margaret Noble was the daughter of a somewhat poverty-stricken Congregationalist minister. On becoming a Hindu, she was renamed 'Sister Nivedita'. In her writings and lectures she castigated Christianity and likened the British in India to a gang of thieves. Gandhi's disciple, Madeleine Slade, daughter of an admiral, was more restrained in her views and stayed in the background as, she thought, a well brought up Hindu woman should. She became 'Mira Behn' or 'Sister Mira' and served the Mahatma ('Great Soul') for many years. The Theosophist Annie Besant who after separation from her husband, the Reverend Frank Besant, had been the partner of the atheist Charles Bradlaugh MP, was once an advocate of free love and birth control. She arrived in India in 1893 and set up a Theosophical centre at Adyar, in Madras. She started the Home Rule League as well as the Hindu College in Benares which later became Benares Hindu University. A fervent advocate of self rule for India, she was elected the first woman president of the Indian National Congress in 1917.

Annie Besant's close association with Madame Blavatsky, whom she succeeded as the high priestess of Theosophy, made many question her judgment and sense of proportion. Matters came to a sorry pass when she declared that a young south Indian named Jiddu Krishnamurti was mankind's new Messiah. India was, quite naturally, overjoyed; here was a great woman of the west who had recognised an Indian as the Messiah. Krishnamurti was sent to England but in the new environment his eyes, as it were, opened. Endowed as he was with a greater degree of commonsense than his mentor, Krishnamurti disowned his divinity and dissolved the Order of the Star of the East which she had founded. He lived the life of an English gentleman and wrote books on philosophy. After his death a member of his family made the disturbing revelation that in his private life, and in his dealings with others, Krishnamurti was far from gentle.

In a very short time the independence movement had marginalised Annie Besant. In 1919, only a few days after the massacre at Amritsar's Jallianwala Bagh, she made an astonishing statement that stupefied her former acolytes which included Nehru and even, surprisingly, the not too easily impressed Jinnah who was later to create Pakistan. She wrote that after a mob had pelted troops with brickbats, it was "merciful for soldiers to fire a few volleys of buckshot". She had not even bothered to ascertain the facts. The troops had not been pelted with brickbats; the crowd was unarmed; the peaceful assembly was mowed down mercilessly with rifle bullets, not buckshot, without prior warning.

Subhas Chandra Bose, who took up arms against the British during the 1939-45 war, had possibly got the measure of Annie Besant. He wrote of her not without a touch of cynicism: "Even the errors and absuses of Hinduism she would explain away, rather than attack."

Like her fellow firebrand, Bal Gangadhar Tilak, Annie Besant brought Hinduism into the very mainstream of the independence struggle. She asserted that Home Rule was inextricably intertwined with religion "by the prayers offered up in the great southern temples" and by the preaching of Hindu holy men up and down the country. Obviously, she did not realise that she was alienating the Muslims by removing them from the equation.

Tilak, in his paper *Kesari*, had preached violence after studying the Gita and taking his authority from it. A week after the publication of the offending articles, a British district head and an army officer were murdered by two brothers who, like Tilak, were Maharashtrian Brahmins. The brothers were executed and Tilak was arrested and sentenced on the charge of sedition.

Economic exploitation had racial aspects. The Empire provided the legal framework for the deployment of human resources to the ultimate benefit of British capitalism. The abolition of slavery resulted in the Empire turning to India. Shiploads of indentured labourers, known as 'coolies', left India's shores to work in British-owned plantations in South Africa's Natal Province, the British West Indies, the Fiji Islands, Mauritius, Ceylon, and Malaya. To East Africa they went to work on the railways.

These labourers, composed largely of people from the lower castes, were obedient and possessed the proper attitude of meekness and subservience. So far as the white managers and foremen were concerned, the 'Indian coolies' were infinitely better than the 'lazy Malays', the 'drunken Negroes' and the 'arrogant Fijians'. The whites knew that the Indians, who had been ground down for centuries by the caste system, were grateful and happy to be given the chance to improve their economic and social position. Many 'coolies' grabbed the opportunity with both hands. Enduring privations, they managed to educate their children and soon created an intermediate class that existed, often uneasily, between the whites and the Blacks.

The descendants of Indian indentured labourers who constituted a sort of lower middle class in the British colonies sided, on the whole though not exclusively, with the British exploiters. And so, when the British left and the Blacks were in power, the Indians paid the price of collaboration. Idi Amin threw the Indians out of Uganda and today the native Fijians are carrying out a similar policy of persecution against the Indians. The Muslim Malays have effectively made the Tamils third class citizens, after the Chinese. In the new South Africa the Indians are generally content though unpleasant incidents occur occasionally. The Muslim communities in Natal enjoy the 'protection' of the Aga Khan and the oil-rich Muslim states; but the Hindus have no such 'protection'.

In the islands of the Caribbean, the hegemony of the Blacks is firmly established and the Indians (or East Indians, as they are called) are either on the defensive or are being culturally assimilated. Hindu revivalists have, however, been busy for some time. Naipaul records that during the 1946 election campaign in Trinidad, a Hindu campaigner with a loudspeaker reminded Indians that they "were of Aryan blood". The inevitable happened for, to quote Naipaul, "all the animosity that might have been directed at the whites has been channelled off against the Indians".

Unfortunately, even among fellow 'coolies', many caste restrictions were maintained and the old Hindu-Muslim problems continued. There was also colour discrimination. Labourers from north India, who were less dark, did not associate with the very dark labourers from south India.

In his detailed study of East Indians living in the Trinidad township of San Fernando, Colin G. Clarke examines the religious, racial, caste and colour divisions that still afflict East Indian society. Those who claim to be Brahmins are at the apex of Hindu society and the caste system of India stubbornly persists. Thus, the *dougla* (the offspring of an East Indian father and an African-Caribbean mother) tends to drift towards Creole culture. In Trinidad, the Blacks and the East Indians "internalised white racist stereotypes of one another" and so at one time it was not uncommon for East Indians to refer to Blacks as 'niggers' and for Blacks to call East Indians 'coolies'.

The *douglas* of India – the 'Eurasians' – were raised in status by the British rulers during the early years of the 20th century and, to the consternation of the original Anglo-Indians, they also came to be called Anglo-Indians. In their day-to-day contact with Indians it was now the newly-created Anglo-Indians who tended to be overtly arrogant, aggressive and downright rude.

The First World War brought to the surface many latent racial and religious attitudes and prejudices. The larger Indian states had their own armies and in a scramble to prove their loyalty to George V, their King and Emperor, the princes placed themselves and their forces at his command. In 1911, only three years before the war began, the princes of India had bowed before George V in an act of fealty during the elaborate proceedings of the imperial Delhi *durbar.* That they rallied to Britain's cause was understandable for they believed, naively as it turned out, that Britain would stand by them against the radical demands of Indian nationalism.

But why did the Indian nationalists, who had not sworn oaths of allegiance, now issue statements supporting the British war effort? Among these was none other than Tilak who said that his country's loyalty to Britain's cause was "inherent and unswerving". This, coming from a man who had written that the British presence in India was a "predatory foreign incubus", was unbelievable. Tilak had fought for *swaraj* (freedom and self government) and during his trial for sedition had famously uttered: "*Swaraj* is my birthright and I will have it!"

Malaviya told the viceroy that India would help ungrudgingly with men and money in the hope that "British armies shall triumph". Gandhi, who in the Boer and Zulu wars had actively served the British as a stretcher-bearer, advocated that India must offer her "humble assistance" for she had a responsibility on account of being a member of "a great Empire". Both the Congress and the Muslim League issued earnest declarations in favour of the British war effort.

Earlier, Gokhale who was Jinnah's model, had assured Lord Hardinge that if he and his British administrators took ship and abandoned India, he (Gokhale) would immediately telegraph them at Aden and implore them to turn back. Clearly, leaders of all shades and opinions had an extremely lofty opinion of British justice and fair play. They were convinced that once the war was over and the militaristic Kaiser had been defeated the British, in recognition of Indian loyalty, would grant

India self-government. However, an incident occurred at the very beginning of the war that set a few people thinking.

Some Sikhs had settled in British Columbia on Canada's western coast where they worked largely as lumberjacks and in the sawmills. A number of Sikhs, therefore, decided to join their fellows in Canada and an old Japanese steamship, the *Komagata Maru*, was chartered to take them there. The reasoning was that since the Sikhs were loyal members of the British Empire there would not be any problem for Sikhs to work in, and assist in developing, an under-populated part of that vast empire. It was recalled that during the 1857 insurrection, the Sikhs had sided with the British and since then Sikh regiments had fought for Britain in China, Abyssinia, Egypt and the Sudan. After all, they reasoned, there were already many Indians working in the West Indies and other far flung parts of the British Empire. But the Sikhs had misread the Empire's agenda.

The Indian 'coolies' had gone as indentured labourers, or substitute slaves, to the 'black' parts of the Empire. The Sikhs, as free men, wanted to go to a 'white' part of the Empire and to work there as the equals of white men. This was unacceptable to the government of British Columbia.

The ship anchored off Vancouver but the Sikhs were not allowed to disembark; they were turned away without food or water. The *Komagata Maru* sailed back thousands of miles to Calcutta where the Sikhs were ordered to board a train and return to the Punjab. Those who refused (they were unarmed) were fired upon by soldiers. Eighteen Sikhs were killed, many more were injured but a number managed to make good their escape.

The slaughter occurred at the end of September 1914. At that very same time two divisions of the Indian army, including Sikh regiments, were disembarking at Marseilles to defend the honour of the British Empire on European soil.

The military authorities in India carefully censored all letters and so prevented news of the Calcutta shooting from leaking out to any of the Indian units serving overseas. If it had, the repercussions, certainly among the Sikh regiments, might have proved disastrous. However, in India many got to know of what had happened and yet not one of the established political parties (Congress, Muslim League, Hindu Mahasabha) took any action against the killing in cold blood of unarmed Indians.

There are four possible explanations for this: firstly, the political parties were unaware of what had happened; secondly, the Sikhs were a minority, smaller than even the Indian Christians, and therefore did not matter; thirdly, the cosy accommodation with the British government could not be put in jeopardy during the course of a world war; fourthly, both Hindus and Muslims had been slaughtered after the collapse of the 1857 uprising and the Sikhs were the ones who had profited, and so it was a just retribution that the Sikhs should now suffer at the hands of the British with whom they had so gladly collaborated.

The first explanation is the only one that must be rejected. Calcutta was a hotbed of political activity and it was impossible for the killings to have been kept quiet. Also, many Sikhs escaped the carnage and would not have kept their mouths shut. Moreover, as ordered, about sixty people had boarded the train for the Punjab. They must surely have spread word of the dismal fate of those they had left behind.

The other three explanations stand up to scrutiny. They are correct; if not wholly, certainly in large measure.

The First World War was a conflict of competing European powers each of which had empires, possessions and colonies. The combatants were all racists and all regarded themselves as superior to what were then called 'people of colour'; that is, blacks, browns, and yellows. In simple terms, the feelings of many in the British War Office – ministers as well as generals – could be summed up thus: We hate the Germans; but only whites must kill them. We must not let blacks kill Germans because that will give blacks the idea that they can kill white men with impunity, and that would be disastrous for the British Empire.

It was because of such beliefs that many in London were adamantly against the deployment of the Indian Army in Europe. In China, Africa, Egypt, South East Asia, the North West Frontier and even the Middle East, the Indian Army was fighting 'lesser breeds'. Europe was for Europeans. In Europe it was a white man's war and only white men had the right to kill white men.

Nevertheless, the reality of war had to be faced. The British Second Corps had been almost annihilated in the first battle of Ypres and there were no trained white troops, British or Canadian, available. In desperation Indians were rushed to the front after being issued with their new Lee-Enfield rifles. On the last day of October, Khudadad Khan, a Punjabi Mussalman, displayed conspicuous valour in the face of a heavy German attack. He became the first Indian to win the Victoria Cross. His impressive features are portrayed in a painting at Sandhurst.

In earlier wars and campaigns the VC was only awarded to white men. Indians, no matter how brave or valorous, were debarred from the ultimate accolade. The presence of the Indian divisions in Europe now forced the War Office to change its racist regulations. The Germans also were soon to alter their ideas about non-white people. News spread in the German trenches that the Indians were not the pushover that they had imagined. The story of how a whole company of Dogras was wiped out fighting to the last man made a distinct impression. The Indian officer, Jemadar Kapur Singh, shot himself with his last bullet rather than surrender. Another Dogra named Ganga killed five Germans in a hand-to-hand encounter and, after his own bayonet had broken, grabbed a German officer's sabre and continued the attack.

A German soldier reported: "At first we spoke with contempt of the Indians. Today we learned to look on them in a different light ... at a hundred metres we opened a destructive fire which mowed down hundreds but in spite of that the others advanced ... in no time they were in our trenches and truly the brown enemies were not to be despised. With butt ends, bayonets, swords and daggers we fought each other and we had bitter hard work."

The freezing cold and rat infested trenches were not ideal conditions for men used to dry, hot climates. Moreover, they were taken off the troopships and sent almost immediately to the front. There was no period of acclimatisation to prepare them for an icy winter on the western front. Also, many had not even been provided with the appropriate clothing. In late November a cavalry regiment – the Poona Horse – was still clad in khaki cotton uniforms; ideal perhaps for Poona but not for Flanders. Many Gurkhas were seen walking bare footed; when asked where their boots were they replied that their feet were frost-bitten and it was impossible to get their boots on. Pneumonia took a heavy toll. The mismanagement of the general staff was colossal. When the Germans used mustard gas it was the Indians who had not been issued with gas masks. In the face of heavy casualties, immense suffering and vast bungling, it is surprising that there was not a wholesale mutiny. The British who commanded these men were, by and large, good officers and it is most probably due to them that serious trouble was avoided.

Military hospitals for Indian troops were set up in Britain and even the Brighton Pavilion was converted into a hospital. Though a lot of money and effort went into the running of these hospitals, there was always an undercurrent of caution. There was, for example, the vexed question of allowing white nurses into the Indian wards and whether it was advisable to allow those patients who could walk to roam about Brighton at will. The overriding fear was, of course, that these men would become friendly with English girls. Many military memos were issued warning about the dangers of fraternisation. Walls and fences were erected and topped with barbed wire. The hospitals took on the appearance of prisoner-of-war camps. Even some British people began to express surprise that war heroes who had fought for Britain were being treated as if they were prisoners of war.

Visits to the town and the shops were allowed in groups within specified hours and these were strictly rationed and supervised. There was always a 'guide' to show them the sights and to make sure that they all returned. This practise continued in spite of the Chief Constable's report that he had no reason to complain about the behaviour of the Indians. So rarely were the Indians seen in Brighton and the surrounding area that the townsfolk took to sitting on the top decks of buses so that they might look over the walls and see the strange natives of India. The Sikhs, with their long hair and beards, attracted the most attention. Soon, those who had lost limbs or had been wounded in the service of their Emperor began to understand the meaning of the word discrimination. One soldier wrote home to say that though he was fed and clothed adequately, England was very much like the Andaman Islands. The comparison with the Andamans is telling; the British used to banish the worst criminals of India to those remote, inhospitable islands situated to the south of Burma in the Andaman Sea.

Even the junior doctors, who were Indians, had to have passes to leave the hospital precincts and they were lucky to get a pass once in two months. A sub-assistant surgeon named Godbole, a Maharashtrian Brahmin, got so frustrated that he attempted to kill the colonel who was responsible for the restrictions. Godbole got seven years for his pains.

Indian officers (in those days Indians could aspire only to a Viceroy's Commission which was graded up to three ranks) had plenty of time on their hands and wrote a lot of letters to their friends and families in India. The letters were censored and those that were considered too outspoken were suppressed. What these letters show is an honest and truthful assessment of Britain; the good and the bad, the dimples and the warts. Some were grateful to Britain; some realised what was wrong with India, its society and its religions; others saw through the sham of imperialism. There were also letters entreating brothers and cousins not to join the army on any account. A few letters had a distinctly poetic flavour. One half-educated soldier, Ram Jiwan Singh, was perhaps more perceptive than all the leaders of India put together, including Gandhi and the Aga Khan. He wrote that the British people were appreciative of India's war effort on behalf of the Empire and of what India was doing for England. However, he concludes: "But I do not know what they will do for India after the war".

What is particularly interesting is the impression the Indians formed of France and the French as opposed to Britain and the British. Largely from rural communities, these men could be pardoned for presuming that all whites were the same. Nevertheless, without realising it, they were drawn to the Gallic temperament rather than to the Anglo Saxon. Many said that in France they were treated with kindness and consideration by ordinary French people.

The war brought to the attention of the world, and especially to India, the issue of Pan-Islamism. This is a matter that to this day exercises the minds of Muslims and non-Muslims alike. In 1914, the King Emperor George V (known in India as *Jarj Punjim*) headed an intercontinental empire that contained more Muslims than any other country or empire. Shafi, who presided over the Muslim League in 1913, conceded that the British Empire was "the greatest Muslim power in the world". Now this presented a big problem. A Christian emperor who was the proclaimed 'Defender of the Faith', that is the Christian faith, was expected to oversee and protect the interests of hundreds of millions of the world's Muslims. The situation was further complicated by the variety of the Empire's Muslim subjects. Muslims from Nigeria, East Africa, Aden, the North West Frontier, north and central India, Bengal, the Deccan, the Arakan in Burma, and Malaya were vastly different from each other in culture, language, costume and cuisine.

Both Christians and Muslims knew that, certainly since the time of the Crusades, the adherents of the two religions were not on the best of terms. India's Muslims were painfully conscious of the fact that a Christian power from the west had destroyed a Muslim empire on the Indian subcontinent.

Muslims have always been uncomfortable living in a country that is not ruled by Muslims and this problem existed even when the British ruled India. Several efforts were made, through armed insurrection, to bring India back to *Dar-ul-Islam*, that is, Muslim rule and law. Saiyid Ahmad Barelvi, a notable leader of the jihad, fought not only the Sikhs but the British as well and to this end joined hands with the plundering Pindaris (Pathan horsemen largely born and brought up in India). In 1831, Ranjit Singh succeeded in bribing some of Barelvi's Pathan allies to keep out of the conflict and then, at Balakot, massacred hundreds of *mujahidin* (jihad warriors). Barelvi was among those killed. Others followed Barelvi's example, the best known of whom were Titu Mir and

Dadu Miyan. Throughout British rule there were extremist Islamic groups, many underground, dotted all over India but particularly virulent in Bihar and Bengal.

There was, unbelievably, a movement among Muslims to leave India and settle in Muslim countries where they would, they optimistically thought, live happily among their co-religionists. Many did attempt to emigrate but were disillusioned. In 1920, for example, nearly 20,000 Muslims sold their homes and possessions and headed for the Afghan border. Amanullah, the king of Afghanistan, had initially invited his 'Muslim brethren' but when the refugees from 'idol worshipping Hindustan' actually appeared on his borders he refused them entry into his country. Many perished in this unfortunate enterprise.

The Aga Khan, head of the Ismaili Shias, relates that his mother insisted that when she died she be buried in a Muslim country, in Muslim soil. She was therefore buried in Iraq near Karbala, a site particularly sacred to Shia Muslims. The Aga Khan was himself buried in Egypt. This sense of alienation took on alarming proportions with many Muslims believing that India was not their homeland and the more they wallowed in alienation, the more they espoused Pan-Islamism.

The tottering and corrupt Ottoman Empire became for the Muslims of India the centre of their world. The sultans of Turkey had, since 1517, assumed the title 'Khalifa of Islam, Commander of the Faithful and Shadow of God on Earth'. It is significant that the Mughal emperors of India never took the claims of the Ottoman Khalifas seriously. In fact, the Mughals regarded themselves as the Khalifas of the subcontinent's Muslim population. But now, at the start of the 20th century, the Muslims of India, the vast majority of whom were converts from Hinduism, began looking to the Sultan of Turkey for succour, relief and consolation. The forlorn dream was for a Pan-Islamic empire under the Khalifa, the Turkish sultan.

During the war, the British cleverly manoeuvred the disunited Arabs, who were all Muslims, to revolt against their Turkish masters. The exploits of Colonel Lawrence, 'Lawrence of Arabia', in this regard are well known. When, in 1916, Britain elevated her ally Hussein, the emir of Mecca, to kingship, the Muslims of India were furious. Hussein was seen as a puppet who was playing into British hands by waging war against the Khalifa. Many pious Muslims were extremely distraught that the holiest city of Islam was now within the sphere of influence of a non-Muslim European power.

With the defeat of Germany the Kaiser was forced to abdicate. Germany's partner, Turkey, 'the sick man of Europe', was in shambles and the future of the Khalifa was in the balance. India's Muslims took up the cause of the Turkish sultan with righteous fervour in what came to be known as the Khilafat Movement.

In a sadly misdirected move to gain mass Muslim support for the Congress Party, and in an effort to forge Hindu-Muslim unity, Gandhi threw his weight behind the Khilafat Movement. He encouraged and supported the Muslim leaders of the movement to pursue an essentially non-national religious goal and issued several strongly worded statements to the effect that India's Muslims were right to uphold the spiritual and temporal power of the Khalifa. What he succeeded in doing was to drag Pan-Islamism into Indian politics and to plant firmly in the minds of millions of Muslims that their concerns and aspirations lay not in India but elsewhere.

The Khilafat Movement exhibited the worst kind of Muslim bigotry and Gandhi, in a major miscalculation, supported it. Jinnah, though theoretically supporting the movement, had little time for its Muslim leaders. All of them, he believed, were being opportunistic and were playing the Congress card.

Turkey, in the meantime, was moving on. The revolutionaries – the Young Turks – were sick and tired of the ineptitude and corruption that surrounded the Ottoman court. Kemal Ataturk, obviously ignoring the efforts of India's Muslims on behalf of the Khalifa, abolished, in 1924, the very institution of the Khalifate. Turkey was declared a secular state and social changes were pushed through by edict.

Many Indian Muslims, however, still hankered after the Khalifa and the glories of the Ottomans. Even as late as the mid-1940s, for instance, Muslims in Lahore and Delhi wore the fez which had been outlawed in Turkey since the mid-1920s.

During the Balkans war, Indian Muslims donated with great religious fervour huge sums for the Turkish war effort. More money was collected for distant Turkey than was ever collected for worthier Muslim causes, such as education, in India itself. A medical team was despatched to minister to the Turkish wounded. Ansari, the doctor who led the mission, said that it was "difficult for any non-Muslim Indian to realise what Pan-Islamism means to Indian Muslims". Therefore, when Turkey joined Germany in October 1914 the British, understandably, questioned the loyalty of Muslims in the Indian Army.

A few Muslim soldiers in France did desert to the Germans but they were Afridi tribesmen from the mountain belt between India and Afghanistan. Their only loyalty was to their tribal chiefs. Therefore, they did not linger in France to fight for the Germans; they were happy instead to be quickly repatriated to their homes via Turkey and Iran. Mir Mast, the man who led his platoon of fourteen deserters was decorated with Germany's Iron Cross. His brother, Mir Dast, who stayed loyal to the British, won the Victoria Cross for gallantry against the Germans.

Two Muslim units, one in Singapore and the other in Bombay, did mutiny after their *maulvis* (learned clerics) had incited them by saying that they had no business to fight the Turks who were brother Muslims. On the whole, it has to be said, the Muslim troops – most of whom were Punjabi Mussalmans – stayed loyal to *Jarj Punjim* (the Christian 'Defender of the Faith'). This was evident in Gallipoli, in Mesopotamia and in Palestine where Indian Muslims fought the Turks face-to-face at close quarters. In one memorable encounter near Damascus hundreds of Turks surrendered to Risaldar Nur Ahmed, a Viceroy's Commissioned cavalry officer and a Muslim.

When Allenby took Jerusalem, Lloyd George hailed it as a great Christian crusade that had been successfully accomplished although he must surely have known that two-thirds of the soldiers in Allenby's army were Muslims.

During the war years the nationalists in India competed with each other in expressing their loyalty to Britain. The Congress affirmed its "firm resolve to stand by the Empire, at all hazards and at all costs". In early 1918, Gandhi offered his services to the viceroy to assist with the recruiting drive. The Muslim League, not to be outdone, promised the British government "support to the Imperial cause by the Mussalmans of India". The government responded by interning those Muslim leaders whom they considered to be extremists.

The war ended when the Americans decided – albeit tardily – to bail out their English-speaking cousins on the other side of the Atlantic. After the collapse of Germany, President Wilson's famous Fourteen Points envisaged a better and fairer world based on the "principle of justice to all people and nationalities and their right to live on equal terms of liberty and safety with one another". Indian politicians were elated when they read Wilson's declaration; they were convinced that Britain would now work out a plan for Indian self-government. They were to be disappointed.

A draconian measure known as the Defence of India Act operated during the period of the war. Since the Act was soon to expire because the war had ended, the government now framed another Act to replace it. The Rowlatt Act, named after the judge who headed the committee which drafted it, was repressive and ran counter to all the high-minded principles enunciated in Wilson's Fourteen Points. According to this Act the government had the power to arrest and confine people without warrants and could, without providing any reason, confine a person to a particular locality. The authorities claimed that these powers were necessary for the control of sedition and terrorist activity. Thousands of Indians had just laid down their lives in the war and Indian political leaders had been reciting litanies of loyalty to Britain. India expected benevolence and reward; she received, instead, the Rowlatt Act.

There was universal uproar; every Indian spoke out against the new law. Jinnah, Malaviya and Mazhar-ul-Haque resigned in protest from the Imperial Legislative Council. Jinnah warned that the new Act would "create in the country from one end to the other a discontent and agitation, the like of which you have not witnessed". It was also a time of unusual harmony between Hindus and Muslims and this caused the government a great deal of discomfort. However, the feeling in the government and the Anglo Indian community was that if Britannia could see off the jackbooted Kaiser she could see off the likes of the dhoti-clad Gandhi. He was, in Churchill's words, "posing as a *faqir* of a type well known in the East, striding half naked up the steps of the Viceregal Palace… to parley on equal terms with the representative of the King Emperor". Gandhi, moreover, was a *bania* (a member of the Hindu shop-keeping caste) and the British had debarred *banias* from military service because they were regarded as congenital cowards. The racial arrogance of the upholders of the Raj had reached unprecedented levels. Gandhi was no coward. S.M. Burke, joint author with Salim Al-Din Quraishi of *The British Raj in India: An Historical Review* writes, "Much as he disliked violence, Gandhi disliked cowardice even more… He rejected the suggestion that non-violence was the weapon of the weak, arguing that its practice was founded on strength of character and required courage, physical endurance and strict discipline."

There were strikes and closures (*hartals*) all over the country and things got out of control. The police firings provoked bloody riots. There were scenes of extreme violence and the government became convinced that another 1857 uprising was in the offing.

In April 1919, matters came to a head in Amritsar, the sacred city of the Sikhs.

MASSACRE AND MURDER

"'I was confronted,' says General Dyer, 'by a revolutionary army'. What is the chief characteristic of an army? Surely that it is armed. This crowd was unarmed."
(Winston Churchill)

If April is the cruellest month then April 13, 1919 was the very worst day in the whole history of Indo-British relations. It could be said that the Raj committed suicide that day. The atrocity in Amritsar defies description. In an enclosed area, known as Jallianwala Bagh, a gathering of Hindus, Muslims and Sikhs, all unarmed, were subjected to continuous rifle fire for no less than ten minutes. A total of 1650 rounds were fired; 379 people were killed, three times that number wounded. These are official figures. There is little doubt that the actual figures were much higher. No warning was issued before the troops opened fire.

Amritsar is the holiest city of the Sikhs and April 13 happened to be Baisaakhi, New Year's Day in the Punjab and a day particularly special to all Sikhs. It was on Baisaakhi day in 1699 that Gobind Singh, the tenth and last guru, inaugurated the Khalsa, the 'society of the pure'.

How and why did the massacre occur? Why was the situation allowed to deteriorate to such an extent? Who were the victims and who were the villains? What was the result?

The country-wide hostility against the Rowlatt Act, which curtailed the civil rights of Indians, convinced many in the government that an insurrection on the 1857 scale was about to erupt any day. It was this fear that made them react with bewildering venom and ferocity. It also happened that at the time two men in the Punjab believed without doubt that destiny had chosen them to be the saviours of the Raj. Neither was English. One was Michael O'Dwyer, the governor of the province, and the other was an army officer named Reginald Dyer. Both believed that they knew best how to deal with Indians and declared that all Indians, especially the educated ones, only respected you when you cut them down to size and made them understand that the British in India were there to rule; by force, if necessary.

The governor was born near Tipperary, Ireland, the scion of a land-owning family. He was one of fourteen children. Educated first by the Jesuits in Ireland, he went up to Oxford and then joined the Indian Civil Service. In the Punjab he gained a reputation as an officer who could 'get things done'. This bolstered his self-esteem. The people of the Punjab, he said, needed strong government; India, as a whole, was a country unsuitable for democracy. He claimed that the democratic process in India would soon degenerate to become "but a sham, a façade".

In one well known conspiracy case, O'Dwyer had persuaded a tribunal to pass the death sentence on twenty-four of the accused when only six had actually been proved guilty of murder. It was only the timely intervention of Lord Hardinge, the viceroy who had escaped an attempt on his life, that prevented a gross miscarriage of justice.

The governor held the view that the peasants' interests, rather than the politicians', were the chief responsibility of the Raj and it was on this account that he sneered at reformers like Edwin Montagu, the Secretary of State for India who was a member of the British cabinet. Montagu had toured India to discuss the prevailing situation with all shades of opinion – British and Indian. He complained of O'Dwyer's intransigence to Prime Minister Lloyd George. The governor was "opposed to everything", reported Montagu and "determined to maintain his position as the idol of the reactionary forces"; he aimed to "govern by the iron hand".

During the war years the Punjab governor had to keep a keen watch on elements in the province who were continually stirring up trouble. He came down heavily on anyone suspected of sedition. The Khalifa of Islam, in the person of the Sultan of Turkey, had joined Germany and many Indian Muslims were uncomfortable with the idea of opposing their Khalifa. There was also the Ghadr Party (Revolutionary Party), based in the then neutral USA, which was busy negotiating anti-British deals with Germany. The Oxford-educated Hardayal had founded the party in 1913 with the express purpose of carrying the war to India through procuring German military assistance and even intervention. Some arms were smuggled into the Punjab and many dissidents had become adept at making and throwing bombs. O'Dwyer, therefore, distrusted all Indians who had been abroad; they had, he believed, picked up ideas beyond their station. On the other hand, he considered himself a stern guardian angel whom the Almighty had placed in the Punjab; his task was to help and guide the illiterate peasantry provided they came to him in the proper attitude of submission. His family had treated the Irish peasantry in exactly the same manner for generations.

Reginald Dyer was born in Murree, now in Pakistan, where his father had established a brewery. The Dyers were originally from Ireland, a country which for centuries was well acquainted with the ways of English colonialism and exploitation. When Reginald, or Rex as he was known, was very young, Dyer senior started another brewery at Solan, near Simla, the summer capital of British India. The family moved to Simla and there Rex was sent to Bishop Cotton School which was, in every respect, an English Victorian public school. (This boarding school flourishes now as never before; the boys come from some of north India's most affluent families.) Rex and his elder brother were then despatched to Ireland where, as Anglo-Indians, they had problems adjusting to Anglo-Irish society. Though his family was hoping he would study medicine, Rex decided on soldiering and went to Sandhurst.

As a subaltern in a British infantry regiment, Dyer first served in Ireland and then in Burma. On transferring to the Indian Army, he made a name for himself as an aggressive battalion commander on the North West Frontier and in Persia. From the time when he was a schoolboy, Rex was prickly and pugnacious; he had inherited a stammer from his mother and was ever-ready to resort to fisticuffs. On at least three occasions, he ought to have been court-martialled and dismissed the service for physical violence and conduct unbecoming an officer and a gentleman; but his misdemeanours were condoned and therefore covered up by his superiors. Their cover-ups cost the Empire a heavy price in 1919 when Dyer, then a brigadier general, a rank still used in the US army but no longer used in either the British or Indian armies, was commanding a brigade, the 45th, headquartered at Jallandhar cantonment.

Throughout March and early April, the law and order situation in Amritsar had deteriorated. The city, smaller than Lahore and a place of pilgrimage for the Sikhs, had a sizeable Muslim population and what worried the British administration most was the unusual sight of Sikhs, Muslims and Hindus displaying their religious and political unity openly and arrogantly. In 1857, it will be recalled, the Sikhs had sided with the British. But now leading members of the three communities shared the same platform and made fiery speeches; religious and caste considerations were thrown to the winds when, in nationalistic zeal, all drank water from the same vessel; Muslims joined Hindus in celebrating Ram Navami, the birthday of the Hindu god Rama; huge crowds took vows to achieve unity and harmony. Loud slogans were chanted proclaiming national unity and ultimate victory over British imperialism.

Such scenes had never occurred before. British officials had always believed that it could never happen. Miles Irving, the deputy commissioner of Amritsar who headed the entire district administration, clearly lost his nerve and let the situation slip from bad to worse.

The two Indians who were instrumental in welding together the citizens of Amritsar were Saifuddin Kitchlew, a Muslim, and Satyapal, a Hindu. The former, a successful lawyer, was at Cambridge with Nehru and after qualifying for the Bar at Lincoln's Inn had taken his doctorate at Munster university. Satyapal, a first class physician, graduated from Lahore's Forman Christian College, an American missionary college, and then read medicine at King Edward Medical College which was the leading medical institution in north India. Both these men were exactly the type of 'wogs' that O'Dwyer and Dyer detested. Apart from the undoubted racial aspect, there was also a clash of personalities.

Neither Kitchlew nor Satyapal advocated violence but the rowdier elements soon got out of control. One British bank manager and his assistant were murdered in cold blood, another's skull was brutally smashed, banks and other buildings were burnt down and even the mission hospital for women was attacked. A missionary doctor, Marcia Sherwood, was badly beaten by a mob of hooligans and narrowly escaped being killed. A Hindu family hid her in their home, treated her wounds as best they could and at night, when the crowds dispersed, had her conveyed to safety. The city, particularly the older parts which were densely populated, became no-go areas for anyone who looked even vaguely European.

There were outbursts in other cities as well and, so far as the British were concerned, there were further bad omens. Shradhanand, an orthodox Hindu religious leader, was made welcome at the Jama Masjid, the great mosque of Delhi. In Bombay, Gandhi and Sarojini Naidu, the poet and woman activist, were invited to a mosque on a Friday to address the Muslim congregation. Never before in the history of India had a Hindu woman addressed Muslim worshippers in a mosque. On several occasions the army and police had to resort to firing on rioters and arsonists.

On April 9, Gandhi, who was on a train bound for the north on a peace mission, was turned back to Bombay. On the same day, the Punjab government issued a confidential ordinance for the deportation of Kitchlew and Satyapal from Amritsar. Whereupon, deputy commissioner Irving devised a stratagem. He invited the two men to his residence in the Civil Lines, ostensibly for talks. They went in good faith but once they were inside the guarded residence they were detained and informed of their fate. Under armed escort they were taken out of the city. They became the city's heroes and, not unnaturally, the people of Amritsar clamoured for their return. Public disorder erupted immediately and the police lost control. Irving called for the army's intervention and O'Dwyer sanctioned the use of military force.

Dyer arrived at Amritsar from Jallandhar on the evening of the 11th and the next day, in a show of strength, he paraded an armed column round the city. There was no reaction and he thought that he had cowed the citizens. On the morning of the 13th he issued a stern warning to the people of Amritsar. In short, the following was spelt out: (1) No one could leave the city without a special pass. (2) No one was permitted to leave his place of dwelling after 8 pm. (3) There were to be no processions or public meetings of any kind whatsoever. (4) Four or more persons standing together would be considered an unlawful assembly and would be dispersed by force of arms if necessary. The last two words, "if necessary", were appended by the ineffectual Irving. It was probably his last act as the civilian head of Amritsar district before he handed over to Dyer. Little did he imagine that his two words, flowing so naturally from a bureaucrat's pen, would hound Dyer till the day he died.

It was Baisaakhi and people from the outlying rural areas had already congregated in the city. That afternoon, therefore, a huge crowd, many ignoring and some perhaps unaware of Dyer's warning, collected in an area that was called a *bagh* (garden). It was actually a piece of enclosed waste ground, uncultivated and poorly kept. In former times during the hey day of Sikh rule it might have been a pleasure garden but for decades it had served as a venue for public meetings and as a site for *melas* or fairs. There are varying estimates as to the number of men, women and children that had collected there; some figures range from 6000 to 20,000, others from 15,000 to 50,000. Whatever the exact number, several thousand had congregated and there is absolutely no doubt that they were unarmed.

What is mystifying is that though Dyer's prohibitions were read out loudly by the police in several parts of the city, the two most obvious places where they should have been proclaimed, not once but several times, were left out; namely, the Golden Temple and the Jallianwala Bagh itself. This glaring omission points to the dark suspicion that it was not an oversight; perhaps a sick military mind eager for recognition and reward had coldly calculated that a sizeable crowd would, being unaware of the warning, assemble at the appointed spot.

The crowd collected at about four and before five the speeches and protest poems in Urdu and Punjabi were being delivered enthusiastically from the makeshift wooden platform. There were loud slogans against martial law and British oppression. Demands were made for the release and return of Kitchlew and Satyapal. Volunteers with buckets of water were providing for the thirsty. Children were running around playing hide and seek. Many of the old and infirm, scores of them women, were squatting on the ground.

An aeroplane appeared overhead. It caused a ripple of excitement since many in the crowd had never seen an aeroplane before. A little later, at about a quarter past five, the beat of soldiers' boots was heard. Fifty riflemen, twenty-five Gurkhas and twenty-five Balochis, quickly entered the *bagh* at the double through the narrow entrance. They were followed by forty Gurkhas with *kukris* (short curved swords) at the ready. The troops spread out in orderly formation and occupied an advantageous position on a strip of high ground. Dyer gave the order to fire.

At short range the fusillade of .303 bullets cut deep into the crowd. Bodies fell limply like corn before the scythe. For the first few seconds most of the people in the *bagh* didn't know what was happening. Then, amid the wailing and shrieking, pandemonium broke loose. Many were trampled and those who tried to scale the walls were shot down. Corpses piled on corpses and several fell into an old well, some even jumped in to escape the hail of bullets.

Dyer, unruffled and unconcerned, directed the soldiers to shoot into the densest part of the fleeing crowd. He then ordered them to reload and continue firing at will to bring down those who were still running or trying to escape. Briggs, Dyer's brigade major, watched the senseless slaughter with distaste. His face contorted with pain; he pulled at Dyer's sleeve but Dyer did not notice. Only when there was just enough ammunition left to cover a retreat did Dyer gave the order to cease fire.

The people of India were paralysed with disbelief. Even the most rabid nationalist had, till that afternoon, a lingering belief in British justice, decency, honesty and fair play. Now, within a span of ten minutes, British bullets, fired by Indians, had sealed the fate of the British Empire. "The massacre that ended the Raj" is the assessment of Alfred Draper who has, to date, written the best book on Jallianwala Bagh.

The poet Tagore, in a memorably passionate yet controlled and civil letter to the viceroy, renounced his knighthood of the British Empire. He could not, he said, be a member of an order of knights which served an empire that slaughtered its unarmed subject peoples. London was first shocked and then divided; many hailed Dyer, but a few realised that the Empire had proved to the world and, more importantly, to itself that it was morally bankrupt.

To make matters worse Martial Law was proclaimed in the province and backdated to March 30. Gujranwala, now in Pakistan and at the time a small district town, was bombed and machine gunned from the air and a *salaaming* (saluting) order was issued whereby Indians had respectfully and correctly to salute any European within sight. Humiliations were meted out every day. If riding on horseback an Indian had to dismount and salute a passing European. If an Indian were using an umbrella he was to close it, lower it and salute. In one particular instance, an Indian who had failed to salute a European was whipped and publicly made to kiss the white man's boots.

Most notorious of all was Dyer's crawling order. Pickets of British soldiers in the Kutcha Tawarian, the lane in which Marcia Sherwood had been beaten, saw to it that any Indian who wished to pass through the lane was made to crawl; not on all fours but rather by having to scrape across, lizard-like, on his stomach. Rifle butts came down on the heads and backs of those who did not comply with the correct crawling procedure. A whipping post was set up and six youths suspected of being involved in the attack on the missionary were flogged; each got thirty lashes.

The spectacle of public floggings became common all over the Punjab but especially in Lahore, the capital. People were arrested, detained and beaten by both the police and the army on the slightest excuse. The very few brave British voices that were raised against the atrocities were soon silenced. Horniman, who edited the *Bombay Chronicle*, was highly critical of what had happened in Amritsar. Within days he was shipped back to Britain. By and large, however, O'Dwyer and Dyer were treated like heroes and saviours of the Empire.

In early May, the Afghan king, Amanullah, made an attempt to take advantage of the hatred for British rule in India. His ambitions were foiled by Dyer at Thal where he defeated the Afghans and gained further commendations. India, however, was in such a state of ferment that the government was forced to investigate the whole Amritsar affair.

The Indian National Congress had already set up a commission to interview witnesses and prepare a report. This made it necessary to constitute an official committee. Lord Hunter headed the committee which conducted its initial proceedings at Lahore. Though the majority of the members were British, there were three Indian members: Jagat Narain, Sir Chimanlal Setalvad and Sultan Ahmed Khan. They were experienced lawyers and grilled Dyer meticulously. During the period of Martial Law, Dyer had forced Indian lawyers in Amritsar to perform the most menial tasks and now, unbelievably, Indian lawyers were cross examining him as if he were a criminal in the dock. He had never imagined that he, a senior British officer, would ever be spoken to in this manner by mere Indians. Dyer, visibly rattled and disturbed, often rambled and repeated himself when replying to the unemotional, silkily-delivered barbs that were heavy with innuendo and sarcasm. His stammer was no help and he was trapped several times.

It was largely his own fault. He had been advised by his military superiors to retain Counsel and there is no doubt that some of the best KCs in London would have come to his assistance without charging a fee. But in his arrogance he felt that he himself could easily send the Indian interrogators scuttling. He made a serious error from the very start. On entry he saluted Hunter and addressed him respectfully with a "Sir" but did not extend that courtesy to the Indians even though Setalvad was a knight. This was noticed and commented upon.

Dyer insisted throughout that at Amritsar he had done his duty as a soldier; his sole aim was to rescue the Empire from dangerous seditionists. He could not, however, provide satisfactory explanations for several features of his conduct, the chief of which were: (1) His failure to have the proclamation banning processions and assemblies read out and posted at the Golden Temple and at Jallianwala Bagh; (2) His failure to order the crowd to disperse before ordering his riflemen to start firing; (3) His failure to make provision for medical aid for the hundreds which he knew would be wounded; (4) His failure to ascertain the guilt of the youths before having them flogged in the Kutcha Tawarian.

He claimed that the firing had saved the situation in Amritsar, that the law-breakers had been punished and that order had been restored. If the situation had been saved and law and order restored, why was Martial Law imposed later and why was it backdated? To this he had no convincing explanation. Under relentless pressure, Dyer admitted that he had made up his mind to kill as many as possible in order to teach Indians a lesson they would never forget. He said that if he could have got his armoured cars into the *bagh* he would have turned their mounted machine guns on the crowd. The armoured cars had to be left outside because the entrance was too narrow for them.

When asked to confirm whether he had continued directing his fire into the thickest part of the crowd when the people were already fleeing after the first shots, he replied: "That is so." He admitted that he could have dispersed the crowd without actually firing a single shot. Whereupon Hunter asked, "Why did you not adopt that course?" Dyer replied that the crowd "would come back and laugh at me ... I would be making myself a fool."

Dyer had damned himself out of his own mouth. Somewhat naively, he was pleased, even triumphant. He thought that he had done well in making himself clearly understood in his brusque military manner. Lawyers, he believed, needed to be taught a few lessons. Unfortunately, many of his friends and admirers, such as Maclagan the new provincial governor, convinced him that he was right in what he had done and in the testimony he had given. Dyer left Lahore for Delhi by the night train.

All the berths in the first class compartment were occupied by Europeans, but in one of the top berths, unknown to them, lay an Indian and this is what he recorded: "In the morning I discovered that all my fellow passengers were military officers. They conversed with each other in loud voices which I could not help overhearing. One of them was holding forth in an aggressive and triumphant tone and I soon discovered that he was Dyer, the hero of Jallianwala Bagh, and he was describing his Amritsar experiences. He pointed out how he had the whole town at his mercy and he had felt like reducing the rebellious city to a heap of ashes, but he took pity on it and had refrained. He was evidently coming back from Lahore after giving his evidence before the Hunter Committee of Inquiry. I was greatly shocked to hear his conversation and to observe his callous manner. He descended at Delhi station in pyjamas with bright pink stripes, and a dressing gown."

The Indian in the top berth was Jawaharlal Nehru, Saifuddin Kitchlew's Cambridge friend, who in 1947 became independent India's first prime minister.

O'Dwyer, on his recent retirement, had relinquished the governorship of the Punjab. He also appeared before the Hunter Committee and justified the imposition of Martial Law. He not only exonerated Dyer but praised him in the loftiest terms. It transpired that when news of the shooting was conveyed to O'Dwyer in Lahore, the first question he asked was whether Indian troops had been used. The governor had previously made it clear to Dyer that only Indian troops were to be used against the Indian population. O'Dwyer wished to prove that Indians were treacherous by nature and Indians massacring Indians was proof of their treachery. Also, by not using British troops the government intended to avoid the charge of racism.

Dyer did not use Punjabi soldiers, either Sikhs or Muslims, at Jallianwala Bagh. He knew full well that if he had they would most probably have mutinied and turned their rifles on him and the handful of British officers with him. The use of Gurkhas and Balochis was carefully planned. Both nationalities, the former largely low caste, meat-eating Hindus and the latter beef-eating Muslims, were not in the strictest sense 'Indian Indians'. What bonded the Gurkhas and the Balochis was a deep-seated hatred for all north Indians, especially Punjabis, and this is what Dyer traded on. During the firing there is evidence that the riflemen, while carrying out their orders, were actually relishing the massacre. Dyer, it seems, had afforded them the rare opportunity of spilling blood in the very heart of Amritsar, the sacred city of the Sikhs.

Many Indians were convinced that the real culprit was O'Dwyer and that Dyer, an unthinking soldier, was his tool. One Sikh boy who was at Jallianwala Bagh made it his life's mission to wreak revenge. He was a volunteer serving water to the thirsty when suddenly the firing started. While men, women and children were falling about him, he crouched in fear. Though his arm was wounded and he was in great pain, he lay quiet and still under the corpses and managed to escape death. His name was Udham Singh.

Dyer had been promised promotion to the rank of major general with the possibility of a knighthood and so, in an effort to prove his credentials, he made a dramatic gesture of reconciliation with the Sikhs. He decided to make a public profession of his respect for the Sikh religion by being initiated into Sikhism. The corrupt manager of the Golden Temple had a hand in this so-called conversion which was condemned and declared invalid by all practising Sikhs. Sikh theologians pointed out that Dyer had never renounced Christianity and could not, therefore, be accepted into the Sikh faith.

From that moment it was downhill all the way for Dyer. His promotion was cancelled and, after lengthy official deliberations in India and London, he was made to retire from the army. Many, especially Indians, thought he had got off too lightly. The British press was, however, on the whole, hysterically defensive of Dyer. It was claimed that a soldier who had devoted his life to king and country had been cast aside by the politicians. Montagu, a Jew, was the politician who was singled out for the worst abuse. A fund was set up for Dyer by the *Morning Post* and thousands of pounds were collected; he was even presented with a sword of honour. Kipling, to his discredit, subscribed to the fund.

Nevertheless, Lord Meston lamented in the House of Lords that at Amritsar "... British traditions of fair dealing and of humanity and justice to a weaker people were broken, and no casuistry can mend that." Curzon, then Foreign Secretary, added that if the government were to endorse Dyer's action "... we shall lower our own standards of justice and humanity, we shall debase the currency of our national honour."

Dyer's health broke down and he died in 1927. Up to the end he claimed that he had no remorse or regrets over what he had done; he would, if necessary, issue the same orders again. It is perhaps worth letting Churchill, no lover of Indian nationalism, have the last word. At the time, Churchill was Secretary of State for War. He said: "It is an extraordinary event, a monstrous event, an event which stands in singular and sinister isolation ... 'I was confronted,' says General Dyer, 'by a revolutionary army'. What is the chief characteristic of an army? Surely it is that it is armed. This crowd was unarmed."

Even after Dyer had died the campaign to clear his name and to commemorate his services to the Empire was continued. O'Dwyer worked hard lobbying MPs, ministers, peers, generals and bishops. So far as he, personally, was concerned O'Dwyer thought that in England he was perfectly safe. England, after all, was not lawless India. In this presumption he was mistaken.

Udham Singh had been brought up in an orphanage; at an early age he had lost both his parents as well as his elder brother. He was a bright pupil with an enquiring mind and his scrape with death in the *bagh* had made him something of a fatalist. His life had also found focus and he pursued his aims single-mindedly. The various revolutionary groups, such as the Hindustan Socialist army in India and the Ghadr party in the USA, appealed to him and he made contact with them.

His hero was Bhagat Singh, leader of the Hindustan Socialists, who had famously said that he had no need to get married since he had already taken death as his bride. In 1928, Bhagat Singh had shot dead a British police officer named Saunders and had later thrown a bomb into the Central Assembly while the house was in session. Bhagat Singh and two of his fellow assassins were sentenced to death. They accepted the hangman's noose with equanimity, secure in the belief that they had been chosen by destiny to die for their country.

Udham Singh operated under various aliases and busied himself smuggling arms into India; he brought in revolvers and ammunition from the States and was, on one occasion, caught and convicted. On his release in 1933, he made his way to England where he established contact with the Irish Republican Army. By then he had shaved off his beard and cut his hair and became 'a bit of a swank', a term then used for smartly-dressed show-offs. Describing himself as an engineer, he developed a taste for fast cars and motorcycles and liked to talk of his white girlfriends.

Continually changing his name and address, he is known to have lived in Southampton, the Midlands, the East End and north London. Most significant of all, he had stayed in Thurlestone in Devon. O'Dwyer lived at Sunnybank, Thurlestone. Udham Singh had obviously traced the former governor's country retreat and had followed him there. There for a time he became O'Dwyer's driver.

The Punjabis, mostly Sikhs, whom Udham Singh met in the Shepherd's Bush *gurudwara* (temple) or in the Indian eating places – then rare in London – were impressed with his English and his wide knowledge of politics. However, some thought that he bragged a bit too much especially when he told them that he was on a great mission. No one took him seriously although he often told them that he would one day rock the great empire that the British had built through the exploitation of his country.

In 1940, Britain was literally fighting for its life. The Germans seemed invincible. However, in spite of Hitler's frightening superiority, British *sang-froid* did not waver. A meeting convened by old India and central Asia hands, assembled at the Caxton Hall to hear a retired army officer reminisce about Afghanistan. Men in their seventies were to recall their adventures in a distant, backward and landlocked country during the 19th century when only a few miles away, across the Channel, an invasion of Britain was being planned by a modern, technically advanced world power.

Conspicuously present at the Caxton Hall were the Marquis of Zetland, Secretary of State for India; Lord Lamington, retired governor of Bombay; Sir Louis Dane, a former Indian civil servant and best remembered for his house north of Simla which was dubbed 'Dane's Folly'; and, of course, O'Dwyer who was, in the eyes many Indians, the chief villain of Amritsar.

It was March 13, exactly a month before the anniversary of the Amritsar firing. Udham Singh had entered the hall quite normally and stood by the wall near the front listening to the speeches. At the end, just as the audience stood up, he moved purposefully towards the platform and pulling out a heavy revolver fired six bullets at short range. Two struck O'Dwyer killing him on the spot. Zetland, Lamington and Dane were wounded. The assassin made no effort to get away. In fact, he was stunned. He could not figure out why the others had not been killed as well. An arms expert later testified that Udham Singh had used the wrong bullets.

The previous night, Udham Singh had invited his friends for a meal and had handed out *luddoos* (yellow sweets shaped like golf balls) which are distributed on blessed, happy and festive occasions.

When arrested by the police, Udham Singh gave his name as Ram Muhammad Singh Azad. What the officers at Cannon Row police station did not understand was that Udham Singh had provided this unlikely name (incorporating Hindu, Muslim and Sikh names and the word for 'free') to proclaim that O'Dwyer had been killed by him on behalf of all the Hindus, Muslims and Sikhs who had perished at Jallianwala Bagh.

One of Udham Singh's defence lawyers was Krishna Menon, later to play an important role in independent India. After facing the due processes of law at the Old Bailey he was condemned to death. Before leaving the dock he made a defiant speech, shouted out his hatred of British rule in India and, as he was being led out to the cells, he turned and showed his contempt by spitting into the court. He was hanged at Pentonville and buried near the prison wall in an unmarked grave. He had, at the age of 37, finally taken death as his bride.

The war was at a critical point and Britain could have been invaded at any moment. India, just as at the beginning of the First World War in 1914, was in this war also on Britain's side. Men and materials from India were vitally important to the war effort. Even Churchill knew that. Gandhi and the Indian political parties, always conscious of being constitutional and hence against Fascism, terror tactics and assassinations, condemned the gunning down of O'Dwyer. A compromise, in the best British tradition, was worked out. In the national interest it was decided to play down and smother the whole Udham Singh trial.

Had the facts of the assassination been recounted and the full court proceedings published there would, undoubtedly, have been riots and disturbances in India. The country would have gone up in flames which not even Gandhi could have controlled. Crucially, the war effort would have been disrupted. Moreover, army recruitment in India, and particularly the recruitment of Sikhs, would have been seriously affected and Britain could not afford that.

The statement made in open court by Udham Singh was, therefore, suppressed by the trial judge and the Press was instructed not to report it. Pressure was put on Reuter's to ensure that only extremely sanitised, low-key reports of the trial were transmitted to India. The British government made it clear to the viceroy that the newspapers in India were to be subjected to censorship. All India Radio, a government department, only put out vetted and carefully worded communiqués.

The people of India, however, have always held the revolutionaries to be *shaheeds* (martyrs). The Urdu word *shaheed*, a warrior who lays down his life for Islam, has clear Muslim references and connotations. Yet, even today, in an increasingly Hinduised and Hindi-dominated India, people refer to Shaheed Bhagat Singh and Shaheed Udham Singh.

In 1961, Jallianwala Bagh was declared a national memorial in honour of those who had died there. A garden was laid out and in the middle was erected a red symbol of liberty, a permanent reminder of the blood that was shed there. The Indian government made representations to Britain asking for the remains of Udham Singh to be sent to India and, after confidential high level discussions, they were exhumed from the Pentonville grave and flown to Delhi. In 1974, Nehru's daughter, Indira Gandhi, then prime minister, received the remains with fulsome homage that would have embarrassed Gandhi, the Father of the Nation. In an effort to arouse national fervour and to placate Sikh sentiment, she announced that Shaheed Udham Singh had "sacrificed his life for the independence of the country".

The coffin from London, now draped with the tricolour flag of the Indian republic, was taken through the Indian Punjab to Amritsar which is almost on the border of Pakistan. Hundreds of thousands thronged to pay their respects. The hero had returned in triumph. He had, at the very least, proved Sir Michael O'Dwyer, Knight of the British Empire, wrong. The tyrant was never safe, not even in London.

Indira Gandhi, daughter of the revolution whose father and grandfather had fought the good fight for India, managed to commit an outrage that neither the Mughals nor the British dared to envisage even in their wildest moments of madness. In 1984, she ordered the Indian army – in what was called Operation Blue Star – to enter the Golden Temple and punish Sikh separatists who were lodged there under the leadership of a fanatic named Bhindranwale. Tank shells blasted the edifice and machine guns rattled mercilessly. The army of independent India, now officered entirely by Indians, massacred more Indians inside the Golden Temple than Dyer had at the nearby Jallianwala Bagh.

After the desecration of the temple, many Sikhs, even those of moderate views, lamented that a Brahmin woman had done what no fanatic Muslim ruler or racist British governor had ever done in the entire history of India.

Indira Gandhi, too, met a fate similar to that of O'Dwyer; not in London but in New Delhi. Her own Sikh bodyguards laid her low in a hail of bullets. To her credit, however, it must be said that she absolutely refused to change her Sikh bodyguards even though her closest advisers had insisted that she must. "Why should we change them! Aren't we supposed to be secular?" she famously demanded.

The day she was assassinated there were celebrations in the streets of Southall, in west London, which has a sizeable Sikh community. Loud-speakers blared out music and Sikhs, both young and old, joined in the celebratory *bhangra* (dancing). People embraced and congratulated each other. *Luddoos* and other sweets were distributed to passers by. The British police looked on in disbelief.

In Delhi and the other cities of India where Sikhs were in a minority, the atmosphere was very different. Hindus, mainly of the Jat caste from Haryana, were hunting down Sikhs and butchering them. The writer-journalist Khushwant Singh, once accused of being the dead prime minister's sycophant, had to leave his home in a hurry, and with the help of foreign friends sought safety in the Swedish Embassy. "I felt a refugee in my own country," he records. Thousands of Sikhs perished, many burnt to death in their own homes.

A friend of mine who is a *mona* (clean-shaven) Sikh, always wore his *kara* (steel bangle) more for sentimental reasons than any other. It was a vestige of Sikhism that still lingered on his wrist. When I visited Delhi a couple of years after Indira Gandhi's death I noticed that the *kara* was missing and asked why. He said that he had had to get it cut and removed. If he'd been spotted wearing the *kara* he risked having his hand severed at the wrist. He, a senior airline pilot, was in constant fear of being attacked even in one of the better parts of the capital. The fate of his fellow Sikhs in the poorer districts can be imagined.

The much-quoted constitution of India guarantees all citizens justice and the freedom to practise their religion. In Delhi, in 1984, constitutional guarantees meant nothing. Khushwant Singh again: "I have not the slightest doubt that a few armed jeeps with armed policemen, with orders to shoot at sight, would have seen to it that there was none of this. The goons were deliberately allowed to get together. They were directed by the people of the Congress Party. They gathered people armed with rods and brought them in trucks with gallons of petrol. These people then went about looting shops and killing Sikhs, burning them alive with the police watching."

After reading this, the corrosive comment of the hated O'Dwyer comes to mind. He had said that the democratic process in India would soon degenerate into a sham, a façade. Over twenty years have elapsed since the slaughter of the Sikhs in Delhi; not one of the influential politicians, the ringleaders of the killings, has been brought to justice.

Indira Gandhi's son, Rajiv, succeeded her as prime minister. He, too, was assassinated, but not by Sikhs. His handling of the Tamil problem in Sri Lanka had angered many Tamils and a militant organisation – the Tamil Tigers – became active in both Sri Lanka and the Indian state of Tamil Nadu. While on a visit to south India, Rajiv Gandhi was killed by a woman suicide bomber. His body was blown to smithereens and was identified by parts such as his fingers, which were white. His father was a Parsi and his mother a Kashmiri; both white so far as most Indians are concerned. The remains of his Italian-made shoes were also found some yards from where he stood.

The breweries started by Dyer's father, like most of the institutions started by the British, such as the gymkhana clubs and race courses, are still flourishing. The one at Murree in Pakistan is owned by a Parsi family, and though alcohol is forbidden to Muslims in a Muslim country, Islamic law is easily circumvented. Non-Muslims are issued permits to buy alcohol; the drinks are purchased quite legally but then sold on.

In India, the brewery at Solan, near Shimla (in British times spelt without the 'h') is owned by an Indian family named Mohan. A small railway station on the narrow gauge line that goes up to Shimla serves the business. The station is known quite simply as Solan Brewery.

In the late fifties, there was a white Anglo-Indian family in Ambala cantonment which is not far from either Amritsar or Solan Brewery. They lived in somewhat reduced circumstances. Their surname was Dyer. Although I knew them, I was too embarrassed to ask whether they were connected with the monster of Jallianwala Bagh.

THE LEADERS; WARTS AND ALL

*It is significant that at their very first meeting it was Gandhi
who brought the religious question into their relationship.
Later it was Jinnah who concentrated on religious
differences – with a vengeance it has to be said.*

In the whole of south Asia hero worship can reach ridiculous dimensions. Deification is a common phenomenon; even more common is the raising to sainthood and guruship of men and women who have carefully cultivated a reputation for holiness. God-men of various persuasions, Hindu *sadhus*, Muslim *faqirs*, and Sikh *sanths* stalk the land spreading, what they like to call, goodness and positive vibrations. India can certainly claim to be the country which possesses the majority of the world's living gods, goddesses and gurus.

The mentality of placing leadership on a pedestal of sanctity and reverence manifested itself from the very start of political consciousness in the subcontinent. It was not only the people who wanted this; the political leaders, themselves, soon realised that the only way to get a popular following was to invest oneself with the aura of greatness and goodness. Unfortunately, once a leader was canonised a saint or became undisputed head, his followers could find no fault in him. This stifled criticism, comment, analysis and assessment so far as his fanatical followers were concerned. Two men – Mohandas Karamchand Gandhi and Mohammad Ali Jinnah – immediately spring to mind: one, the Mahatma ('Great Soul'), the other, the Quaid-e-Azam ('Supreme Leader').

Both were outstanding men. Both made errors and both, being London-trained lawyers though neither had been to university, played politics till the bitter end. One led his country to independence; the other, almost single-handedly, created a country. Gandhi's followers could see no good in Jinnah and *vice versa*. The two, however, on account of their similar backgrounds, understood each other perfectly, though over the years their paths diverged.

Gandhi, born in 1869, and Jinnah, born in 1876, died in the same year, 1948. Gandhi was assassinated in Delhi in January; Jinnah died in September in Karachi, then Pakistan's capital, a victim to decades of heavy smoking. They had much in common. The hero of both men was the Moderate leader, Gopal Krishna Gokhale. Their respective families hailed from the same area of Kathiawar in western India; Gandhi's from Porbandar, Jinnah's from Paneli; they had the same mother tongue, Gujarati.

Both hailed from merchant-trader backgrounds. Gandhi was a Hindu *bania*, Jinnah a *khoja* of the Ismaili sect of Shia Muslims. The *khojas*, who recognised the Aga Khan as their spiritual head, were Hindu converts to Islam and had retained many elements of their original Gujarati culture. Their names were Hindu-sounding though, on account of intermarriage with Persian Ismailis, many of them were quite fair complexioned and sharp featured. Jinnah's father was Jinnahbhai Poonja and his mother's name was Mithibai. Jinnah's original name was Mahomedalli Jinnahbhai; he later changed it to Mohammad Ali Jinnah. Both were called to the Bar in London; Gandhi at the Inner Temple, Jinnah at Lincoln's Inn. Both were married to very young girls chosen by their respective families. Gandhi's wife, Kasturbai, followed him faithfully throughout his political career; Jinnah's fourteen-year-old wife, Emibai, died soon after he had left for London. Both men adored their mothers who died while they were abroad. Neither was a brilliant student.

When Gandhi was married, he was a thirteen-year-old schoolboy; his wife was slightly younger. She was illiterate. He bullied her but, at the same time, became sexually obsessed with her. This affected his studies. He himself records that when he was sixteen he was having sexual intercourse with Kasturbai while his father lay dying. Consequently, when the pregnant Kasturbai gave birth and the baby died within a few days, Gandhi was grief-stricken and racked with guilt.

Thereafter, he started to regard sex, even within marriage, as sinful. He came to believe, perversely as it happens, that he and his family were being severely punished on account of his carnal pleasures with his young wife. Gandhi's sense of guilt made him a most unusual Hindu because guilt, sin and punishment chiefly preoccupy those from monotheistic faiths such as Judaism, Christianity and Islam.

When he joined college he could not cope and wished to drop out. It was then that his family decided that he must go to England to be educated even though they could hardly afford such a luxury. They were by no means rich even though Gandhi's father and grandfather had been *dewans* (chief ministers) to minor local rajas. They were honest, hardworking bureaucrats; scrupulously careful in money matters and abstemious in their habits. Gandhi inherited these qualities in full measure. He wished to go to England and train to be a doctor but the very idea shocked both family and friends. To become a doctor he would have to touch dead bodies and handle specimens of blood, sputum, urine and excrement. To orthodox Hindus this was unthinkable. In the end it was decided that Mohandas should study law which would qualify him for a good government job.

The *banias*, Gandhi's trader caste, are low in the pecking order of the Hindu caste system. They are just above the Shudras, the manual workers; but then, as in other societies, it is the in-betweens who are particularly conscious of their status. In class-ridden Britain it is the lower middle class, the *petit bourgeoisie*, that differentiates itself most markedly from the working class. Gandhi could never have imagined that with the passage of time and the demolition of the British Empire – due in no small measure to him – many of his fellow *banias* and other even lower caste Gujaratis such as the Patels would own corner shops and run sub-post offices in Britain itself. These Asians now constitute the very backbone of the British lower middle class.

It is interesting that not a single person in Gandhi's sprawling family had studied Sanskrit, the sacred language of the Hindus over which the Brahmins had a near monopoly. They were unaware of the ebb and flow of India's cultural development and the higher ideas embodied in vedantic speculations. Religion, as they practised it, was what they were brought up to do or not to do as a matter of custom. Ritual was predominant and was overlaid with much superstition and hedged about with caste restrictions. As a schoolboy, for example, the young Gandhi became friendly with an older boy who happened to be a Muslim. The father disapproved of the friendship on the grounds that Mehtab, the bigger, stronger boy would lead his son astray. Moreover, he was a meat-eater and, hence, unclean. As it happened, the future Mahatma did start eating meat with Mehtab and discovered, unhappily, that he liked it.

He thought also that eating meat would make him physically stronger and sexually more active and Mehtab had assured him, "If you eat meat you will be brave like me". It was the classic case of a younger boy following his hero; but to Gandhi's father it was the Muslim who was entirely to blame.

Kasturbai was pregnant again and this time their son, Harilal, survived; it is interesting to conjecture that Mohandas's secret meat-eating sessions with the boastful Mehtab might have had something to do with it. Anyway, before he was nineteen, Gandhi set sail for England. His mother, Putlibai, made him swear that he would not touch meat, that he would not drink wine and that he would not sleep with other women. England, it was widely thought, was a land soaked in sin. Putlibai was the fourth wife of

Gandhi's father and several years younger than her husband. When in 1995 the Bombay writer Ashok Row Kavi said in a television interview that the Mahatma was a bastard, there was, it should come as no surprise, a furore in India. Kavi, though reviled and threatened, stoutly maintained that Gandhi was illegitimate since he was born before his father had married Putlibai.

During his almost four years in London the law student had a very trying time. He was chronically short of money; it was cold and foggy; vegetarian food was hard to come by; the uniform of the English professional gentleman, with stiff collar and necktie, was uncomfortable. Gandhi took to walking. Originally, it was to save the bus fare but then he discovered that the exercise was good for him. He became a dedicated walker which held him in good stead in the years ahead.

In those days vegetarianism was not fashionable. Vegetarians were regarded with amused derision by most Europeans but Gandhi enthusiastically joined the Vegetarian Society of England which, as a part of its general principles, extolled the virtues of simple living and non-violence. He soon started writing articles for their magazine. He then went a step further than his fellow Gujarati *banias* back home; he gave up spices, chillies, cloves and even ginger. Later, he forsook cow's milk in favour of goat's milk. Any food that was 'heatening' and which, he believed, aroused the baser passions was to be avoided.

Gandhi did, however, have his period of flirtation with western ways. He attended elocution classes to improve his accent, he began violin lessons and actually started to learn ballroom dancing. In an effort to improve his chances with the ladies, he once even suppressed the fact that he was a married man with a son. The suppression did not result in any conquest because his conscience bothered him and he soon confessed to his deception.

It was also in London that he read the Gita (in English) seriously and was tremendously attracted to the Authorized Version of the New Testament, especially the Sermon on the Mount. British law impressed him greatly and he came to the conclusion that India could do no better than to achieve Dominion Status and stay securely within the British Commonwealth. So far as his studies went he failed the London matriculation. Latin was his stumbling block; but he managed to get through at the second attempt. The law examinations he passed at the first attempt.

He was popular with the other aspiring barristers for no other reason than that he was a teetotaller. During the compulsory dinners that the students had to eat at the Inns of Court, each group of four was supplied with two bottles of wine. This meant that the three students who could persuade Gandhi to join their group would each get a larger share of the wine, and so he was always being invited to join one group or another.

Two days after he was admitted to the Bar he boarded a steamer for India. On landing in Bombay the first news he received was that his mother had died some while ago. The family had not informed him as they did not want him to grieve; it would have affected his studies.

As a lawyer he was a disaster; the first time he appeared in a Bombay court he was tongue-tied through shyness and retired from the case in embarrassment. He was forced to eke out a living doing clerical work before his half-brother, Laxmidas, who had largely financed his education in London, helped him to get a job in his native Gujarat.

It was now that Gandhi got his first taste of British imperial arrogance in India. Laxmidas had lost his job as secretary to the raja of Porbandar's heir on the grounds that he, Laxmidas, had given wrong advice. Laxmidas, therefore, asked Mohandas to plead on his behalf with the British political agent who was the real power in Porbandar. Gandhi had met the British official briefly when the latter was in London on leave. In London the officer had been very civil and Gandhi thought that the political agent would at least give a patient hearing to Laxmidas's version of events. The official, however, rudely informed Gandhi that if Laxmidas had prepared a proper enough defence he ought to submit it through the usual channels. He then summoned one of his servants and ordered him to eject Gandhi.

The young lawyer's future was bleak, when out of the blue he received a letter from a local company which traded with South Africa. Dada Abdulla & Co, owned by a Muslim merchant family, had a law suit pending in a South African court and required the services of a trustworthy Indian lawyer to represent them there. They offered Gandhi the job. It was a godsend because the law offered Gandhi no future in India. He left for South Africa in April 1893 leaving his family for the second time. By now he had become a father again; his second son was named Manilal.

The situation in South Africa was confused and fractured, and riddled with racial and colour discrimination. Gandhi was in for a number of very rude shocks. Though the vast majority of the population was Black, or 'Negroes' as they were then called, they were at the very bottom of the pile. Unfortunately, the Blacks were, themselves, bitterly divided along tribal lines, for example, Zulus versus Bantus.

The whites, the masters, were also divided along racial lines; the British administrators and settlers had little or no time for the Afrikaners, those of Dutch descent who were mainly farmers; hence, the term 'Boer', the Dutch word for peasant. The Dutch had colonised huge areas of southern Africa long before the British came on the scene. Indeed, the 'Boers' maintained that they had moved into some unpopulated tracts of Africa before even the Black tribes. It is for this reason that the Afrikaners proclaim themselves to be a white African tribe.

There were also people of mixed race, called 'Coloureds'; they were usually the progeny of 'Boer' men and Black African women.

The Indians who had been brought to South Africa as indentured labourers, were universally labelled as 'Coolies'. They, too, were divided amongst themselves; firstly, along religious lines and then along caste lines. A few Indians, particularly in the British administered province of Natal, were doing well as merchants and shopkeepers and this aroused envy not only among the Blacks but also among the whites.

Gandhi landed in Durban correctly attired in trousers, coat, shirt and tie. On his head he sported a turban in the Kathiawari style. In court, however, the judge instructed him to remove his turban. It transpired that though Arabs were permitted to wear turbans in the courtroom, Indians were not. He resented being called a 'Coolie barrister' and disliked even more the fact that he was often treated like a Black African. Indeed, Gandhi himself referred to the Africans as *kaffirs*, the derogatory term that the whites used. However, the great moment of truth came when he was thrown off a train for the offence of travelling first class even though he had bought a first class ticket.

Gandhi's eyes were opened on the train to Pretoria just as Paul's were on the road to Damascus. He decided to stay on in South Africa and fight for the rights of the Indians who had settled there. He got his wife and small sons to join him. In South Africa he and Kasturbai had two more sons, Ramdas and Devadas. He decided to educate his sons himself but their education was desultory; not only did he lack patience but he was not often at home. He was either too busy with his legal work or away in distant townships delivering speeches and organising demonstrations.

For the very first time, Indians of all religions, castes and classes rallied together, for here was a man they could trust and respect. Many found him eccentric, even somewhat dictatorial; none could doubt his integrity. Dada Abdulla & Co were happy with the way that Gandhi had handled their case; rather than let the proceedings drag on for years in the courts he got the opposing sides to assent to arbitration. A compromise was agreed upon and both sides went away content in the knowledge that each had won a partial victory. The Muslim traders of Natal, many of them *khojas*, were more than happy with the slightly built Gujarati *bania.* Many Indian business houses hired him as their legal adviser and attorney and he set up a busy practice. His income was now considerable but he distributed most of it to worthwhile causes. All the while, however, he worked to galvanise the Indian community to stand up for their right to be treated like human beings and to oppose the blatantly unjust and discriminatory laws.

Gandhi instinctively sensed that ordinary uneducated people could achieve great results with dramatic effect. When every Indian over the age of eight was required to be registered and fingerprinted and made to carry on his person a certificate or 'pass' that could be checked at any time, Gandhi decided on action. He called a mass meeting in the grounds of the Hamidia Mosque in Johannesburg. A resolution to burn the 'passes' was adopted and men, women and children came forward and consigned their government decreed documents to the flames. An English newspaperman who was present compared the event to the Boston Tea Party. He was right, perhaps more right than he realised. The incensed people of Boston were protesting against unjust taxation; the 'Coolies' of Johannesburg had discovered their dignity.

Years later, in India in 1930, Gandhi brilliantly organised and stage-managed the celebrated Salt March which caught the world's attention not so much because it was a protest against an iniquitous tax, which it certainly was, but because it assumed the magnitude of a moral crusade. In a letter to the viceroy, Gandhi had said that the salt tax was the most unjust of all "from the poor man's standpoint" and as the movement for representative government was essentially for the poorest in the land the countrywide civil disobedience would begin with the breaking of the salt law. He and his followers marched about 240 miles from his Sabarmati ashram near Ahmedabad to a village called Dandi on the Arabian sea. As the procession progressed through the hot, dusty countryside, thousands left their mud hovels and joined him. It was as if Moses were leading the Hebrew slaves to freedom.

At Dandi the sea water was evaporated under the blistering hot sun and, in contravention of the law, salt was collected. The police moved in and charged the unarmed crowd; hundreds were injured and arrested. Nehru and other members of the Congress who were initially sceptical of the Salt March were now, in Nehru's words, "abashed and ashamed for having questioned the efficacy of this method". They marvelled at Gandhi's ability "to impress the multitude and make it act in an organised way".

Greatly influenced by the writings of Tolstoy and Ruskin, Gandhi set up self-supporting settlements based on the principles of simple living and mutual help. People had to keep their austere living quarters spotlessly clean and were responsible for cleaning out their own toilets. On this last requirement he had endless rows with his long-suffering wife; she, an orthodox woman, was brought up to expect Untouchables to perform menial and polluting tasks.

Though he believed in *ahimsa* (non-violence), he coined another concept *satyagraha*, the irresistible force that springs from truth and love. "*Satyagraha* hates the evil deed but has only love for the doer of the deed. We will overcome our enemies with love, not with hate or violence. We will convert them from wrong-doing to right-doing."

It is obvious from the above that Gandhi took Jesus seriously; more seriously in fact than most people who liked to call themselves Christians. It is no wonder that some Christian priests, such as C.F. Andrews, became his most fervent friends and that the Quakers, in particular, loved him. Even the British police chief of Durban, a man named Alexander, took it upon himself to protect Gandhi. Once, when Gandhi was being beaten-up by some white thugs, Mrs Alexander appeared, parasol in hand. Opening the parasol she asked him to join her under it. The gang melted away since they could not continue kicking Gandhi without pushing aside the white woman who happened to be the police chief's lady wife.

In 1899, South Africa was torn asunder by a hard fought war between the dominant whites. Called the Boer War by the British, the contest between the Afrikaners and the British was bloody and vicious. Gandhi, ever conscious of 'British justice and fair play' and his abiding duty to the empire of which he considered himself to be a loyal subject, raised an ambulance unit made up of over a thousand men. Of these, no less than 800 were indentured labourers who had volunteered in response to Gandhi's exhortations.

The Indian Ambulance Corps did useful work which the British military recognised; Gandhi and some of his colleagues were awarded medals for their war services. However, though the British empire had triumphed over the doughty Afrikaners, the humiliating conditions under which the Indians had to live continued as before. Later, during the Zulu War, Gandhi raised and led a stretcher-bearer unit.

After many years of agitation, jail sentences and tortuous negotiations, Gandhi managed to extract only two concessions from Smuts, the South

African leader. The government agreed to recognise non-Christian marriages as legal and withdrew the tax on indentured labourers. All other discriminations continued, in fact became worse under other Afrikaner leaders more severe than Smuts.

Smuts had declared, "We will eradicate the Asiatic cancer which has already eaten so deeply into the vitals of South Africa." The South African authorities held Indians in utter contempt and argued that Indians ought first to treat each other decently before demanding better treatment from the whites. The iniquities of the caste system gave them all the ammunition they needed. The British government in London did not wish to upset the rulers of self-governing South Africa, especially when a lot of British capital was invested in that country; and so Gandhi's visits to London to plead his cause met with cold indifference.

Gandhi had certainly made his reputation as a leader during his two decades in South Africa, but the long struggle had achieved little. It could be said that it was a period of preparation for the real work that lay ahead in India itself. If that is so, then it was entirely fortuitous because Gandhi had not planned his long apprenticeship in agitation. It could also be said, however, that *satyagraha* had failed against the stubborn, hard-hearted Afrikancr regime as it would most certainly have failed against the likes of Mussolini, Franco, Hitler, Stalin, Tojo and, later, Mao and Idi Amin.

It was during his last months in South Africa that Gandhi stopped wearing European clothes. The great man discovered he was an Indian while on foreign soil. The same happens today to hundreds of thousands of Indians. The clamour for Indian culture, Indian values and Indian philosophy is heard loudest in places such as London, New York, Los Angeles, Toronto and Sydney.

In July 1914, the Gandhi family left South Africa – but not for India. They boarded a ship for London *en route* to Bombay. It was certainly an odd way of returning to India. The world was on the brink of a world war and everyone knew that a catastrophe was imminent. The family arrived in the capital of the empire a day before the declaration of war. In London, Gandhi energetically involved himself with the raising of an Indian ambulance training corps and made speeches urging Indians to assist Britain in her hour of need. This was puzzling behaviour in view of the fact that he had obtained nothing from the British after proving his loyalty in the two wars in South Africa.

Those who hate Gandhi and all his works have propounded the following conspiracy theory: The perfidious British, knowing that India was at boiling point, needed someone to cool things down there. Gokhale was dying and they saw Gandhi as the best man to replace him. They also knew that Gandhi had failed in South Africa and had no future in that country. It was the British, therefore, who did a deal with Gandhi; in exchange for his moving to India and restraining the extremists they would bestow a degree of autonomy to the Indian people. These theorists claim that Gandhi was summoned to London and briefed by the British government before being despatched to India. They point to statements made by British politicians such as Ellen Wilkinson who said that "Gandhi was the best policeman" that Britain had in India and to the fact that Gandhi figured in the 1915 New Year's honours list when the viceroy awarded him the *Kaisar-i-Hind* (Czar of India) gold medal.

The proponents of the conspiracy theory have never produced a shred of evidence; only murky rumours and innuendoes. Gandhi was certainly misguided in believing so blindly in British justice; but to accuse him of being hand-in-glove with those who were exploiting his country is quite simply not credible.

After spending the first few months of the war in London, Gandhi sailed for India. He arrived in Bombay in early January 1915 and was feted by the Gujarat Society, the chairman of which was none other than Jinnah. In response to Jinnah's speech of welcome, Gandhi remarked that he was "glad to find a Mohammadan not only belonging to his own region's Sabha (Society), but chairing it". At the time, Jinnah was a leading member of the Congress Party and a secular nationalist. Gandhi had only just arrived on the Indian political scene. He was a novice in India and, hence, his patronising tone and his harping on religion irritated Jinnah. It is significant that at their very first meeting it was Gandhi who brought the religious question into their relationship. Later it was Jinnah who concentrated on religious differences – with a vengeance it has to be said.

Gandhi, keen to participate in the uplift of his country, went to see the ailing Gokhale who advised him to get to know his motherland if he wished to be of use to her. Whereupon, Gandhi founded an ashram on the banks of the Sabarmati river near the industrial city of Ahmedabad. The rich and the poor, the high caste and the outcaste were made welcome here. Funded by local mill owners, it was a social experiment of the utmost significance. However, Gandhi's close association with leading Indian industrialists such as G.D. Birla was always held against him, especially by those in the Congress Party who professed socialism. Indian mill owners, it was pointed out, treated their workers far worse than their counterparts in Britain.

In 1915 (Bombay) and 1916 (Lucknow), Gandhi attended the sessions of the Indian National Congress but did not figure prominently in the deliberations. It was at Lucknow, however, that he first met Motilal Nehru and his son Jawaharlal. They were not particularly impressed by Gandhi. Jawaharlal, in fact, could not understand why Gandhi seemed so keen to go about inspecting and cleaning the camp latrines; Gandhi, on the other hand, was greatly impressed by the white and wealthy Kashmiri Brahmins with their superior airs.

Nehru's remark about Gandhi's obsession with latrines requires some elaboration. Gandhi was blessed in this regard because he had no sense of smell. In India, particularly, this is no mean boon. Gandhi could, therefore, spend hours in the most malodorous places where the bravest might fear to tread. He also had, it was widely noticed but rarely talked about, a fixation about bodily functions, especially what he liked to call "bowel movements". Most illnesses, he believed, could be eradicated by salt water enemas. He, himself, would often administer these health-endowing enemas to his friends. It is no wonder that he has been accused of anal fetishism. He also had a great belief in human excrement. 'Night-soil' used as a fertiliser, he often proposed, could increase food production and thus transform India's rural economy.

Gandhian economics were tailored for the Indian peasant and, hence, emphasised village arts and handicrafts such as spinning, weaving, basket-making and cane-work which would not only generate income but also promote self-reliance and dignity. Gandhi had seen the degrading mill towns of Lancashire as well as the squalid slums of Bombay and Ahmedabad. He fervently believed that factories and mills caused human beings untold misery. Nevertheless, some of India's most rapacious capitalists were his friends; they not only financed Gandhi's pet projects but also gave liberal donations to the Congress Party. They realised that his campaign to stop the import of British textiles into India was in their interest. As soon as the fervour for homespun cloth (*khadi*) subsided, the Indian masses would become a ready market for Indian mill-made cloth. In this way Gandhi, somewhat naively, served the cause of India's increasingly powerful industrialists.

Gandhi's horizon had its limitations, especially where his own family was concerned. He put his foot down when his son, Manilal, wanted to marry a Muslim girl, and when his eldest son, Harilal, became a Muslim he cut him off without the slightest hesitation accusing him of selling out to the highest bidder. When Motilal Nehru's daughter, Vijaya Lakshmi (Jawaharlal Nehru's sister), fell in love with Syed Hussain, editor of the

Independent newspaper which was owned by Motilal, and announced her intention of marrying him, there was panic in the family. Motilal was well aware that if his elder daughter were to marry a Muslim the image of the Nehrus would be permanently tarnished so far as orthodox Hindus were concerned and, more to the point, Jawaharlal's political future would be ruined.

The Mahatma was consulted and he suggested a simple solution: the wayward young woman should be sent to his ashram where simple living and high thinking would soon cure her of her silly infatuation. In her autobiography, Vijaya Lakshmi reports that she was appalled by what she saw there. Conditions were primitive and some of Gandhi's ideas shocked her; he actually advised young newly-weds to abstain from sexual intercourse.

The Mahatma certainly had odd theories about sex and these were developed at a very early age. They culminated in 1906 when he was busy carrying wounded British soldiers who were fighting the Zulu nation. He became a *brahmacharya*, that is, took a vow of celibacy. "I will live with my wife as though we are brother and sister," he declared. But then he went further: "I must declare ... that sensual attraction, even between husband and wife, is unnatural." With regard to birth control he emphasised that "the adoption of artificial methods must result in imbecility and nervous prostration".

Gandhi was always prepared to test himself and to conduct, what he believed, were experiments with truth. He slept naked with young girls, one of them his own great-niece, Manu, in order to prove his chastity and self-control. He undertook these tests in 1945 and 1947 when he was aged, respectively, seventy-six and seventy-eight. In any other county this would have been the cause of endless mirth and held up as an example of an old man's eccentricity. Not so in India. Humourless Gandhians, even today, cite these experiments as proof of the Mahatma's greatness.

A great Hindu like Gandhi appears to have been blissfully innocent of the *Kama Sutra* which celebrates the several pleasures of love-making and copulation. He may not have visited and worshipped in the temples that are covered with erotic sculptures of sexual intercourse but he most certainly would have heard of them. He of all people ought to have known that sexual abstinence within marriage is not only un-Hindu but anti-Hindu.

Although he made a point of staying in 'Bhungi colonies' (inhabited by Untouchables), there is no evidence that he ever ate food prepared by them. His eating habits became increasingly frugal and idiosyncratic and his fasts caused endless concern to his faithful followers. Sarojini Naidu, poet and freedom fighter, once remarked in despair that the country had to pay a high price to keep the Mahatma in poverty.

Once, when Gandhi was asked whether Hindus and Muslims should eat together and inter-marry in order to promote a sense of national unity, he made the astonishing remark that the idea was preposterous and a superstition borrowed from the west.

When pressed on the Hindu-Muslim divide, Gandhi always maintained that it was largely a creation of India's British masters and that once the country was independent and free from malign foreign influences the Hindus and Muslims would soon sink their differences and learn to live side by side. Gandhi was patently wrong; after well over half a century of independence there are still Hindu-Muslim clashes in India. In Pakistan there are no Hindu-Muslim clashes for the simple reason that there are hardly any Hindus left in Pakistan.

At that time, however, the Congress and the Muslim League were not as antagonistic to each other as they later became. The parties often held their annual meetings at the same time in the same cities. Many Muslims were members of the Congress while at the same time being members of the Muslim League. When the Muslim League met in Lucknow in 1916, during the week of the Congress session, its president was Jinnah who made no secret of the fact that he had been a member of the Congress for many years and still was, in 1916, a Congress member. The leaders of the two parties met, argued and bargained and then signed an agreement which came to be known as the Lucknow Pact. The Congress agreed to the principle of separate electorates based on religion with special weightage for Muslims. Jinnah, who had previously opposed separate electorates, now saw this as the only hope of harmony between the two communities. The Congress Party, too, since it had signed the pact, agreed with Jinnah.

Gandhi's ideas were, as far as can be seen, confined to improving the lot of India's peoples by freeing them from British rule. So far as the British onslaught against the Zulu people is concerned, Gandhian scholars and apologists have failed to come up with a rational explanation as to why Gandhi did not espouse the cause of the Zulus who were, like the Indians, only fighting for their legitimate rights, culture and way of life. Is it because they were Black, mere 'Negroes', that they did not matter?

Jinnah, too, in his way, had his blind spots, though he never tried to garb himself in saintliness. He was extremely western in his dress and lifestyle. In fact, it was very late in his political career that he started wearing Muslim-style clothes. Knowing little Urdu, the language that the Muslims of north India regarded particularly as their own, he spoke English forcefully and with conviction. One would have thought that Jinnah, of all people, would have encouraged inter-marriage between members of the various communities of India. But not so.

By the time he was thirty-nine, Jinnah had become a highly successful lawyer in Bombay. He had also, by this time, joined the Asna Ashari sect of the Shias who did not accept the Aga Khan's authority. In fact, the Asna Asharis rejected the very idea of a religious head. The sophisticated Jinnah now moved in the best circles and it was then that he fell in love with Rattanbai, the sixteen-year-old daughter of the wealthy Sir Dinshaw Petit, a distinguished Parsi. Petit was against the marriage and took out an injunction forbidding Jinnah from approaching Rattanbai, known to her family as Ruttie, who was a minor. However, as soon as Rattanbai was eighteen, Jinnah married her; but not before she had become a Muslim.

The marriage ended in separation, though it must be pointed out that Jinnah always treated his young wife with kindness and consideration. She was not wayward but was, in today's terms, feisty. She dabbled in Theosophy and spiritualism and spent a lot of time with her cats and dogs. She lost her appetite, became extremely thin, couldn't sleep and endured bouts of deep depression. Kanji Dwarkadas became her dearest friend and she assisted him with his social work. According to Dwarkadas, Jinnah and Ruttie became very close during the last days of her life. One can only conjecture that had she lived on, there might have been a reconciliation. However, she died aged twenty-nine, on her birthday as it happened, and was buried in Bombay. The tearful Jinnah attended the Muslim funeral. Her father, who never forgave her, did not.

Dina, the only child of their marriage, fell in love with a Christian named George Wadia who came from a well-to-do Parsi family. Jinnah was horrified and did his best to stop them marrying simply because he wanted his daughter to marry a Muslim. The man who succeeded in creating a country failed with his own daughter. Dina married the man she loved and had two children; a girl, also named Dina, and a boy named Nusli. The Wadias migrated to the USA.

Jinnah's daughter never entered Pakistan and her son, Nusli, an entrepreneur who often travels to Mumbai, has not been made welcome in the country that his grandfather created.

After the establishment of Pakistan, efforts were made to present Jinnah as a fervent, uncompromising Muslim who had disowned his daughter for disobeying him. Nothing could be further from the truth, as is evident from the following written by Dina Wadia: "My father was not a demonstrative man. But he was an affectionate father. My last meeting with him took place in Bombay in 1946. He had come from New Delhi, in the midst of the most heavy preoccupations with crucial negotiations ... He was very happy to see us – Dina was five and Nusli, two. We mostly talked about the children and politics. He told me that Pakistan was coming. Despite his pressing engagements in New Delhi he had found time to buy presents for us. As we said good-bye, he bent down to hug Nusli. The grey cap he wore so often that it now bears his name, caught Nusli's fancy, and in a moment he had put it on his grandson's head saying, 'Keep it, my boy'. Nusli prizes the cap to this day. I remember the gesture because it was characteristic of his sensibility and consideration for me and my children."

Jinnah was never a fanatical or even a practising Muslim. An inveterate smoker, his preferred cigarette brand was the English-made 'Craven A' and he liked a drink or two in the evening. Also, while in Bombay, he certainly liked ham sandwiches. Always elegantly dressed, he sported a monocle. His immaculate suits and two-tone shoes, then known as co-respondents, were the height of fashion.

Aloof in demeanour – some even accused him of arrogance – Jinnah was not easily moved. Only three times in his life did his eyes brim with tears; when his mother died, when his wife died and, finally, in 1948, just before he himself died. His friend, Jamshed Nusserwanjee, a Parsi, recorded that Jinnah wept when he saw the plight of a group of displaced Hindus in a camp in Pakistan.

On a man-to-man basis, Gandhi had Muslim friends and Jinnah Hindu friends. Abdul Ghaffar Khan, the Pathan leader, and the brothers, Muhammad Ali and Shaukat Ali, who spearheaded the Khilafat movement, were close to Gandhi. Amongst his friends, Jinnah numbered Kanji Dwarkadas and the Punjabi laywer Dewan Chaman Lal.

Jinnah had been a disciple of two leading Moderates; Dadabhai Naoroji, the first Indian to sit in the British House of Commons, and Gopal Krishna Gokhale. The former was a Parsi and the latter a Maharashtrian Brahmin. He emulated Gokhale and wanted to become a 'Muslim Gokhale'. To a large extent he did and that was why Sarojini Naidu, who seems to have had a soft spot for Jinnah, eulogised him and hailed him as "an ambassador of Hindu-Muslim unity".

The idea of a separate homeland for the Muslims of India was an old one and was based on the theory that the Hindus and Muslims were two different nations. This came to be called the Two Nation Theory. Apart from a large number of Muslims, several leading orthodox Hindu leaders also espoused the theory. Most Indian intellectuals, especially those with socialist views, despised the Two Nation Theory on the grounds that it was a capitalist-imperialist ploy to divide and exploit the masses. They argued that the common man, irrespective of his religion, was more concerned about his bowl of rice than his neighbour's faith and beliefs. Nehru belonged to this camp as did a large number of his secularist followers. They believed that once poverty had been abolished, and the proletariat educated, communal harmony would assert itself as a natural consequence.

The historian Panikkar, quoted earlier, had made the pertinent remark that Islam had split Indian society "from top to bottom" and that two separate nations came into being "from the beginning", that is from the time that Islam entered India. Later, two important Hindu leaders – Lajpat Rai and Veer Savarkar – openly accepted the Two Nation Theory. In 1920, the former even advocated the partitioning of the Punjab; a West Punjab with a Muslim majority and an East Punjab with a non-Muslim majority made up of Hindus and Sikhs. At the time, the Muslim majority, led by a cabal of influential Muslim feudal families such as the Tiwanas, the Noons and the Daulatanas dominated the Punjab, and so Lajpat Rai's proposal made sense to many Hindus and Sikhs.

As later events were to prove, the Two Nation theory was a gross over-simplification, the result of a blinkered misreading of India's demography, chequered history and amazing cultural diversity. India was never made up of only two nations but was, rather, always a conglomerate of many nations or, more precisely, nationalities. There are many nationalities within the loosely spun Hindu fold and, likewise, several nationalities within the admittedly tighter Muslim fold. The very notion of a 'Hindu nation' or, for that matter, a 'Muslim nation' is untenable. The Rajputs and the Marathas were always at each other's throats even though each of them claimed to be upholders of true and pristine Hinduism. The Mughals and the Afghans detested each other though they were fellow Sunni Muslims.

If all Muslim people, the *ummah*, constituted a single nation, there would be in existence today one vast Muslim nation state stretching from the Atlantic to the Pacific instead of the scores of politically volatile Muslim states often at loggerheads with each other. Within Afghanistan – a predominantly Muslim country – Muslims of different tribes have been slaughtering each other for generations. Nearer home, if the Bengali

Muslims of East Pakistan belonged to the same nation as their fellow Muslims of West Pakistan, there would have been no need for them to fight for a separate homeland. The very name of their country, Bangladesh, derives from Sanskrit rather than from Arabic or Persian.

In Pakistan today, there is bitter rivalry between the four provinces that make up the country, while there is constant friction between Sunnis and Shias. One wonders what Jinnah might have felt had he known that one day his minority community of Shias would be at the receiving end of discrimination in the country he had fought for and won. The Urdu-speaking Muslims, whose parents and grandparents fled from India to the new Muslim state sixty years ago, are still encountering problems in Pakistan. They are even today called *mohajirs* (refugees).

India, too, is afflicted with the problem of containing within its borders the various diverse nationalities, religions and castes. Lajpat Rai's proposal for the establishment of East Punjab was fully realised when India itself was partitioned. He believed, somewhat optimistically, that Hindus and Sikhs could live peacefully, side by side. Under unhappy circumstances, East Punjab had to be partitioned. In one part, known as Punjab, the Sikhs form a majority; in the other, known as Haryana, the Hindus are in the majority. What the British ruled as one province – the Punjab – has been divided, like Caesar's Gaul, into three parts: the Muslim Punjab in Pakistan, the Sikh Punjab and the Hindu Haryana. Nationalities in other parts of India are continually demanding, and are succeeding in getting, their own states. There is, moreover, the Muslim majority state of Kashmir which is a millstone round India's neck.

Even in the 19th century, the Muslims feared that in an independent India, with its overwhelming Hindu majority, the Muslims would always be under what they labelled 'Hindu Raj'. In the 1880s, Syed Ahmed Khan, who was then the undisputed leader of the Indian Muslims, voiced his feelings on this sore subject; he preferred British Raj to Hindu Raj on the grounds that the British were, after all, 'People of the Book'. He was also aware of the fact that not only were Hindus in the majority but that they had produced an educated middle class which would take up the important administrative posts vacated by the British. So concerned was he for the future of the Muslims of India that he once said he would prefer the British to rule India forever rather than see it handed over to the Hindus. Because of this, he has often been called unpatriotic, anti-national, and a toady of the British by Hindu nationalists and both Hindu and Muslim secularists. Aligarh College, which he founded and which later became Aligarh Muslim University, was always in fierce competition with Benares Hindu University and produced the men who later worked for the creation of Pakistan. Both universities are still flourishing in India.

When the British government mooted the idea of local and provincial self-government, Syed Ahmed Khan insisted on not only communal electorates but also on special weightage for Muslims. In other words, though Hindus voting for Hindu candidates and Muslims for Muslim candidates would ensure parity of representation, he wanted more than parity. Through his demand for special weightage, the Muslims – the minority – would be favoured and the Hindus – the majority – would be penalised. Syed Ahmed Khan, who hailed from a noble family and had been knighted by the British, could never forget that India had been ruled by Muslims before the British ever came on the scene. Hence, he believed that the Muslim community had some sort of a right to privilege. He declared with passion that the Hindus and Muslims were two separate nations, although for some inexplicable reason, he always used the abhorrent term 'Muhammadans'.

A leader of distinction who has not been given his proper place in the pantheon of leadership is the Aga Khan. Aga Khan III, for that was his real title, was the internationally known hereditary leader of the Ismaili sect of the Shia Muslims.

The Aga Khan, apart from being a renowned owner and breeder of racehorses, was popular with the aristocracy of Europe. A *bon viveur*, the women he married were breathtakingly beautiful. His appreciation of loveliness could reach poetic heights as in this passage: "The most beautiful woman whom I ever knew was without doubt Lady D'Abernon ... the brilliance of her beauty was marvellous to behold: the radiance of her colouring, the perfection of her figure, the exquisite modelling of her limbs, the classic quality of her features, and the vivacity and charm of her expression. I knew her for more than forty years, and when she was seventy the moment she came into a room, however many attractive or lovely young women might be assembled there, every eye was for her alone. Nor was her beauty merely physical, she was utterly unspoiled, simple, selfless, gay, brave, and kind."

In India, because of his philanthropy and personal contacts with political leaders and British administrators, his influence was enormous. In 1937, he was elected President of the League of Nations. Without a shred of bigotry, he strove for Hindu-Muslim understanding and to that end believed that Hindus and Muslims must have separate electorates for harmony to prevail.

When the Muslim League was founded in 1906, the Aga Khan was elected its first president and continued be the League's president until 1912. At the time, however, Jinnah was against the very idea of separate electorates. In his *Memoirs*, the Aga Khan refers to Jinnah in the following words: "We had always been on friendly terms, but at this juncture he came out in bitter hostility towards all that I and my friends had done and were trying to do. He was the only well-known Muslim to take up this attitude, but his opposition had nothing mealy-mouthed about it; he said that our principle of separate electorates was dividing the nation against itself, and for nearly a quarter of a century he remained our most inflexible critic and opponent." Later, in 1947, the Aga Khan's cash kept Pakistan afloat.

Jinnah's image has been a poor one due, in part, to his own fault. He has been portrayed as cold and calculating, vain even. Many accuse him of lacking the warm moisture of humanity. He did not write an autobiography and there have been very few biographies of him. He did not wear his heart on his sleeve and kept his private life exactly that, private.

Jinnah was a self-made man who, through sheer hard work and professional integrity, had become a leading member of the Bombay bar. The city's advocates, mostly Hindus and Parsis, regarded him highly. To be respected by one's peers is perhaps the highest accolade that a man can earn. In 1918, as an active leader of Annie Besant's Home Rule League, he succeeded in scuppering a plan to build a memorial to the British governor of Bombay. The city's citizens were so approving of his success that they collected the necessary funds by public subscription and erected a Jinnah Memorial Hall. The building was opened by Mrs Besant who came to Bombay from Madras for the occasion. Later, in the 1926 elections to the central legislative assembly, Jinnah's rich Hindu friends used their cars to get Muslim voters to the booths. Many non-Muslims, mainly Hindus, openly declared that because of the system of communal electorates it was a pity that they themselves could not vote for Jinnah.

Ever since his father's business had collapsed, Jinnah had become the sole breadwinner for the entire family. He also took on the responsibility of educating his relatives; he saw his sister, Fatima, through dental school. This meant long hours of gruelling work in his chambers. He, therefore, had no time to write books or to cultivate the great and the good. Moreover, he did not believe in courting arrest and going to jail; that, he thought, was not what a professional gentleman ought to do. If he had spent years in internment, like the Congress leaders, he would have had the time to read, think and write. On the other hand, he was supremely self-reliant and did not suffer fools gladly. Possessing a fine mind, he disdained the second rate. It was this disdainful air that made him forbidding even to members of the Muslim League. They made him their leader because they knew full well that none among them had the intellectual acumen to confront the giants – Hindu and Muslim – of the Indian National Congress.

Many strict Muslims were most uneasy with the fact that a lax Muslim was leading the Muslim League. Jinnah held that what India's Muslims needed was a good advocate who could win their case and not a strict Muslim who would lose it. One evening, it is said, while he and his deputy, Liaquat Ali Khan, were drinking their scotches in Jinnah's hotel suite, some admiring Muslim students knocked at the door. Jinnah enquired who it was and invited the students to come in. As soon as the group entered, Liaquat Ali Khan whipped his tumbler off the table and placed it under his chair. Jinnah saw what his deputy had done but ignored it. He spoke to the young men and signed their autograph books. They soon left in a flurry of thank-yous. Liaquat Ali Khan stretched down, picked up his whisky and replaced it on the table. At this, Jinnah took up his glass and put it on the floor. Liaquat Ali Khan was perplexed and enquired what was wrong. "Liaquat Ali," said Jinnah, "you're not a man that I'm prepared to drink with any longer."

Even if this story is apocryphal it gives an accurate idea of Jinnah's character.

The British disliked the man intensely, chiefly because they could not patronise him. Here are two examples of how Jinnah dealt with the British. Once, at a dinner party at the governor's residence in Bombay, Jinnah's wife, Rattanbai, was wearing a daringly low-cut dress which was then fashionable in Paris but not in Bombay. Lady Willingdon, the governor's wife, a strait-laced woman, felt that her young guest was attracting some attention and diplomatically asked the ADC to fetch Mrs Jinnah a wrap as the evening sea breeze was a bit chilly. Without a hint of emotion, Jinnah thanked Lady Willingdon for her concern and said that if his wife required a wrap she would ask for one.

Mountbatten was angling to become the governor general of both India and Pakistan, a sort of super governor general who would keep an eye on both countries. Jinnah would have none of it and secured the governor generalship of Pakistan for himself. On August 14, 1947, Mountbatten had to go to Karachi for Jinnah's swearing in ceremony.

There were rumours that dissatisfied groups might attempt assassination and security was tightened. However, the two shared the same ceremonial horse-drawn carriage. When the inauguration was over and both had returned to government house, Mountbatten remarked that he had done his duty by getting Jinnah back safely. "On the contrary," said Jinnah coldly, "it was I who got you back safely".

As can be imagined, Jinnah was not feted by the British establishment. He did not solicit their good opinion and neither did he seek testimonials from foreign powers and the international press. He was, in short, unaware that the world was being increasingly swayed and shaped by the power of the media. That legacy of media ignorance lives on in the country he created and so, over the decades, the image of Pakistan has progressively deteriorated.

Even in Pakistan, few know some of the basic facts pertaining to Jinnah's life. When he left India as a young man in November 1892, he was bound for the London offices of Graham's Trading Company where, as a paid apprentice, he was to be trained in book-keeping and accountancy. His father had dealings with Graham's and the apprenticeship had been arranged through the influence of Frederick Croft who headed the company's Karachi branch. Like Gandhi a few years before him, Jinnah was cold, miserable and lonely. And, like Gandhi, he found lodgings in West Kensington. "The severe cold and the dreary drizzle chilled me to the bone. I felt miserable but I steeled myself and with much effort settled down to take on London on its terms," he told Fatima.

The day after his arrival in London, he had to start work in the City and took an immediate dislike to his desk-bound job. He found it repetitive, unchallenging and boring. He decided to become a lawyer and joined Lincoln's Inn because it had a fresco depicting humanity's greatest lawgivers among whom was featured the prophet Muhammad. Jinnah's father was far from happy at his son's decision and ordered him to return home. Jinnah refused and assured him that he would make no additional financial demands on his father.

He worked hard and, in two years, passed the law examinations. But he had to stay on in London to complete the formalities of attending the Inn dinners. He was called to the Bar in 1896. While in London, Jinnah took an active part in student politics and came under the spell of Dadabhai Naoroji whose speeches in the Commons he often went to hear. He also developed a passion for Shakespeare and went to the Old Vic as often as his slender means would allow. He even nursed an ambition to tread the boards and to play Romeo but, writes his sister Fatima, "the only offer he got was to play a minor part with an unimportant theatrical company". Nevertheless, his love for the poetry of Shakespeare stayed with him all his life.

Back in Karachi, his father informed him that the family business had failed with creditors on all sides clamouring to recover their debts. Jinnah, who at the time was a briefless lawyer, calmly told his father not to worry. Without a moment's hesitation he undertook to support the family and to pay off all the creditors. Two firms of Hindu lawyers were keen to take on the London-qualified barrister but his sights were set on bigger things. He had made up his mind to go to Bombay even though he hardly knew anyone there. Quite naturally, his father and family were fearful.

The unknown Jinnah was ambitious almost to the point of absurdity. He took a room at the well known Apollo Hotel in Bombay and set up a one-man law practice. For several months he did not get a single client though he managed to give out the impression that he was a busy barrister. He joined the right clubs and made some important contacts. The Advocate General of Bombay, John Molesworth MacPherson, was so impressed by Jinnah's potential that he allowed him to use the facilities in his chambers and even passed on some cases to him. By this time, however, Jinnah's financial position was getting desperate and MacPherson recommended him to Sir Charles Ollivant who headed the government's judicial department. Ollivant appointed Jinnah a temporary magistrate.

Reports of the young magistrate's dispensation of justice soon began circulating all over the city and Ollivant offered Jinnah a more senior position on fifteen hundred rupees a month which, in the closing years of the 19th century, was a huge salary. It was a tempting offer but on reflection Jinnah declined the job saying that he intended to earn that much in a single day. How different would history have been if, on account of his family's straitened circumstances, he had accepted Ollivant's well paid job! Jinnah would most probably have retired as Chief Justice of the Bombay High Court. But, most certainly, there would have been no Pakistan.

Jinnah's professional brilliance attracted wealthy clients and he commanded huge fees. He lived in style and, as he had promised his father, supported his large, extended family. Bombay society took Jinnah and his beautiful wife to their hearts. M.C. Chagla, who was a junior in Jinnah's chambers, wrote, "In 1919, Jinnah was the uncrowned king of

Bombay." In later years, after independence, Chagla himself became Chief Justice of the Bombay High Court and was later appointed Chief Justice of India's Supreme Court.

Chagla, a Muslim from the Kutch area of Gujarat, worked very closely with Jinnah not only as a lawyer but as a political activist. In his autobiography, Chagla addresses the awkward question: "Did Jinnah eat pork?" The answer Chagla gives is, quite simply, "Yes".

In 1930, Jinnah was a disillusioned man personally and politically. Ruttie had died the previous year and the Muslim League was divided. He left for London with the intention of practising at the Bar and even toyed with the idea of standing for Parliament. In any case, he thought that London was the "centre of gravity" (his words) so far as India's future was concerned. He purchased West Heath House in Hampstead, a large villa with eight acres, from Lady Graham Wood and established his chambers in King's Bench Walk. Every morning his English chauffeur drove him to his chambers in a Bentley. Lunch was usually taken in a fashionable restaurant such as Simpson's.

As well as his legal practice, Jinnah had business interests. At all times, however, his political concerns came first. A Round Table Conference was convened in London by Prime Minister Ramsay MacDonald during the period November 1930 to January 1931, and during his address Jinnah stressed that India be granted Dominion Status without further delay.

While Jinnah was still in England, a somewhat disturbed student at Cambridge, Rahmat Ali by name, wrote a pamphlet (*Now or Never*) demanding the partition of India into two independent states; one for the Hindus and the other for the Muslims. The Muslim state, he said, would be called Pakistan. He claimed that "Allah's guidance" had led him to the name Pakistan. No one took Ali seriously. Respected Muslim leaders dismissed Ali's ideas as "only a student's scheme" and "chimerical and impracticable". In 1933, Jinnah, certainly, had no time for fanatics like Rahmat Ali.

When the two main opposing factions of the Muslim League (the Hidayat group and the Aziz group) eventually settled their differences, it was to Jinnah that they turned. He left London and in 1934 assumed the presidency of the All India Muslim League. After the first meeting of the now united League, Jinnah stated: "Nothing will give me greater happiness than to bring about complete co-operation between Hindus and Muslims."

History, however, was to take a very different course. On August 14, 1947, Pakistan became a reality amidst the cries of torture, rape and bloody massacres. There was no "co-operation between Hindus and Muslims". There was, in fact, bitter hatred.

The question being asked today is: Was Jinnah a secularist? It is surprising that L.K. Advani and Jaswant Singh, Indian politicians of the right wing Hindu Bharatiya Janata Party, have presented Jinnah in the best possible secularist light. The following statement made by Jinnah on August 11, 1947 is often quoted: "We are starting with this fundamental principle that we are all citizens and equal citizens of one State... I think we should keep that in front of us as our ideal and you will find that in due course Hindus would cease to be Hindus and Muslims would cease to be Muslims, not in the religious sense, because that is the personal faith of each individual, but in the political sense as citizens of the state." However, Dr Javid Iqbal, son of the poet Muhammad Iqbal who is widely regarded as the Poet of Pakistan, recently asserted that Jinnah was not secular and did not want to create a secular state. He said that the significance of Jinnah's speech had been highly exaggerated.

Professor Ishtiaq Ahmed of the University of Stockholm, himself a Pakistani, writes: "The noble lie was necessary, Plato argued, in order to obtain complete submission to the ruler from the citizens and thus maintain a stable social and political order... As one born in the Ismaili sect, Jinnah would surely have known that his sect was never considered proper Muslims and therefore had to live on the fringes until the English intervened and had the Aga Khan recognised as a great leader of the Muslims... Consequently if Jinnah did not want Pakistan to be a secular-liberal state, as the wording of his statement suggests and as I believe he did want, then he was telling a noble lie in the best interest of Pakistan. Unfortunately his successors betrayed him either way by introducing initially discriminatory constitutional provisions and then the blasphemy law... the rape law and so on. The result has been brutalised women, Christians, Hindus and Ahmadiyyas. Calls have even been given to declare the Ismailis heretics."

The only leader in the subcontinent to have founded a political dynasty was Jawaharlal Nehru. More accurately, it was his ambitious father, Motilal, who was responsible for the ascendancy of the family.

The Nehrus are, in fact, Kauls who are Kashmiri Brahmins. While on a visit to Kashmir, Farrukhsiyar, the third emperor after Aurangzeb, was so impressed by the Persian and Sanskrit scholar Raj Kaul that he invited him to the imperial capital. Thus, in 1716, Kaul was granted a *jagir* (estate) and a residence in Delhi near the canal (*nehr*); and because the family lived by the *nehr* they came to be called Nehrus.

The family did well under both the Mughals and the Company Bahadur. Ganga Dhar Nehru, the future prime minister's grandfather, was *kotwal* (chief police officer) of Delhi under the last Mughal emperor, Bahadur Shah II. Motilal, born on the same day as the poet Tagore, was the posthumous son of Ganga Dhar who died three months before his youngest son's birth. A hardworking lawyer, Motilal became a leading member of the Allahabad Bar; his earnings were immense as were his expenses. He believed that when a man saved money he was only making a pathetic confession that he didn't have the confidence or capacity always to earn enough to maintain his accustomed lifestyle.

Motilal Nehru, strong-willed and autocratic, rode and wrestled and admired the English immensely. He moved into a large mansion which he called Anand Bhavan, 'Abode of Joy', and fitted it with furnishings and gadgets bought in Europe. He once ordered that only English was to be spoken in his presence but this didn't work as many of the ladies of the household and most of the servants couldn't speak the language. As a leading citizen of Allahabad and a freemason, he was invited to attend the grandest parties and receptions. In the Nehru family memorabilia is a photograph of Motilal resplendent in court dress with breeches, buckled shoes and ceremonial sword. During George V's visit to India in 1911, Motilal and his wife were presented to the king emperor at the Delhi *durbar*.

Motilal Nehru was an Englishman in the Curzon mould and, in his son's words, "had a feeling that his own countrymen had fallen low and almost deserved what they had got". For nationalist politicians, whom he considered worthless windbags, Motilal Nehru had the profoundest contempt.

Being a pragmatist, he had no time for religious rituals and observances; these he thought were best left to the women of his household. Whenever he returned from a visit to Europe, he absolutely refused to undergo the prescribed purification ceremony and this caused a rift in the Kashmiri Brahmin community. He did, for a short period, consider Theosophy but then the interest petered out. "I do not believe in the Divine Revelation of any scripture whatsoever," he said. He rejected the concept of 'Mother Cow' by saying jokingly that he couldn't call his father a bull. He did, however, concede that as codes of moral behaviour the religious books of the various faiths were "quite good".

Motilal suffered a double tragedy when his first wife died in childbirth; this was followed by the death of the only child of the marriage, his three-year-old son, Ratanlal. Motilal then married the fifteen-year-old Swarup Rani. Their first child, also a boy, died. Later, in 1889, another son, Jawaharlal, was born. He was followed, after eleven years, by a daughter named Sarup Kumari, or "Nan", but known more widely as Vijaya Lakshmi Pandit. Five years later, Swarup Rani gave birth to another son but he died when only a month old. Still later, after two years, another girl, Krishna, was born.

The Nehrus, who spoke chaste Urdu, the sophisticated language of aristocratic north Indian Muslims and Hindus, were secular and cosmopolitan. Their home in Allahabad became a sort of intellectual salon frequented by Europeans and Indians of all religions. They celebrated Holi, Dewali, Eid and even Christmas. The girls had an English governess, Miss Hooper (affectionately called 'Toopie') who, when she married, was given away by Motilal Nehru. The somewhat spoilt Jawaharlal's resident tutor was F.T. Brooks. The garden superintendent was an Anglo Indian and the seeds for the flowerbeds were imported from England.

Life in Anand Bhavan was very different from that which most Indians and indeed most British people were exposed to. Vijaya Lakshmi Pandit summed up the conundrum when she confessed that, as a girl, she believed that all upper crust Indians spoke Urdu and those whom they employed spoke English. She gained this childhood impression when the British ruled India. Perhaps it is only in India that such beliefs can take root.

Though Jawaharlal admired his father, he feared him and was always in awe of him. Motilal was overbearing and while showering his son with good advice managed, in effect, to dent his son's self-confidence. The relationship between the two was fascinating and peculiar. Nehru relates how when he was a small boy his father beat him mercilessly for the offence of taking a fountain pen without permission and then, even worse, for not owning up to it. "Almost blind with pain and mortification at my disgrace I rushed to my mother, and for several days various creams and ointments were applied to my aching and quivering little body." It was his mother who adored him; she would condone his lapses and he often tried to "dominate over her a little". Describing her he says, "She was *petite* ... I admired her beauty and loved her amazingly small and beautiful hands and feet."

The man whom he was closest to was Mubarak Ali, his father's *munshi* (clerk) who hailed from a good Muslim family which, since 1857, had fallen on hard times. Nehru remembered how he used to snuggle up to the grey-bearded *munshi* and "listen, wide-eyed, by the hour to his innumerable stories" and accounts of what had happened in 1857-58. Intellectual stimulation he got from Brooks who had been recommended to Motilal by Annie Besant. An introverted scholar, Brooks instilled in his pupil a passion for reading, poetry, science and Theosophy.

In his early teens, Nehru became a member of the Theosophical Society and was initiated into its mysteries by none other than Mrs Besant herself. Later, both Nehru and his tutor left the society. Nehru discovered socialism and agnosticism and Brooks could not accept Mrs Besant proclaiming Krishnamurti as the New Messiah. The disenchanted Brooks died soon after; his body was found floating in a river. No one discovered the cause of his death, though it was most probably suicide.

Motilal was keen that his son should go to a leading English public school, and so the family left for England where Jawaharlal, then sixteen and well over the usual entry age, was admitted to Harrow. There can be no doubt that the resourceful father had pulled strings and had the right words whispered into the right ears. Sir Harcourt Butler, who became governor of the United Provinces (now Uttar Pradesh), was a great friend of Motilal Nehru and one of Butler's relatives had been Headmaster of Harrow. In fact, a Butler was Master of Trinity College, Cambridge, when Jawaharlal was admitted there after two years at Harrow. Many years later, 'Rab' Butler, the Conservative minister who instituted Britain's Butler Act and who was born in India, also became Master of Trinity. Trinity's connection with India is still strong; a recent Master was an Indian.

At Harrow, Nehru was thoroughly homesick but buckled down to work. He was not a brilliant scholar, but then the school boasted that it was not in the business of producing bookworms but rather a far better human species, namely gentlemen. 'Joe', as Jawaharlal was soon nicknamed, did not make much of an impression. He was a reserved sort of boy though courteous and well-mannered. He played cricket and football and joined the Harrow School Corps. The Rev Edgar Stogdon, his housemaster who also commanded the Corps, noted that the young Nehru had "quite good capabilities as a soldier" and that "he worked well, and seldom (almost never) gave trouble". He also "very specially liked the Harrow school songs". Stogdon made a point of mentioning the following episode: When the Harrow team won a shooting competition, the victors rode back to Harrow in a horse-drawn carriage. However, some of the senior boys were so elated that their team had brought home the trophy that they decided to relieve the horses of the task. A group of them enthusiastically hauled the carriage with the shooting team in it up Harrow Hill. In the group, recollects Stogdon, were Nehru and the future field marshal Lord Alexander of Tunis.

What is revealing is the cascade of correspondence that 'Joe' received from his father. Full of suggestions, advice and lectures it is a wonder that young 'Joe' did not cut and run. Motilal tells his son that he must "patronise the creameries" and get on good terms with members of "the rowdier element" of the school by entertaining them; he was not to worry about expenses so long as he became "a general favourite". The father wishes to know if 'Joe' got into fights "even if you get the worse out of it". He then assures his son, "It will by no means be discouraging to me to hear about it."

Motilal could never be accused of an excess of modesty as the following will prove: "I think that I can without vanity say that I am the founder of the fortunes of the Nehru family. I look upon you, my dear son, as the man who will build upon the foundations I have laid and have the satisfaction of seeing a noble structure of renown rearing up its head to the skies... Be perfect in body and mind and this is the only return we seek for tearing ourselves from you."

'Joe' never became the darling of the school though Harrovian camaraderie remained with him in spite of his incarcerations in British jails. When he was prime minister, he used to escape from the cares of office by collecting his nephews, nieces and grandchildren around him and teaching them his old school songs such as *Jerry, you duffer and dunce* and *When Grandpapa's Grandpapa was in the Lower Lower First.*

In 1952, while he was at the Commonwealth Conference in London, Nehru attended the Old Harrovian dinner. Another Harrovian, Winston Churchill, was also present and neither man was oblivious of the fact that it was Churchill's government that had sent Nehru to his longest spell in jail. Together they sang *Forty Years On* and many handkerchiefs dabbed eyes when they came to the following verse:

> Forty years on, growing older and older,
> Shorter in wind as in memory long,
> Feeble of foot and rheumatic of shoulder,
> What will it help us that once we were strong?

Churchill actually confessed that it was difficult to believe that a man who had languished for years in confinement imposed by the British had not an iota of hate or revenge in him.

At Trinity College, Nehru read for the Natural Sciences tripos which meant chemistry, geology and botany. Trinity, Newton's alma mater, had a tremendous academic reputation and Nehru did not find the course easy. Moreover, his interests were wide ranging and took in political philosophy, economics and psychology. He managed to get a second class degree and did not become "the most popular young fellow and the most distinguished graduate" that his father had urged him to aim for. He had a natural shyness and though he sometimes went to the meetings of the Cambridge Majlis, a forum for Indian students, he could never muster the courage to speak there. Motilal, incidentally, disapproved of his son mixing with Indian students; he did not want him to be tainted with notions of agitation or nationalism. But Nehru had already been bitten by the bug. Garibaldi, the Italian patriot, had become his hero.

It was the family that first mooted the idea that Jawaharlal should prepare for the Indian Civil Service competitive examination; but it was dropped and, moving to London, the science graduate joined the Inner Temple. He was not thrilled at the thought of following his father's profession and "the technicalities and trivialities of the law", he said, held no interest for him. His wish to study at the London School of Economics was quickly brushed aside by the father who was footing the bills. Motilal knew only too well that the LSE was a breeding ground for left-wingers. The law student, with a penchant for Bond Street suits, nevertheless, fell in with the Fabians one of whose leading lights was George Bernard Shaw, scathing intellectual, successful playwright and polemicist for socialist causes.

In London, Nehru came out of his shell and adopted a somewhat dandyish, extravagant and expensive lifestyle. He mixed with old friends from Harrow and was keen on champagne and partying. A Pathan student named Khan Sahib, who was at St Thomas's, became one of his closest companions. After a few drinks there was always fun and frolic and Nehru invariably took a ride on Khan Sahib's broad shoulders. Khan Sahib's half-brother, Abdul Ghaffar Khan, later known as the 'Frontier Gandhi', started the Khudai Khidmatgaran (*Servants of God*) movement. This anti-British movement, allied with the Congress, was popularly called the Red Shirt Movement because its members wore red *kameezes* (long shirts). Khan Sahib himself was drawn into politics; he headed two Congress governments (1937-39 and 1945-47) in his native North West Frontier Province. After India's partition, he became a minister in the Pakistan cabinet and later Chief Minister of the whole of West Pakistan.

Once, when his father wrote suggesting that he concentrate on his studies and watch his spending, Nehru replied waspishly: "May I know if I am supposed to keep you informed of every penny I spend on a bus fare or a stamp?" This waspishness stayed with Nehru all his life and marred a character that was otherwise warm and sensitive.

He passed his law examinations, in his own words, "with neither glory nor ignominy" and was called to the Bar in 1912. At the end of that year he landed in Bombay. Writing much later, he confessed that as a young man he was "a bit of a prig with little to commend me."

Nehru senior had, in the meantime, been drawn into politics. He could not stand the extremist views of men like Tilak and felt that it was his duty to raise the voice of moderation. Motilal had not only cultivated the highest levels of the British administration but also knew all the important Indian political leaders. Consequently, his son had easy access to public life; he became a full time politician without the burden of having to earn a living. Jinnah, from the very beginning, scorned the younger Nehru on the grounds that he was a rich man's son who had no notion of life's struggles. He also accused Jawaharlal of being a dreamer of sorts who had no first hand experience of the cut and thrust of political debate. In both assessments Jinnah was right.

Jawaharlal, on the other hand, had formed certain opinions of Jinnah which were far from complimentary. Jinnah had not been to Harrow or Cambridge, or in fact to any university, was not well read in any of the world's philosophies and literatures and, above all, was not an Urdu-speaker, the language which the Nehrus believed encapsulated elegance and culture. In short, Nehru believed Jinnah to be, at best, only half-educated. However, what no one could deny was the brilliance of Jinnah's advocacy. Theirs was a clash of personalities.

What made any *rapprochement* impossible was revealed in a passage in Nehru's well known book *The Discovery of India*, published in 1946, in which he described his visit of homage to the dying poet Muhammad Iqbal. Nehru wrote: "I admired him and his poetry, and it pleased me greatly to feel that he liked me and had a good opinion of me. A little before I left him he said to me: 'What is there in common between Jinnah and you? He is a politician, you are a patriot.'"

Nehru also wrote: "Iqbal was one of the early advocates of Pakistan and yet he appears to have realised its inherent danger and absurdity." Bringing in the British left wing social historian Edward Thompson as a witness, Nehru recorded: "Edward Thompson has written that, in the course of a conversation, Iqbal told him that he had advocated Pakistan because of his position as president of the Muslim League session, but he felt sure that it would be injurious to India as a whole and to Muslims specially."

All this was, of course, dynamite. The Muslim League under Jinnah's iron leadership held Iqbal in great esteem and believed that his intellectual and poetic vision had, without question, demanded an independent state for India's Muslims. And here was Nehru trying to make out that the philosopher poet had had second thoughts at the end of his life. The very idea of this was anathema to all those Muslims who believed passionately in the ideology of Pakistan.

Jinnah and Gandhi could, at least, talk to each other; there was hardly any dialogue between Jinnah and Nehru. Jinnah despised particularly those Muslims, largely Urdu-speakers, who belonged to the Nehru camp; he regarded them as puppets of the Hindu-dominated Congress. Men like Maulana Abul Kalam Azad, Rafi Ahmed Kidwai, Syed Mahmud, Zakir Hussian and Chief Justice Chagla were hardly likely to be anyone's poodles and Jinnah's dismissive attitude towards the 'Nationalist Muslims' was undeserved and unjust. Not surprisingly, the Muslim Leaguer who would willingly converse with Nehru was the Urdu-speaker Liaquat Ali Khan, Jinnah's deputy, who became Pakistan's first prime minister. A man of only above average ability, Liaquat Ali Khan hailed from a land-owning family on the Indian side of the border. His efforts to establish some semblance of democracy in the new state were a miserable failure. He and Nehru signed a concord called the Nehru-Liaquat Pact which terminated with Liaquat's assassination in 1951.

With a certain flourish, Jinnah's daughter Dina once wrote, "No Jinnah, no Pakistan." She meant, of course, that had her father not been born, there would have been no Pakistan. However, these four words are music to the ears of those Pakistan-baiting Hindu fundamentalists who look forward to the day when the estranged provinces comprising Pakistan will be reunited with Mother India. Echoing Dina they say that since there is no longer a Jinnah, there should no longer be a Pakistan,

It is Pakistan's great misfortune that Jinnah died only a year after the birth of the new state. However, many Indians feel it is India's greatest misfortune that Jinnah did not die a couple of years earlier.

India had Nehru at the helm of affairs for many years. Though not a resolute or ruthless politician, and no great administrator, he had a grand vision and a blueprint for India based on science, secularism and socialism. He famously called the high dams, the steel mills and the nuclear power plants the new temples of modern India. His compatriots adored him and followed him unquestioningly. His several blunders in the sphere of economics, his muddled foreign policies (particularly in relation to China) and his obsession with Kashmir were willingly forgiven. His passionate affair with Edwina, Mountbatten's wife, was an open secret but no one, not even Mountbatten, was greatly concerned. Indians, at large, felt that he needed the love and solace of an intelligent and understanding woman.

Nehru certainly had charisma; he could, when he wished, charm the birds from the trees. Women found him fascinating because his personality was Hamletian. A fine writer, his *Discovery of India* is a classic study of India's culture, history, religions, philosophies, achievements and failures; his autobiography is honest and hugely readable; his *Letters* to his daughter Indira, a few written when he was in prison, are an education. His 'Tryst with Destiny' address to the nation ranks among history's great speeches.

Nehru was, of course, extremely fortunate in that his deputy, Vallabhbhai Patel, had hands of steel which he clothed in gloves of steel. The opposite of Nehru in every possible way, he was a man of few words who believed in firm and decisive action. Not given to Nehruvian soliloquies, Patel was Minister of Home Affairs and, thus, responsible for internal security and the maintenance of law and order. He was also put in charge of integrating the hundreds of princely states into the Union of India. With the assistance of V.P. Menon, an outstanding bureaucrat, he drafted what they called an Instrument of Accession – more an Instrument of Surrender – which the princes were expected to sign without asking too many unnecessary and awkward questions.

Many a proud Rajput ruler quaked with fear when Patel, a Gujarati, summoned him to Delhi. Those who were recalcitrant, like the Nizam of Hyderabad, were subjected to 'police action', a nice term for military invasion. Others, like the Maharajas of Travancore, Jodhpur, Dholpur and scores of other lesser potentates, were blackmailed and bullied and signed meekly on the dotted line. Patel achieved what neither the Mughals nor the British were able to do. He broke the back of India's age-old princely order. He is rightly celebrated as the Bismarck of India.

A POSTSCRIPT

The enigma that is India is not easy to penetrate. Understanding India, therefore, has to be a lifelong passion, a magnificent obsession. The enigma is what makes the enterprise so interesting, so fascinating. I have been fortunate; my learning curve has been long and, I hope, not entirely fruitless. From an early age I have been something of a traveller. I have visited many parts of the subcontinent and have met and interacted with all sorts of people. People – high, low, rich, impoverished, powerful and powerless, some highly educated and others illiterate – have taught me more than books will ever do. This might show me up as simplistic, naïve and purposefully anti-intellectual. Not so; I have read many books and even written some. What I am trying to say is that I have no time for those who churn out weighty tomes from safe and lofty ivory towers. Neither do I have time for those who recline in comfortable libraries or for those who know only how to surf the Internet. Shakespeare was a jobbing scribbler and a 'player'. In Elizabethan times, 'players' were equated with vagabonds and vagrants. There were no knighthoods, peerages, Padma Shris or Sitaras-e-Pakistan for mere actors in those bad old days. But the world remembers Shakespeare. The world does not know the thousands of drudges and scholars who wrote, and still persist in writing, erudite doctoral theses about Shakespeare's life and plays.

No book, such as the one you have just read, would be worth writing if it were not suffused with the warm moisture of humanity. But love for humanity or a country or a culture must never be allowed to blind us or blinker our vision. Our hearts must be hot and pulsating but our minds must never be misted. We are all infected with the virus of intense hates, dislikes, personal prides and prejudices. The uncivilised man is governed by these; those who attempt to transcend them are among the elect, the civilised.

To me, it seems that the clash of civilisations, so much discussed and debated today, is a misnomer. The clash is certainly there. But it is between the uncivilised and the civilised. As always, it is the uncivilised that are on the offensive. The uncivilised are widely spread and encompass those who, on the surface, seem or pretend to be enemies. Shrill rightwing evangelists in the American Bible Belt are no better than frenzied Middle Eastern mullahs or fiery Hindu zealots in Haridwar. They are all in the business of marketing various brands of hate wrapped in enticing packages that promise the pleasures of paradise. In short, the uncivilised of all persuasions are brothers-in-arms.

The question is: How do the civilised cope? If they do not take effective measures, not tomorrow but today, rest assured that the uncivilised will triumph and humanity will be doomed. There will, then, be no recovery from the resulting era of darkness which the Hindus call Kal-yug.

The assertions and statements made in this book have been rigorously researched. It is not an anti-India, anti-Pakistan, anti-Hindu or anti-Muslim book. It is not anti anyone or anything. All I have endeavoured to do is to present facts and opinions not necessarily generally known or, if they are, have been wilfully suppressed by governments, religious establishments, political extremists and those with evil and hidden agendas.

Human beings, no matter of what colour, class, caste, religious persuasion or nationality, are basically decent. *Azaadi !* – my collection of stories and histories is a celebration of this fact. Then why the discord? This is because human beings, precisely because of their innate decency, are also vastly and tragically gullible. They are easily taken in by charm, sweet-talk and propaganda. The advertising industry understands this very well indeed and, therefore, flourishes in every country on earth. The war for the minds of men is now waged by the media moguls. Sophisticated spin can neatly justify any criminal or unjust act. It is no wonder that amongst the young, cynicism is so widespread.

Joseph Goebbels, an unsavoury character who was Hitler's Minister of Public Enlightenment and Propaganda, wasn't far off the mark when he said that people were happy with slogans. Governments did not have to provide bread and butter so long as they provided good slogans. All established authorities, political, religious, economic, social and educational, have always coined and handed down heady slogans. They still do. And these slogans are then chanted by millions who obviously believe them fervently and passionately. Throughout the centuries, men have died for slogans. This happens all over the world, even today, but since this book is about the subcontinent of south Asia, I shall confine my comments to south Asia only.

When I was a boy in Lahore, the capital city of the Punjab, before Independence and Partition, I could not help but notice the tensions in society. These had their genesis in the prejudices that children were brought up with from an early age. Society, in general, was to blame; but particularly the parents. Children believe their parents, and so when small Hindu children were told that Muslims were bloodthirsty killers (*khooni*) the idea was implanted in their minds. Ideas injected into young minds last a lifetime. The same happened when, for instance, Muslim children were told that Hindus were cowards (*buz-dil*) and crafty (*chalak*). For generations, this poisonous stereotyping led to much bad blood. Therein lay the root cause of the Great Divide.

There can be no doubt, and British district heads were well aware of it, that in the united Punjab the Muslims tended to be the more reactive. The 'PMs' ('Punjabi Mussalmans') were the backbone of the British Indian army. The Hindus, by and large, were comparatively peaceful and non-violent. In a village, for example, even where most of the inhabitants were Hindus it was the minority Muslims who managed to get their way. The Hindus tended to concentrate on trade, education and civil service examinations.

The annual matriculation results used to be splashed in all the newspapers. The first ten in the first division were mostly Hindus; seldom did a Muslim or Sikh name figure in the top ten. The same was the case with the BA and BSc results. Hence the notion that Hindus were 'brainy'. Mathematics, especially, was their forte and this caused envy and ill feeling. However, the poison was spread by men such as Golwalkar, the head of the fascist Rashtriya Swayamsevak Sangh who extolled the Nazis and advocated a 'pure Hindu India'. It was he and those that thought like him who alienated the Muslims of India.

There were economic factors at play as well. All the bankers and moneylenders were Hindus. Bilaki Shah, the notorious moneylender, was owed millions by leading Muslim families. Moreover, the Hindus of Lahore, and of the Punjab in general, laid great store by English and British type education. They, therefore, gained a near monopoly of the professions. They acquired social prestige and status. The Muslims and Sikhs regarded themselves as glorious martial races who could not descend to mere book-learning. Myriads of myths, half-truths and untruths were held by Muslims against Hindus and *vice versa*. Both communities saw the Sikhs as simpletons who, at twelve noon when the sun was high, were bound to do something silly. There were scores upon scores of jokes about dim-witted Sikhs. It must be said that even the Sikhs often related these 'Sikh jokes' with relish.

The future of Lahore was left in limbo when the partition of the Punjab and of India was agreed upon by the three participating parties: the British

Labour government of Clement Attlee which gave Mountbatten a free hand; the largely Hindu Congress Party; and the Muslim League. Most of the property and businesses in Lahore were owned by Hindus, but the population had a Muslim majority. Eventually, the boundary commission awarded Lahore to Pakistan. And then the killing and raping began. It was relentless and ruthless.

It is perhaps those nightmares of sixty years ago that made me, decades later, write the following lines:

> And so I am compelled to take up my pen
> And condemn as criminals all those men
> Who wilfully divide humankind
> With boastful talk of country, culture, religion, race,
> Nation, colour, gender, class and caste,
> And other considerations of wayward chance.
> No man or woman ever chose to be
> In any particular category.
> The unborn never had a voice;
> The unborn never had a choice.

Nevertheless, as a human being, I am proud to report that in spite of the hatreds, the massacres, the unprecedented forced migrations, the flame of humanity – often small and dangerously flickering – was not extinguished.

Courageous individuals from all communities put their lives and families at risk to protect and ferry to safety those whom they, only a few days previously, regarded with suspicion and fear.

Because members of the present generation are not haunted by memories of the 1947- 48 holocaust, they have an inbuilt advantage. They must recognise and reject the sins of their forefathers and, at the same time, accept with open minds and humility the good that has been bequeathed to them. With a fresh, humane and rational 21st century approach they now have an opportunity to forge an entirely new future for the whole region. If they do not, nobody else will.

Inertia will only allow matters to deteriorate. Time is short, for if there is yet another India-Pakistan confrontation, it will surely be the last. The military establishments of both countries have missiles with nuclear warheads ready to be launched. It will take only a few from either side to get through for the whole region to be devastated beyond redemption.

INDEX